HOUSEHOLD FINANCIAL MANAGEMENT

Other World Scientific Titles by Sumit Agarwal

Kiasunomics©: Stories of Singaporean Economic Behaviours
ISBN: 978-981-3233-36-2
ISBN: 978-981-3234-53-6 (pbk)

Kiasunomics©2: Economic Insights for Everyday Life
ISBN: 978-981-121-709-8
ISBN: 978-981-121-839-2 (pbk)

Impact of COVID-19 on Asian Economies and Policy Responses
ISBN: 978-981-122-937-4

HOUSEHOLD FINANCIAL MANAGEMENT

Sumit Agarwal
National University of Singapore, Singapore

Yeow Hwee Chua
Nanyang Technological University, Singapore

World Scientific

NEW JERSEY • LONDON • SINGAPORE • BEIJING • SHANGHAI • HONG KONG • TAIPEI • CHENNAI • TOKYO

Published by

World Scientific Publishing Co. Pte. Ltd.

5 Toh Tuck Link, Singapore 596224

USA office: 27 Warren Street, Suite 401-402, Hackensack, NJ 07601

UK office: 57 Shelton Street, Covent Garden, London WC2H 9HE

National Library Board, Singapore Cataloguing in Publication Data
Name(s): Agarwal, Sumit, 1970– | Chua, Yeow Hwee, author.
Title: Household financial management / Sumit Agarwal, Yeow Hwee Chua.
Description: Singapore : World Scientific Publishing Co. Pte. Ltd., [2024]
Identifier(s): ISBN 978-981-12-6712-3 (hardback) | 978-981-12-6767-3 (paperback) |
978-981-12-6713-0 (ebook for institutions) | 978-981-12-6714-7 (ebook for individuals)
Subject(s): LCSH: Finance, Personal. | Home economics.
Classification: DDC 332.024--dc23

British Library Cataloguing-in-Publication Data
A catalogue record for this book is available from the British Library.

For any available supplementary material, please visit
https://www.worldscientific.com/worldscibooks/10.1142/13165#t=suppl

Desk Editors: Poornima Harikrishnan/Jiang Yulin

Typeset by Diacritech Technologies Pvt. Ltd.
Chennai - 600106, India

We would like to dedicate this book to our children.

To Siddharth and Maya with love – Sumit
To Clare and Caleb with love – Yeow Hwee

Contents

Preface

The goal of this book is to improve households' financial well-being from the lens of academic research. In recent years, there has been much progress in the field of household finance. Particularly, extensive research work has been conducted on households' usage of financial instruments and markets to achieve their goals.

From these academic studies, we have increased our understanding of households' financial decision-making processes and identified mistakes commonly made. Additionally, economists have developed tools and techniques that individuals can use to overcome these errors and challenges.

It is our firm belief that the research carried out in household finance ought to be made widely available and accessible to everyone. Leveraging on our experience in the teaching of economics and finance, we have put together this guide to household financial management.

Through this book, we hope to share the key takeaways of household finance and help individuals improve their personal finances. By distilling the various challenges that we face in different stages of our lives, we further provide suggestions on how to avoid making recurrent blunders in our financial decisions.

Drawing from international examples and case studies, we realize through a global lens of household finance that we are all not that different. Households in different countries tend to make similar suboptimal choices when it comes to managing their finances.

Rather than overwhelming our readers with the large number of research papers which have been developed in household finance, we center our attention on a few studies in each topic. This will serve as a primer for each subject and allow us to dive deeper into the details of each study.

Notwithstanding, inspired by the 30 topics presented in this book, we ended up with more than 100 research papers involving more than 20 countries! While we seek to provide a comprehensive understanding of household finance, the spectrum of households' decisions is just too wide. Therefore, we have chosen to focus on research articles that best represent the needs of our readers and those that we are most familiar with. For these reasons, you will see many of our research work being featured.

We strongly believe that the research work conducted in household finance can help us make more informed financial choices. As Mark Twain once said, "History never repeats itself, but it does often rhyme." As we learn from the experiences of others, we can avoid making costly financial mistakes and better manage our household finances.

The study of household finance is also highly related to behavioral economics. In the chapters ahead, we will provide additional insights on the different types of heuristics and cognitive biases that individuals are prone to. By recognizing our own behavioral biases, we will then be able to better develop strategies and overcome them.

While discussing the research articles, we seek to shed light on how economists approach and analyze problems. The growth of household finance in recent years has been attributed to advancements in technical methodologies and the availability of high-quality datasets.

As each of the featured papers exemplifies how economists employ different techniques and data to gain insights into households' financial decision-making, we will be taking this opportunity to introduce state-of-the-art economic methodology that has been developed over the recent years.

Another goal of this book is thus to help readers make sense of economic models, policies, and data. Hence, this can be an entry level guidebook for students who are interested in the field of household finance. For more advanced readers, we invite you to review the research papers cited in the references for more in-depth analysis.

The Road Ahead

We have carefully selected topics that play an integral role across the lifetime of households. Drawing on lessons from academic research, readers from all walks of life can enhance their financial proficiency and develop a greater understanding of how households make financial decisions across different markets.

The topics are classified into eight parts. In Part I, we introduce financial literacy and financial planning for households. We also give an overview of the behavioral biases and the role of the macroeconomic environment. This will put us in good stead for the rest of the book.

The book then flows into Part II: Savings, which highlights the challenges that we face as we save for the future. Here, we focus on the importance of saving for retirement and the different retirement income support programs. Thereafter, we examine the retirement savings puzzle and investigate whether households are saving enough.

We shift our attention to consumption in Part III and analyze unexpected factors that could influence our spending. These include the weather and our peers. We then discuss how digital payments have reshaped our spending habits. As the digital economy assumes greater importance, we also address online fraud and identify ways to steer clear of them.

Part IV is where we explore the importance of borrowing. We center our discussion on how credit markets work and break down the following consumer debt: overdrafts, payday loans and credit cards. As interest rates differ across various types of loans, understanding the role of borrowing costs will help us make more informed financial choices.

In Part V, we dive into investing. We will discuss the stock market participation puzzle and common pitfalls encountered during market participation. These pitfalls include the lack of diversification, portfolio inertia, overtrading, as well as mental accounting. Subsequently, we will highlight how investors often misinterpret their investment performance.

We then move on to the housing market in Part VI. The housing market plays a key role in our lives as purchasing houses and deciding on mortgages are crucial financial milestones. In this context, we identify pointers to look out for when we buy and sell our houses, and point out some common errors when financing/refinancing mortgages. We will also highlight the role of intermediaries, namely, housing agents, mortgage brokers, and appraisers.

Part VII turns to the role of risk management in our lives. By focusing on life insurance, health insurance, and annuity, we evaluate the role of different financial instruments that we can use to manage our risk. Depending on our financial goals and circumstances, we might choose to use different forms of protection.

We conclude by discussing the role of gender in household financial management. An appreciation of gender differences and intra-household financial decisions is important as it helps us make better collective decisions. This will ensure that the households' resources are used effectively and help promote financial stability in the family.

About the Authors

Sumit is Low Tuck Kwong Distinguished Professor of Finance at the Business School and a Professor of Economics and Real Estate at the National University of Singapore (NUS). He is also concurrently the President of Asian Bureau of Finance and Economic Research, and the Managing Director of Sustainable and Green Finance Institute at NUS. In the past, he has held positions as a Professor of Finance at the Business School, Georgetown University. Before that, he was a senior financial economist in the research department at the Federal Reserve Bank of Chicago and a senior vice president and credit risk management executive in the Small Business Risk Solutions Group of Bank of America.

Yeow Hwee is an Assistant Professor in Economics at the Nanyang Technological University (NTU). He is also the Deputy Director of the Economic Growth Centre at NTU and the Assistant Honorary Secretary of the Economics Society of Singapore. Prior to his current appointment, he was a visiting postdoctoral scholar at the Stanford Graduate School of Business. An award-winning educator, he has previously taught economics in a junior college and in NUS. Yeow Hwee is a member of the Association Chartered Certified Accountant (ACCA), and a Chartered Financial Analyst (CFA) charterholder.

Part I

Introduction

1

Why Financial Literacy Matters

Financial literacy matters because it can improve our lives. As we are primarily responsible for our own financial security, it is important that we understand the consequences of our financial decisions. Whether we are paying with our credit cards, buying our first home, or preparing for retirement, good decision-making plays a crucial role in ensuring our financial well-being. After all, the choices we make today chart the path for tomorrow.

Nonetheless, making financial decisions is challenging. For instance, there are many factors to consider when deciding to rent or buy a house. We are required to synthesize and interpret a plethora of information, such as the future economic conditions, our expected salaries and other factors related to the housing market, including transaction costs, liquidity and volatility. These tasks involve the use of our memory, computational abilities, and financial sophistication.

With increasingly complex financial products and services, access to these products leave individuals with even more choices to make. An excessive number of choices can be detrimental. In a multifaceted financial environment, economic research has shown that households are making substantial errors in their financial decision-making. These mistakes are being repeated across time in different countries and across different age groups in their life cycle.

Although this might sound disheartening, there is still a way forward as we learn about the intricacies of household finance. It is our belief that financial education can be acquired by everyone and we invite you to join us on this journey. This is best done through the review of research in household financial management.

To kick things off, we will underscore the impact of financial education, which can help navigate challenges that influence us to make poor financial choices.

In this introductory chapter, we seek to accomplish two tasks. First, we will demonstrate how the lack of cognitive abilities is related to suboptimal decision making. Next, we focus on a critical aspect of financial literacy: compounding interest rate and how financial education can help to address this issue.

Through the research study "Cognitive Abilities and Household Financial Decision Making", by Sumit and Bhashkar Mazumder, we analyze the relationship between cognitive abilities and financial decision making.

Published in the *American Economic Journal: Applied Economics* in 2013, this article specifically looks into how quantitative reasoning (and not nonmathematical components) causes individuals to make mistakes.

The study centered around two mistakes that households in the United States made: the balance transfer mistake and rate changing mistake. The former is made by credit cardholders, while the latter is made by mortgage owners.

Balance Transfer Mistake

The balance transfer mistake occurs when households pay a higher interest rate using their credit cards when they transfer their credit card balance to a new card.

Interest is the amount that a lender charges a borrower. To a borrower, the interest rate is the cost of borrowing. To a lender, the interest rate is the rate of return. While we will cover credit cards in greater detail at Chapter 14, let us begin by exploring an example of poor financial decision making in the context of credit card balances.

When individuals are unable to pay off their credit card bills at the end of the billing cycle, they will end up with a credit card balance. This is the total amount of money that they owe to the credit card company.

In the United States, the average credit card interest rate is around 20 percent, which is much higher than other forms of debt. In an effort to attract a larger customer base, credit card companies occasionally offer promotions that include below-average annual percentage rates (APR) to encourage existing cardholders to switch to a new card.

The teaser rates are temporary and can range from six months to a year. While it is clearly beneficial to take up the offer as our cost of borrowing will be lowered, there is usually one trick. In fine print, we often have the following statement: "We apply your payments to balances with lower APRs first".

To understand how the trick works, let us consider the scenario where you have transferred existing balances from your previous credit card to a new one. As such, the new card, card B, has a lower teaser rate than your previous card, card A.

Given that payments are applied to balances with lower APRs, which card should you use to make new purchases? The answer is Card A! This is because payments that are made to card B are applied to the transferred payments (with lower interest rate) first. Payments can only be applied to new purchases on card B when the transferred balance is paid off.

Therefore, borrowers should use card A to make new purchases, and only use card B to make purchases when their transferred payment is fully paid off. In doing so, they can take advantage of the lower interest rates offered during the teaser rate period.

However, borrowers might not realize this optimal strategy immediately. In fact, there is evidence of credit cardholders who use the new card for "convenience" transactions.

This research study by Sumit and Bhashkar Mazumder examined how fast the cardholders managed to figure out the trick, otherwise referred to as the "eureka moment". It was estimated that one-third of all customers implemented the optimal strategy straight away and one-third of all customers never experienced a "eureka moment."

Rate Changing Mistake

We now discuss the rate changing mistake. The rate changing mistake occurs when borrowers do not estimate the value of their houses accurately, resulting in higher interest rates.

One key determinant of loan pricing (i.e., interest rate) is the loan-to-value (LTV) ratio. This is the loan amount as a percentage of the property's value. With a high LTV ratio, the loan is perceived as being more risky, which will lead to a higher interest rate being charged.

For the financial institution that is being examined in the research article, borrowers first estimate their home values before asking for a credit line. Based on the estimates of the borrowers, the loan will fall into three categories: LTV of 80 percent or less, 80 to 90 percent, and finally, 90 percent.

Subsequently, the financial institution will independently verify the house value and obtain another LTV measurement. Note that the LTV of the financial institution can be different from the borrower.

If the LTV of the borrower is lower than that of the financial institution, the borrower has overestimated the value of the house. Given the riskier nature of the loan, the financial institution's estimation will prevail. In other words, the borrower will be given a higher LTV, and subsequently, a higher interest rate.

Conversely, if the LTV of the borrower is higher than that of the financial institution, the borrower has underestimated the value of the house. In this case, it is better off for the bank to not make any changes to the borrower's estimated LTV and offer a higher interest rate.

We define a rate changing mistake to have occurred when the borrower's LTV category differs from the bank's LTV. It was found that making a rate changing mistake increases the APR of the interest by 269 percentage points for home equity loans. No small change!

Do you think that you will make these two mistakes under the same circumstances? Do spend some time to deliberate on your past decisions, and see if you can do better next time!

Now that we have delineated the two mistakes, let us prove that cognitive abilities play a pivotal role in influencing them.

Cognitive Ability

To measure cognitive abilities, the study leveraged on the American Services Vocational Aptitude Battery (ASVAB) Test provided by the U. S. military. The ASVAB is a comprehensive exam and has been used as part of the selection process for entering the military. The test contains both mathematical and verbal subcomponents.

By matching data of the ASVAB detailed test scores with administrative datasets of retail credit from a large U.S financial institution, it was revealed that individuals with higher math scores are less likely to make both the balance transfer mistake and the rate changing mistake.

Interestingly, non-mathematical skills, such as verbal subtests, do not influence the borrower to make these mistakes. This suggests that quantitative reasoning plays an instrumental role in helping households avoid making suboptimal decisions.

Nevertheless, while ASVAB scores are measurements of cognitive ability, it is crucial to acknowledge that these scores are not immutable and therefore not an indicator of innate intelligence. Rather, the scores reflect many factors, including financial education.

In light of the above, it is highly recommended that we get ourselves equipped with financial literacy skills, as they inevitably enhance our quantitative understanding. This will directly overcome our cognitive constraints.

Moving along, we will focus on an essential component of financial literacy: the study of compound interest.

Compound Interest

With a compounding interest rate, the interest will be charged on the interest that is being earned or borrowed. This is unlike a simple interest rate that only charges interest on the principal amount.

It is essential for us to understand the implications of compounding interest. As compound interest has the potential to expedite the growth of our earnings or borrowings over time, it can be a double-edged sword that helps to grow or worsen our finances.

To illustrate how compounding interest works, consider Figure 1.1. Here, we see that as time passes by, the gap between different interest rates widens. As a case in point, with an interest rate of 15 percent, a \$100 investment would accrue to \$1,400 after 20 years. However, if the interest rate is at 5 percent, we will get less than \$300. That is the power of compounding interest.

One simple way to see the significance of compounding interest is the Rule of 72. To estimate the time taken for an investment to double its value, we can divide 72 by the annual fixed interest rate. For example, if the annual interest rate is 8 percent, it would take nine years to double our investments or debts!

Conversely, we can also examine the interest rate that is required to double the investment value by dividing 72 by the given number of years. For instance, if we would like to double our investment in 10 years, the required interest rate would be 7.2 percent.

Compounding interest is particularly useful to help individuals reach their goals. Suppose you would like to have \$1 million upon retirement, what is the monthly savings amount required? This will depend on two factors: the rate of return and the number of years.

Figure 1.1: The Effect of Compounding Interest

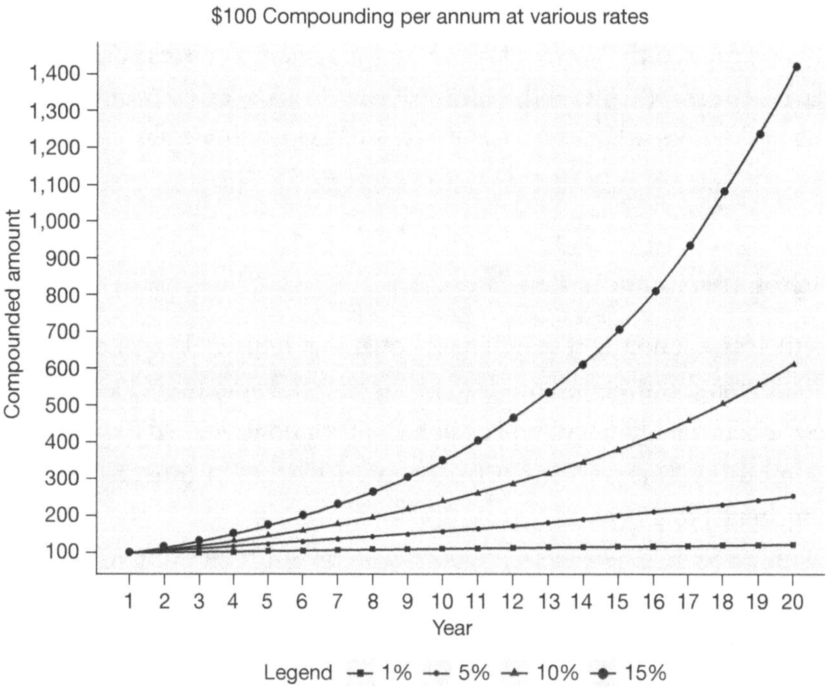

Table 1.1: Monthly Savings to Reach 1 Million

Rate of Return	Years			
	5	10	20	30
3%	15,470	7,160	3,050	1,720
5%	14,750	6,480	2,460	1,200
7%	14,050	5,850	1,970	820
9%	13,380	5,270	1,570	550

Table 1.1 shows how much you should set aside each month. The longer the time period and the higher the rate of return, the more achievable the goal will be. To illustrate, if you are enjoying a rate of return of 9 percent for 30 years, you will need to save $550 per month. In comparison, if you

are only saving for 5 years and experience a rate of return of 3 percent, you will need to save $15,470 each month!

As we can see, the power of compounding interest creates possibilities for savers to grow their wealth quickly. It pays to start saving from a young age. Due to its essential role in wealth creation, some might even proclaim compound interest to be the 8th wonder of the world.

A Field Experiment in China

Nonetheless, economic research has shown that households generally do not understand compound interest. Let us shift our attention to a research article "Financial Illiteracy and Pension Contributions: A Field Experiment of Compound Interest in China," written by one of our co-authors Changcheng Song.

Published in *The Review of Financial Studies* in 2020, Song relied on a field experiment in rural China to show that financial education helps to correct households' misunderstanding of compound interest.

The study is based on the New Rural Social Pension Insurance Program introduced by the Chinese government in 2009. Through this program, farmers 16 years or older (and who are not students) are given the opportunity to take part in a voluntary defined contribution plan.

In the county being studied, individuals are allowed to make a choice out of five annual contribution levels: 100, 200, 300, 400, or 500 Renminbi (RMB). This corresponds to 2 to 8 percent of their net income.

To encourage farmers to save for their retirement, the government provides subsidies that matches the contribution level. For instance, when the contribution level is 100 RMB, the government subsidy is 30 RMB per year. In comparison, when the contribution level is 500 RMB, the government subsidy is 50 RMB per year. Hence, individuals will enjoy more subsidies when they choose to have higher contribution levels.

The offered interest rate is based on the one-year policy rate of China's Central Bank, the People's Bank of China. When the experiment was conducted, the interest rate compounded annually was 2.5 percent.

To examine how financial education of compound interest impacts households' decisions, Song conducted a randomized control trial (RCT). This is a popular method that is used in scientific research to examine the causal impact of a policy change.

During an RCT, individuals are randomly assigned to treatment and control groups. While the treatment groups are exposed to the intervention being studied, no intervention is provided to the control group. Subsequently, through the analysis of outcomes between the treatment and control groups, researchers can establish whether the intervention has a causal effect.

In this study, the farmers are randomized into three groups: control, calculation and education.

For the control group, no additional information was given. For the calculation group, the author calculated the expected benefit of pension to the farmers. For the education group, the author taught the farmers the importance of compound interest, as well as the calculations of the expected benefit of pension. Additionally, through the provision of financial education, misunderstandings of compound interest were corrected.

The results are striking. Pension contributions increased starkly by 40 percent in groups that were educated about compound interest. Furthermore, it was found that financial education can partly correct households' misunderstanding of compound interest. The impact was lower for individuals who received calculations of the compounding interest in contrast to those who received education.

Using a lifecycle economic model, the author estimated that when the misunderstanding of compound interest is removed, consumers' lifetime utility could increase by 10 percent. Consequently, these findings reveal the substantial impact of financial literacy.

Key Takeaways

Through the studies above, we have highlighted the value of financial literacy. Our hope is that this will inspire you to learn more about the different aspects of financial education and empower you to make better financial choices.

We have also drawn your attention to a few common mistakes made by households, such as the balance transfer and rate changing mistake. While this is just the tip of the iceberg, it is crucial to be mindful of our financial decisions. As each (financial) action has a (financial) consequence, we need to be wary of the significance of all our decisions.

Moreover, we have emphasized on the power of compounding. Through the compounding effect, our assets have the potential to grow exponentially. Hence, it is paramount to save and invest as early as possible. On the other hand, when our debts are being compounded, they will increase sharply.

In light of this, compounding could be our friend or foe, best described by Albert Einstein as follows: "He who understand earns it; he who doesn't, pays for it."

2

Understanding Behavioral Biases

Why do we tend to make financial mistakes? Besides cognitive abilities, financial mistakes can also be attributed to behavioral biases, which unconsciously influence our decision making processes.

Everyday, we are compelled to make multiple micro-decisions with an abundance of options. For instance, Amazon US sells more than 606 million products! How do we choose from there?

To manage the increasing amount of information that we process daily, we have developed mental shortcuts or rules of thumb. Known as "heuristics" in the academic literature, these approaches alleviate the mental effort required for decision-making. While heuristics help us make decisions quickly, they often contribute to behavioral biases.

The examination of these biases has been undertaken in the field of behavioral economics, which combines principles from economics and psychology. By examining how individuals' biases are shaped by their environment and emotions, we can have a better understanding of how individuals make decisions.

In this chapter, we will set the stage for the remaining of the book by providing an overview of behavioral biases. Thereafter, we will relate to the role of behavioral biases in the remaining chapters involving consumption, investment, housing and even retirement.

Heuristics

Let's begin by discussing heuristics. There are different types of heuristics including representativeness, anchoring, and availability.

The representativeness heuristic is a mental shortcut that we use to judge how likely an event will occur. As individuals mix up the degree of similarity with the probability of an outcome, they believe that similar events are more closely correlated than they actually are.

One example is the Gambler's Fallacy. Also known as the Monte Carlo fallacy due to its origins from the Monte Carlo Casino, gamblers have the tendency to believe that if an event occurs more often than normal during the past, it would be less likely to happen in the future. Consider a coin toss. The Gambler's Fallacy suggests that if a coin is historically producing "heads" when being flipped, gamblers believe that the probability of coming up with "tails" in the future will increase.

Have you ever experienced this yourself? Unfortunately, this perception is statistically incorrect. As long as the coin flips are statistically independent of one another, the probability does not change!

Next, we turn our attention to the anchoring heuristic, which occurs when we focus on only one specific information (or anchor). By relying too much on one piece of information (such as the first piece of information we are exposed to), it could influence our entire decision-making process.

This includes the use of a fixed reference point in evaluating investments. For example, individuals may delay the selling of their investment because current market prices are lower than the price they had purchased it at. Even if the market is trending downward, we may still hold the investment despite the rational response to sell the investment immediately and cut losses.

Finally, we have the availability heuristic, which is a rule of thumb that is based on information that is readily available to individuals, based on the impact of an event, or its recency. The use of heuristics can often lead to cognitive biases, swaying us toward making suboptimal decisions. For example, if a person had lost his job during an economic boom, he might become more pessimistic about the economy. Hence, the person may halt his investments, even though these investment opportunities may have the potential to bring in good yield.

We will look at a few examples of behavioral biases globally. From America to Europe to Asia, we got you covered.

Mental Accounting

Behavioral biases in individuals have the tendency to impact individuals' ability to make optimal decisions. Consider mental accounting, a concept developed by Richard Thaler, the 2017 recipient of the Nobel Memorial Prize in Economic Sciences.

In mental accounting, individuals sort their funds into separate accounts, which affects the way they spend and repay borrowings. As they classify money differently based on their subjective criteria, it could lead to counterproductive decisions.

Mental accounting suggests that individuals do not regard money as fungibles. Instead, money is categorized into preset mental accounts determined by the individuals. For instance, when they experience an increase in income, they could choose to keep the money for their nest egg instead of paying off credit card debt in the short run.

But in our view, this is counterproductive. If households choose to pay off their credit card debt first, they will have more money for retirement as they do not need to pay additional interest accrued on credit card debt.

We can visualize mental accounting using Figure 2.1. Instead of seeing all our assets as one bucket, we divide them into different buckets, say bank deposits, housing, and credit cards.

Financial inflows and outflows are then considered in each separate bucket. When we allocate our money into the different mental accounts, money is no longer fungible. Consequently, we seek to optimize our decision in each bucket, rather than all our assets. This affects our spending and saving decisions as a whole as mental accounting prevents us from freely moving funds between the different accounts.

Figure 2.1: Mental Accounting as Buckets

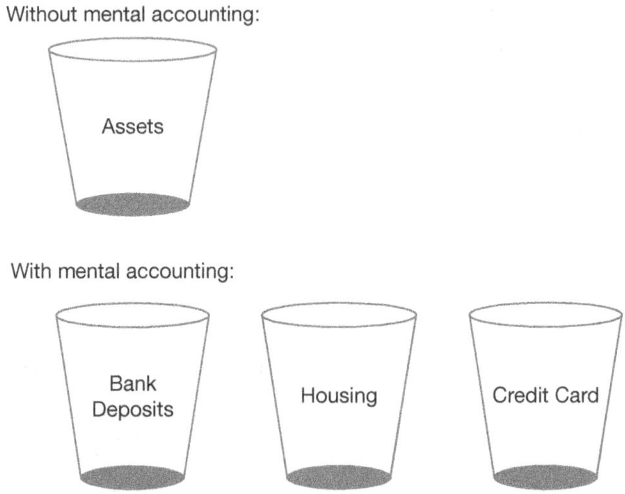

Let us now explore some evidence of mental accounting in the real world. We begin by looking at the gasoline market in the U.S. In a research study by Justine Hastings and Jesse Shapiro titled "Fungibility and Consumer Choice: Evidence from Commodity Price Shocks" that appeared in *The Quarterly Journal of Economics* in 2013, the authors established that U.S. households do not treat gasoline money as fungible with other income.

In general, there are three grades of gasoline in the U.S: regular, mid-grade, and premium. These grades of gasoline are determined by the acceptable octane levels, with regular gasoline having the least octane levels (85–88), and premium the highest (more than 90).

The grades differ in price and perceived quality. The higher the octane level, the higher the gasoline's combustion temperature, which can potentially increase horsepower of the vehicle. Nonetheless, it is unclear whether the buyer really needs it, given that high-octane gasoline is generally perceived as a luxury good, and most vehicles do not require such high performance grades.

How do consumers respond to changes in gasoline prices? The findings of the study indicated that there is an inverse relationship between gasoline prices and quality choice. Households turn to gasoline of lower quality when gasoline prices increase. This means that households switch to different grades of gasoline when prices of gasoline change.

Using transaction levels from a large U.S. grocery retailer with gasoline stations on site between January 2006 and March 2008, Hastings and Shapiro further looked into households' spending decisions and proved that the relationship between gasoline prices and choice of gasoline grade was not caused by changes in income.

For instance, during the global financial crisis in 2008, households experienced a fall in income, resulting in a fall in consumption spending. Overall prices in the economy plummeted, including gasoline prices. But when faced with falling gasoline prices, households ended up purchasing gasoline of better quality!

In other words, when faced with a fall in income, households choose to reduce their spending on different goods and services. But they elect to consume better-quality gasoline. Is it rational to sacrifice spending on food in order to obtain higher quality gasoline?

This signifies that households do not treat money as fungible and provides evidence of mental accounting in consumption. In particular, households maintain a mental budget for "gasoline." When there are changes in prices of the gasoline, they will change the quality of the gasoline such that the total spending for gasoline remains unchanged.

Nonetheless, we can see that this is not ideal. We would be better off if we did not improve the quality of our gasoline during economic downturns. This would allow us to spend more on other essentials, such as food!

Sunk Cost Fallacy

We now consider another behavioral bias: the Sunk Cost Fallacy. Sunk costs are costs that have already been incurred and should have no bearing on our future decisions. However, there is evidence that the costs that we have incurred in the past could impact our future decisions.

In our illustration, we will stick to the vehicles market. But this time, we will move on from the United States to Singapore. Singapore has one of the world's costliest vehicles markets. As an illustration, in 2022, a Toyota Camry costs about US$25,000 in the United States but around US$150,000 in Singapore. In other words, for the price of 1 Toyota Camry in Singapore, we can purchase 6 cars in the United States!

This can be traced back to the car policies in Singapore. As a small and densely populated city-state, the Singapore government has imposed many measures to tackle traffic congestion.

One way is through the introduction of the vehicle quota system. Before we can own a vehicle in Singapore, we are required to obtain a permit, known as the Certificate of Entitlement (COE). This certificate entitles us to use a vehicle on the road, and expires after 10 years.

The price (or premium) of the COE is one of the main contributing factors to the high car prices, as dealers usually include the COE prices when setting the selling price. In any case, we cannot drive a car without a COE.

The price of the COE is driven by market forces. While the Singapore government sets the number of permits, the prices are ultimately determined by demand forces as interested car buyers bid for the COE (usually through their dealers).

Figure 2.2 presents the COE prices of large cars (also known as Category B) in Singapore over the last 10 years. There have been large fluctuations with a particularly sharp increase in the past few years. As of 2022, COE prices exceeded S$100,000 (US$75,000).

How would changes in COE prices and consequently car prices impact an individual's driving behavior? This has been identified in a 2017 *Management Science* article "Sunk Cost Fallacy in Driving the World's Costliest Car" by Teck Hua Ho, Ivan Png, and Sadat Reza.

Echoing the sunk cost hypothesis, the authors discovered that households indeed drive more when car prices are higher. Although car prices are sunk costs, individuals' driving activity change in respond to car prices. Furthermore, car usage also decreased faster as the age of the car increased. The findings can be explained by the influence of mental accounting on car costs.

Figure 2.2: COE Prices

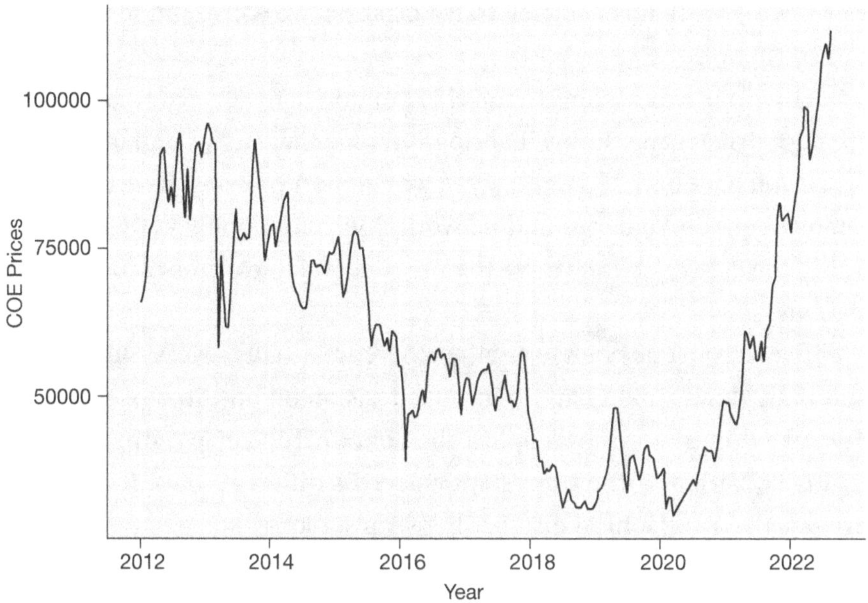

Source: Land Transport Authority, Singapore

Based on the authors' estimates from January 2009 to January 2013, it was revealed that the increase in sunk cost is related to an increase in car usage by 5.6 percent. This is equivalent to 86 km per month.

Status Quo Bias

Finally, we shift gears and examine the status quo bias. Status quo bias occurs when individuals prefer to let things remain unchanged. Due to inertia, they stick to default mental modes and do not wish to change (even though it is beneficial for them to change to other alternatives).

Status quo bias can be related to many reasons, such as individuals choosing to free up mental resources for other tasks when they are overwhelmed by the options available. Besides, individuals are averse to making losses and would prefer the status quo.

There has been much evidence of status quo bias in the real world. Continuing with our theme on transportation, we will examine train/rail transportation.

This time, we are going to travel to London in the United Kingdom: to see how strikes cause individuals to overcome their status quo bias.

If you have been to London, you would most probably have taken the famous London Underground network. More commonly known as "the Tube," the network covers more than 11 different lines across 270 different stations.

To get from one point to another, there are usually several alternatives and individuals would have to make a decision on how to move around. To make things more challenging, the London Tube map only shows the relative position of the train stations across different lines. It does not provide the geographical distance between stations.

Consequently, individuals have a distorted view of the map, and they might have the wrong impression of the actual distance between stations.

This has been highlighted in a 2017 research article in *The Quarterly Journal of Economics* by Shaun Larcom, Ferdinand Rauch, and Tim Willems. Titled "The Benefits of Forced Experimentation: Striking Evidence from the London Underground Network," the authors showed that a large proportion of commuters in the London Underground do not travel according to their optimal route.

However, the optimality of these routes was questioned when strikes in the United Kingdom created major transportation disruptions that compelled commuters to explore new routes.

On February 5 and 6, 2014, strikes in the London Underground network subjected many stations to closure. This forced individuals to experiment and find alternative paths to travel.

What happened when the stations reopened? Did these individuals go back to their usual commuting route? Or did they stick to the new routes?

According to the findings, many commuters preferred their new routes! When the commuters are forced to experiment with new routes due to the strikes, it actually influenced their future decisions.

This implies that their usual route is suboptimal (otherwise they would have gone back to their original route).

Furthermore, the impact is larger for commuters in areas where the Underground map is more distorted, providing evidence that they have misunderstood the map previously. Due to imperfect information, commuters might have made the wrong decision previously.

Hence, these commuters underestimated the value of experimentation as they relied on the status quo.

Key Takeaways

We have introduced the concept of behavioral biases in this chapter. Using different examples in the transportation market, we showed that households often rely on basic judgments to make decisions. While this may seem intuitive at times, it often resulted in worse outcomes.

The next step is to recognize how to prevent suboptimal decisions. In the case of mental accounting, we ought to acknowledge that money is fungible. After all, a dollar is a dollar. Thus, it is highly advisable that we do not evaluate the worth of money differently according to our own personal subjective standards.

When encountering sunk costs, it is useful to proactively recognize that our decisions are influenced by already incurred expenses. Possessing this awareness allows us to avoid spending more to justify these sunk costs. At the end of the day, sunk costs are irrecoverable. It is what we do next that matters.

To overcome the status quo bias, accepting its existence and embracing change is the way forward. When was the last time you experimented with something new? We hope this book will give you the impetus to do something different with your financial planning!

3

Primer to Inflation

Financial literacy also means understanding how the macroeconomy works. This includes our beliefs about inflation in our country.

Inflation refers to an increase in the general price level of an economy. In recent years, there has been an increase in inflation globally. Figure 3.1 shows changes in inflation rates across three countries: Japan, the United Kingdom and the United States from 2015 to 2022.

Evidently, there are huge fluctuations in the inflation rate, which is calculated based on the changes in the consumer price index (CPI). CPI refers to a broad basket of goods and services that is representative of consumer spending. Based on a typical household in the country, the basket includes a wide range of products such as food, housing, clothing and transportation.

An inflation rate of 5 percent will suggest that on average, the prices of the representative basket of goods and services have increased by 5 percent. In comparison, when there is a negative inflation rate, this implies that deflation has taken place, and that things are cheaper than before.

Before we begin our discussion, let us first ask you a hypothetical question. Will you be better off if your income doubles? Intuitively, you will say "Yes!" without any hesitation. But the answer really depends on how much prices have increased. If prices have more than doubled, you will be worse off, as you are able to purchase lesser goods and services.

Figure 3.1: Inflation Rate Across Countries

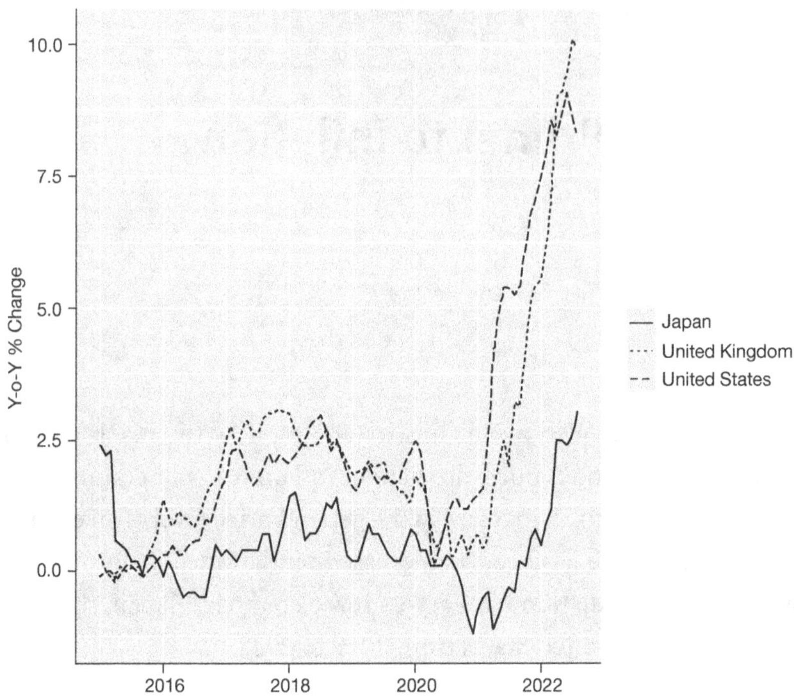

Source: World Bank

Thus, inflation plays a huge role in our well-being as it affects our purchasing power. With an increase in inflation, things become more expensive. As a result, we can purchase lesser goods with the same amount of money, driving up our cost of living.

In the same vein, this means that money loses value when there is inflation. Hence, there is a direct impact on our financial returns.

Money Illusion

To better understand the impact of inflation, let us distinguish between the concepts of real and nominal returns.

Unlike nominal returns, real returns refer to the percentage of profit that is being earned on an investment, after considering inflation.

Mathematically, we have the following: Real Rate of Return = Nominal Rate of Return – Inflation Rate

Consequently, real returns allow us to take into account the actual purchasing power of our money across time. For the purpose of clarity, it will be beneficial to conduct a simple numerical exercise.

To illustrate, if our bank deposits pay a nominal rate of 1 percent, and the inflation rate is 3 percent, our real rate of return will be −2 percent. This means that we have a negative real rate of return and we will end up affording lesser goods and services.

However, many individuals seem to be unaware of this. Economic studies have shown that individuals have the propensity to view their income and wealth in nominal terms, rather than in real terms. This is known as money illusion.

Let us delve into a study by Eldar Shafir, Peter Diamond, and Amos Tversky which was published in *The Quarterly Journal of Economics* in 1997. Titled "Money Illusion," the authors reviewed several survey questions to elicit individuals' responses toward money illusion.

We will now follow one question that is highlighted in this study. The problem is stated as follows:

> *"Suppose Adam, Ben, and Carl each received an inheritance of $200,000, and each used it immediately to purchase a house. Suppose that each of them sold the house a year after buying it. Economic conditions, however, were different in each case:*
>
> - *When Adam owned the house, there was a 25% deflation—the prices of all goods and services decreased by approximately 25%. A year after Adam bought the house, he sold it for $154,000 (23% less than he paid).*
> - *When Ben owned the house, there was no inflation or deflation—prices had not changed significantly during that year. He sold the house for $198,000 (1% less than he paid for it).*

- *When Carl owned the house, there was a 25% inflation—all prices increased by approximately 25%. A year after he bought the house, Carl sold it for $246,000 (23% more than he paid).*

Please rank Adam, Ben, and Carl in terms of the success of their house-transactions."

Who do you think got the best deal? The authors asked this question to 431 respondents. It turns out that the majority thought that Carl got the better deal, and Adam got the worst deal. Do you agree with them?

We hope not. In real terms, this is not true. When we consider purchasing power, Adam was better off. In fact, he was the only one that made a profit (in real terms). Nonetheless, the majority believed that Carl had a better deal as he received the highest amount of dollars (in nominal terms).

Inflation Expectations and Personal Experiences

Once we acknowledge the significance of inflation, it becomes crucial to form our own inflation expectations. However, this is not an easy task, as most of us are swayed by our personal experiences. Allow us to highlight one case study.

Together with Song, Sumit and Yeow Hwee seek to understand the drivers of households' inflation expectations in Singapore. In the article "Inflation Expectations of Households and the Upgrading Channel," that was published in the *Journal of Monetary Economics* in 2022, we find that personal experiences in the form of consumption upgrading is critical in influencing households' inflation expectations.

Through the implementation of a survey experiment, we show how exposure to prices of different types of goods could influence households' inflation expectations. The information treatments are presented in Table 3.1.

For Treatment 1, we provide information of Wall's Ice Cream in 2009 and 2019. For Treatment 2, we provide information of Wall's Ice Cream in

Table 3.1: Information Treatments

	2009	**2019**	**2019**
Treatment 1	$5 Wall's Ice Cream	$6 Wall's Ice Cream	
Treatment 2	$5 Wall's Ice Cream	$14.45 Häagen-Dazs Ice Cream	
Treatment 3	$5 Wall's Ice Cream	$6 Wall's Ice Cream	$14.45 Häagen-Dazs Ice Cream

2009 and Häagen-Dazs Ice Cream in 2019. For Treatment 3, we provide information of Wall's Ice Cream in 2009 and 2019, as well as Häagen-Dazs Ice Cream in 2019.

Both Wall's Ice Cream and Häagen-Dazs Ice Cream are well-known ice cream brands. However, Häagen-Dazs Ice Cream is relatively more expensive per unit weight (and is regarded to be of higher quality). While Wall's seeks to cater to the mass market, Häagen-Dazs positions itself as a premium brand.[1]

In our experiment, the respondents in Treatment 2 and Treatment 3 reported higher inflation expectations than Treatment 1. This suggests that changes in product variety and product replacement have the potential to influence households' inflation expectations. As households are exposed to consumption upgrading in Treatment 2 and Treatment 3, they reported higher inflation expectations due to the different type of goods that they consume.

Besides grocery shopping, there are also many other possible factors that shape our inflation expectations. Among these include our life experiences, our understanding of economic policies, and the media. Therefore, it is essential for us to stay cognizant of the different factors that could impact our individual beliefs of the economy.

[1] A caveat. We love both Wall's and Häagen-Dazs Ice Cream.

In order to mitigate inflation's impact, we can turn to assets that have historically yielded returns surpassing inflation. Such assets include commodities such as gold or real estate. In addition, we could turn to assets that directly adjust their value with inflation.

Treasury Inflation-Protected Securities

One example in the United States is the treasury inflation-protected securities (TIPS). Similar to a treasury bond, TIPS is a form of borrowing from the government. There is a principal amount, fixed interest rate, and tenure (i.e., time to maturity).

But TIPS has an advantage: it directly protects us from inflation. According to the CPI, the principal of TIPS increases with inflation and conversely, decreases with deflation.

With TIPS, we will get our interest twice a year. While the rate is fixed, it is being applied to the adjusted principal. Consequently, when the principal is higher, we will enjoy higher interest payments too.

Consider the following illustration in Table 3.2. Suppose we have two bonds (normal bond and TIPS), with a nominal interest rate of 2 percent and a bond maturity period of 10 years.

Table 3.2: Bond Payments

(a) Normal bond

Assume $r = 2\%$ and bond maturity period of 10 years

Principal	Interest Rate	Interest Paid to You
10,000	2%	200

(b) TIPS

Assume $r = 2\%$ and bond maturity period of 10 years

Principal	Adjusted Principal	Interest Rate	Inflation	Interest Paid to You
10,000	10,100	2%	1%	202

In both cases, the principal amount is $10,000. With normal bonds, we will get an annual interest of $200. On the other hand, we will obtain $202 with TIPS as the principal has increased due to inflation.

Hence, TIPS offer us higher interest payments due to inflation. Moreover, upon maturity, we will get back our principal or adjusted principal (whichever is higher). This is a good deal, isn't it? You would think that TIPS would be very popular among households. Unfortunately, we observe the opposite.

The TIPS market is small and illiquid. The fraction of TIPS relative to the total amount of marketable treasuries has never exceeded 11 percent during the past two decades. This is similar in other countries, such as France and Italy, which offer inflation-protected securities.

Besides, recent work has indicated that Treasury bonds are always overvalued as compared to TIPS!

This is highlighted in a 2014 *The Journal of Finance* study by Matthias Fleckenstein, Francis Longstaff, and Hanno Lustig, titled "The TIPS-Treasury Bond Puzzle." In this study, the authors match the cash flows of both bonds and discovered that prices of Treasury bonds exceed that of TIPS by more than 20 percentage.

It is no small amount. In fact, the authors established that the mispricing between TIPS and Treasury bonds has exceeded US$56 billion! Many studies have since tried to explain the reasons for this mispricing and liquidity puzzles of TIPS.

What are some potential limitations of TIPS? One is its reliance on the CPI. As mentioned earlier, the CPI is based on a representative basket of goods. Thus, it might not fully reflect the inflation experienced by the individual.

Furthermore, while Treasury bonds do not explicitly adjust for inflation, changes in inflation expectations could impact the prices of Treasury bonds as well. A higher inflation expectation would reduce the demand for Treasury bonds, driving down prices and increasing returns. Consequently, some individuals would prefer to hold Treasury bonds, which are more liquid (and tradable).

Notwithstanding the above, it is timely for us to introduce this financial instrument, especially during periods of high inflation volatility. There exists a tool that directly helps us to hedge inflation.

Monetary Policy

Finally, we would like to make a note about monetary policy. In general, the primary objective of central banks globally is to maintain price stability by controlling inflation.

To combat high inflation rate, they rely on monetary policy tools, such as interest rates. When there is high inflation, central banks tend to increase the interest rate so as to increase the cost of borrowing. Commonly known as a contractionary monetary policy, this is intended to reduce the aggregate demand for all goods and services and slow down price changes.

Figure 3.2 presents the Federal Funds Rate in the U.S from 1963 to May 2023. Set by the Federal Reserve, the U.S. central bank, this is the targeted interest rate in which U.S. banks can borrow from one another. Evidently, the Federal Funds Rate has undergone many changes over the past 60 years.

During the early 1980s, the central bank aimed to tackle inflation by raising the Federal Funds Rate beyond 15 percent. Nonetheless, interest rates have remained at a low level since the Global Financial Crisis in 2008 as the focus shifted toward promoting economic growth in a low inflationary setting. As the economy moves across different cycles, inflation will not remain low forever. Thus, an increase in inflation in the future suggests that there could be further increase in interest rates.[2]

A hike in interest rate would have ramifications for households' borrowing. While we would have a detailed discussion about borrowing in Part IV of this book, we would like to emphasize here that changes in

[2] At the point of publishing this book, global inflation has reached around 9 percent in 2022. To combat inflation, central banks worldwide have responded by increasing interest rate. The change can be fast and furious. From near zero in March 2022, the Federal Funds Rate has increased to between 5% and 5.25% in May 2022.

Figure 3.2: Federal Funds Rate

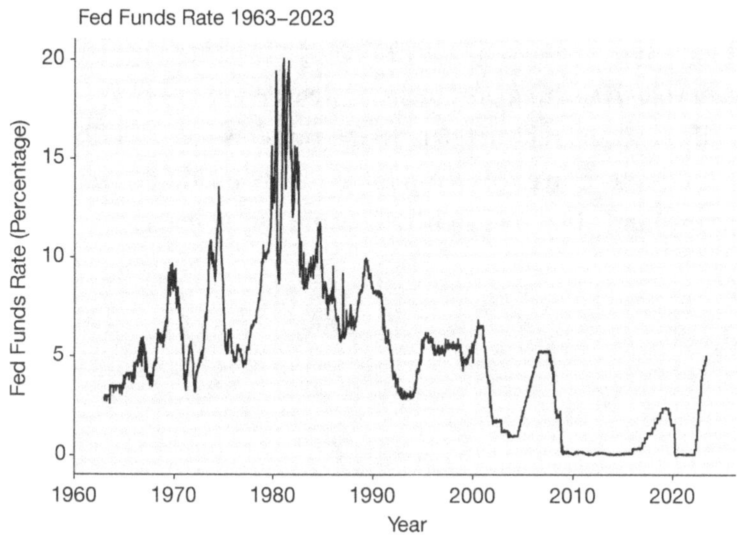

inflation rate could potentially result in monetary policymakers to respond. When central banks increase interest rates, our borrowing costs would directly increase as well.

Key Takeaways

Inflation affects our standard of living. However, blinded by money illusion, individuals end up focusing on nominal values instead of real returns.

Consequently, when planning our finances, it is crucial to be able to distinguish between real and nominal returns. We do not want inflation to erode away the real returns of our savings, which we have painstakingly accumulated over the years.

There are several things that we can do to better prepare ourselves for inflation. One way is to stay informed by keeping abreast of macroeconomic news. In this context, we should regularly read financial news and keep up to date with various economic indicators related to prices. These data are readily available from most government websites and financial news platforms.

In addition, we should regularly monitor government initiatives. This provides us an insight on how the economy is doing. As we will discuss in the later chapters, changes in government policies and regulations play a significant role in shaping our financial well-being.

Finally, we could rely on financial instruments such as TIPS which are designed to protect investors from inflation. By including assets that can hedge against inflation, we can better secure our nest egg.

4

Getting Started with Financial Planning

In this chapter, we are going to talk about financial planning. As Benjamin Franklin once said, "By failing to prepare, you are preparing to fail." This includes preparing for your own finances too.

You are ultimately responsible for your own actions. Just like going for exams, only with proper preparation can we set ourselves up for financial success.

We believe that financial planning should be holistic in nature. It requires lifestyle changes and the support of your family and loved ones. Above all, this will provide you with the impetus to persevere and execute your plans.

This will also make your long-term goals more salient, ameliorating the short-term mindset prevalent in younger adults. In doing so, you can better understand your own needs, and mitigate the mistakes and behavioral biases that we would address in this book.

To initiate your financial planning journey, we would like to outline 4 key steps that you may wish to consider.

Step 1: Know Our Current Financial Status

The first step in financial planning is to ascertain our current financial status. Specifically, we should have a clear understanding of our personal balance sheet and income statement. You may have come across the balance sheets and income statements of corporations, but do you know about the balance sheets and income statements of households?

Just like firms, households have their own balance sheets which include assets and liabilities. Assets are resources owned by an individual, while liabilities are obligations that an individual has. Households' assets typically comprise of cash, bank deposits, financial assets (such as equities and bonds), as well as physical assets (such as property and gold). On the other hand, households' liabilities refer to debts, such as student loans, housing loans, or credit card debts.

Table 4.1 shows an example of a typical household balance sheet for an individual.

Table 4.1: A Typical Household Balance Sheet for an Individual

Assets	Liabilities
Cash: $10,000	Housing loan: $300,000
Bank deposits: $20,000	Credit card debt: $150,000
Stocks: $30,000	
Property: $500,000	

Our household balance sheet provides us with a comprehensive snapshot of our financial position. Through organizing our financial information systematically, we can enhance the quality of our decision-making, as demonstrated throughout the remainder of this book.

A clear grasp of our household balance sheet also helps us set realistic financial goals, which brings us to the next point. If our liabilities are larger than our assets, how do we plan to pay off our liabilities?

To do so, we would turn to our "income statement," which refers to the difference between the inflows that we receive (such as salary, bonuses, or rental income) as well as the expenses that we incur.

Would our current and future income flows be able to pay off our liabilities? This would help us decide on our financial goals.

Step 2: Determine Our Life Cycle Consumption

Next, we should figure out which stage of life we belong to and decide how much we intend to consume throughout our lifetime. By taking these factors into account, we can establish our financial objectives by assessing the required savings or borrowing amount today.

How would you like your living standards to be across different stages in your life? The Life Cycle Hypothesis pioneered by Franco Modigliani, the 1985 recipient of the Nobel Memorial Prize in Economic Sciences, suggests that households seek to smooth their consumption spending over their entire lifetime.

Figure 4.1 presents the Life Cycle Hypothesis. We note that the income level curve has an inverse U shape. This is because as one gets older, our income increases, before reaching a peak. Thereafter, our income falls when we enter into our retirement.

To smooth out our consumption, that is, for consumption to remain constant throughout our lifetime, we need to spend our savings at the start and end of our lives while saving more at the peak of our careers.

Figure 4.1: The Life Cycle Hypothesis

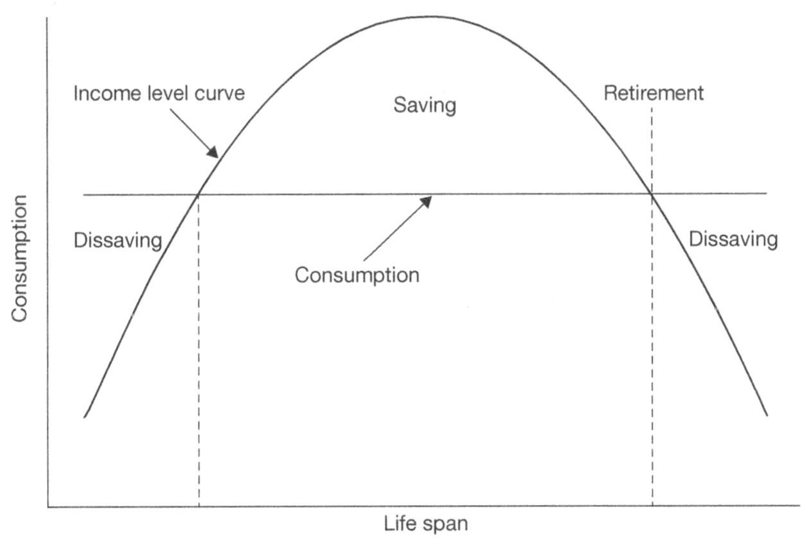

Accordingly, a young adult who has just started working might have different financial needs from an individual that is approaching retirement. In this case, knowing when to save more or less in accordance with our financial life cycle is of paramount importance.

Particularly, we should recognize that saving during our working years is essential for financing our retirement. Only by accumulating our savings throughout our careers will we have sufficient money to sustain our lifestyles in later years when we have stopped working.

Step 3: Set Our Budget and Goals

To reach our goals, we need a budget. A budget is a spending plan that considers both current and future income and expenses. There are many benefits of having a budget.

At the outset, budgeting allows households to methodically track their income and expenses, providing a thorough understanding of their financial capability. Having a holistic view of their entire financial portfolio will further assist households to steer clear of the issues related to mental accounting mentioned earlier.

For instance, households can keep track of different expenses and debt repayment progress, thus helping them find the most optimal way to reduce their obligations across different borrowings. This encourages them to pivot toward loans with lower interest rates.

Besides, this will reduce the over-indebtedness of households. Over-indebtedness occurs when households overspend and end up with debts which they are unable to repay.

To avoid common mistakes in preparing their budgets, households can make use of readily available financial management tools. One example is to make use of online calculators to estimate the recommended debt-to-income ratio, before borrowing money.

With clear rules and guidelines, the likelihood of being subjected to behavioral biases, such as being overly confident of their income and expenditure, is significantly reduced.

We encourage individuals to organize their finances using the SMART goals. This refers to goals that are Specific, Measurable, Achievable, Relevant, and Time-Bound.

Let's examine the scenario of debt repayment. It is evident that plans will fall short if they are not SMART. For instance, having a generic goal such as "I will pay my debt on time", or having an unrealistic goal such as devoting the entire salary toward loans repayments, is bound to fail.

A SMART goal in debt repayment will provide clarity and establish accountability. Here's an illustration of a SMART goal: "Over the next 12 months, I will allocate $500 each month towards debt repayment. Furthermore, this amount constitutes approximately 70 percent of my savings after covering daily expenses, ensuring a safety net."

Step 4: Implement Our Goals

Having defined our goals, the question now arises: How do we attain them? Numerous strategies can serve as sources of motivation to help us achieve our goals. Among them, a simple yet powerful technique involves setting reminders.

Let us now direct our focus to a study by Dean Karlan, Margaret McConnell, Sendhil Mullainathan, and Jonathan Zinman. The title of the article is "Getting to the Top of Mind: How Reminders Increase Savings," which appeared in *Management Science* in 2016.

By conducting field experiments, the authors of this study effectively illustrated the positive impact of reminders on boosting savings. This occurred across different settings, in three different banks in the Philippines, Bolivia and Peru.

To begin with, we have First Valley Bank, a for-profit bank that operates in Western Mindanao, Philippines. With the introduction of a new Gihandom (Dream) Savings product, clients are welcomed to set their own commitment amount and commitment end date. The account is opened with a minimum deposit of US$2.50, and there is no subsequent fixed schedule to meet.

Next, we have Ecofuturo, another for-profit bank in Bolivia. Through a product known as Ecoaguinaldo, Ecofuturo aims to support self employed clients in saving money all year round for their individual year-end pay outs. The term "Ecoaguinaldo" is derived from the word "Aguinaldo", which refers to the year-end bonus that employers are obligated to provide to salaried employees in Bolivia.

Finally, we have Caja de Ica, a government-owned bank in Peru. Through a new product called Plan Ahorro ("Savings Plan"), clients would have to set a commitment end date, a commitment amount to deposit each month, and a specific goal to achieve.

Reminders for the savings goal were provided in different ways. For the banks in the Philippines and Bolivia, random text message reminders to randomly picked individuals were provided. For the bank in Peru, random letters were sent.

With the randomly assigned reminders to their clients, it was found that 20 percent of individuals in the Philippines, 43 percent of individuals in Bolivia, and 3 percent of individuals in Peru exceeded their savings commitments. Therefore, having reminders help, albeit to varying extents.

The authors relate these findings to the limited attention span of households. It is therefore highly advisable for us to have constant checks (such as reminders) so that we can stay vigilant and overcome limited attention, staying focused on our financial goals.

Leveraging on Technology

Looking forward, there are many ways to support our financial planning. One way is by adopting financial technology (FinTech). In a recent article that Sumit and Yeow Hwee wrote, "FinTech and Household Finance: A Review of the Empirical Literature,"[3] we have underscored how

[3] We are happy to share that our paper won the Emerald Literati Awards for Outstanding Paper in 2021, and invite readers to read the research article to have an in depth overview of how FinTech can impact the entire household balance sheet in different ways.

FinTech has transformed the lives of individuals, by equipping them with the necessary tools to manage their consumption, savings, and investments.

According to the International Monetary Fund's Global Financial Stability Report in April 2022, FinTech firms are growing in systemic importance as they offer many financial services, such as lending, payments, insurance, and asset management.

In their operations, FinTech firms work virtually and rely on nontraditional metrics (such as mobile footprints). With lower costs, quicker turnaround times, and higher agility, these companies have managed to come up with creative and customized solutions for individuals.

Leveraging on their innovative tools and large database, we can therefore enlist the help of FinTech companies in all the different stages of our financial planning journey.

In the age of digital payments, we already have the necessary instruments to easily monitor our spending habits and stay informed of our budget balances. For instance, we can make use of expense trackers that track our spending across time.

For a more holistic view of our financial position, we can also make use of financial account aggregators to see all our accounts in one place. By having a consolidated view of our individual accounts, we can enhance our decision-making process and reduce the influence of our behavioral biases.

To manage status quo bias, individuals could make use of reminders through these financial applications that provide them with the relevant information, allaying their fears of making wrong decisions.

We can also make use of goal-based savings and goal-based investing to overcome inertia and mental accounting. In all, these habits could support us to make optimal decisions.

Key Takeaways

To summarize, we have proposed 4 steps that can be employed in managing our finances.

1. Know our current financial status
   – It is imperative to unpack our individual balance sheet and income statement.
2. Determine our life cycle consumption
   – We ought to establish lifetime goals and ascertain our current life cycle stage.
3. Set our budget and goals
   – Goals should be SMART (Specific, Measurable, Achievable, Relevant, and Time-Bound).
4. Implement our goals
   – In order to achieve our objectives, we can rely on external help such as reminders and harness the potential of technology.

As we conclude the introductory portion of this book, we would like to end off with an analogy. We see household financial management as analogous to planting a tree. While we may plant the seeds today, we can only enjoy the shade many years down the road. And as the proverb goes, "The best time to plant a tree was 20 years ago. The next best time is now." It is time for you to take the first step now.

Part II

Savings

5

Intertemporal Choices

In Part II of this book, we would like to discuss about savings. We are sure that you recognize the importance of savings.

Savings provide us with security in our life and we need to save for many reasons. For instance, it is crucial to have precautionary funds set aside to cover unforeseen expenses and unexpected situations, including health-related emergencies. We also need to save for our retirement when we are no longer working.

Moreover, it is beneficial to start saving early. As mentioned in Chapter 1, with compounding interest, our savings can grow into a larger amount over time.

Nonetheless, it has been highlighted that people are saving too little. According to the National Institute on Retirement Saving, 21 percent of Americans are not saving at all. In addition, more than 75 percent of Americans have their retirement savings below the conservative savings target.

This characteristic is not unique to America: The lack of savings has been regarded as a global retirement crisis. While the topic of retirement savings will be covered extensively in Chapter 6, we will first address a fundamental question here: Why are we not saving enough?

Time Preference

Savings are related to an intertemporal choice. Here, the term "intertemporal" refers to the association between past, present, and future decisions. This is because our decision to save today is related to our well-being across different time periods.

Whenever we save, we are giving up current consumption for future spending. In other words, we are forgoing satisfaction today for tomorrow's satisfaction. Hence, there is a trade-off between saving and consuming today.

One of the main reasons for households' poor saving habits is impatience. Individuals prefer to enjoy immediate rewards and deal with costs in the future. Therefore, with this fondness for instant gratification, we might decide to purchase goods and services now instead of saving for the future.

Since most of us prefer consuming goods today rather than tomorrow, we end up choosing not to save. Referred to as time preference in the economics literature, it relates to the inclination of individuals to discount future consumption in favor of current consumption. Thus, we value future consumption lower as compared to current consumption.

Let us look at some examples now. Suppose you are a cookie lover and we provide you with two choices:

Option A: 10 cookies now
Option B: 12 cookies next year

Which option would you choose? If you selected Option A over Option B, you have exhibited time preference. You prefer to have your cookies today (current consumption) rather than next year (future consumption) even though you get more cookies in the future!

Now, if you have chosen Option B over Option A, let us provide you with another decision to make:

Option A: 10 cookies now
Option C: 11 cookies next year

Are you going with Option A this time? By varying the number of cookies you will get next year, we are able to understand how much you value your current consumption relative to future consumption.

Your inclination to discount the future value of consumption plays a crucial role in shaping your current savings decisions. If you place less value on future consumption, your savings will likely be lower. Since individuals have varying perspectives on the future, they save at different rates.

Furthermore, it has been highlighted that our preference for present consumption over future consumption changes over time. This results in us making choices that may seem conflicting through the passage of time, which brings us to the next point: Time Inconsistency.

Time Inconsistency and Present Bias

By definition, time inconsistency suggests that the decisions we make are not consistent across time. Decisions that we make today might not be the most optimal decisions in the future. Let us go back to our cookie examples. This time, we are giving you two other choices:

Option D: 10 cookies 5 years later
Option E: 12 cookies 6 years later

Will you go for Option D or E? If you have selected Option E this time, and chosen Option A over Option B previously, we are going to have a time inconsistency problem. That is because in five years' time, you will decide to eat 10 cookies immediately (even though today, you have committed to eat 12 cookies in the sixth year).

If you have chosen Option E over Option D and Option A over Option B, it is apparent that there will be a conflict between today's preferences and the preferences that will be held in the future. Consequently, you might not stick to your plan over time.

In comparison, if your preferences did not change over time, it is most likely that you will be able to stick to your plan.

Time inconsistency is related to present bias. As we have stronger preferences for consuming goods closer to the present time, we will prefer small rewards that occur earlier, as compared to large rewards that occur later.

Formally, this is known as hyperbolic discounting. The effect of hyperbolic discounting is that our preferences change depending on how distant the reward is in the future. Hence, our valuation of consuming different goods and services changes through the passage of time.

The role of hyperbolic discounting and savings have been explored in a 1997 *The Quarterly Journal of Economics* article by David Laibson, who is Sumit's longtime collaborator.

Titled "Golden Eggs and Hyperbolic Discounting," the article highlights how hyperbolic discounting can explain the relationship between different streams of consumption and income.

With hyperbolic discounting, individuals do not start saving for retirement until it is too late. For instance, we may intend to start our savings plan next year. However, when the next year comes, we might decide to postpone for another year (and so on).

What can we do about it? We now consider the golden eggs. Laibson reasons that illiquid assets, such as pension plans that restrict households from withdrawing early or term deposits, are akin to the goose that laid the golden eggs in Aesop's Fable.

While illiquid assets can generate considerable benefits in the long term, it is hard to realize the benefits straight away. In fact, it is detrimental to cash out the benefits immediately, just like the goose that laid the golden eggs.

Laibson further shows that these illiquid assets provide individuals with a commitment tool. These assets therefore have the potential to overcome hyperbolic discounting and help to increase savings.

Therefore, if households are rather shortsighted with their money management approach, commitment technology could help to achieve financial discipline.

Commitment Savings

Commitment devices for savings have been examined by Nava Ashraf, Dean Karlan, and Wesley Yin in a 2006 article in *The Quarterly Journal of Economics*. The title of the article is "Tying Odysseus to the Mast: Evidence from a Commitment Savings Product in the Philippines," and is inspired by the Greek mythology of Odysseus.

In this account, Odysseus, the legendary king of Greece, expressed a deep yearning to listen to songs from the Sirens. As human like beings with alluring voices, the Sirens are known to employ their captivating voices to convince unwary sailors to leap into the sea. To avoid the temptation of the Sirens while listening to their songs, Odysseus tied himself to the mast, and ordered his men to not change the direction of the ship under any circumstances.

Commitment savings products are similar to what Odysseus did. Once households are committed to savings, they are not allowed to access their savings until their goals are met.

In this article, the authors partnered with the Green Bank of Caraga, a rural bank in Mindanao in the Philippines, and offered some clients a new account called Save, Earn, Enjoy Deposits ("SEED").

This is a pure commitment savings account and there are a few ways that individuals can set their goals. In the beginning, they will select a month that they expect to have higher expenditures. The account will disallow the withdrawal of funds for this month. This includes celebrations, such as Christmas or for school purchases.

Subsequently, they will establish a savings target. Access will only be given to these funds when this goal is reached. While households are given the flexibility to set these restrictions, these choices cannot be changed after the decision is made.

Out of 710 clients who were offered the product, 202 individuals took up the offer. This corresponds to a take-up rate of around 28 percent. Based on the 202 accounts that were opened with the bank, 140 chose a date-based goal, while the remaining 62 took up an amount-based goal.

Who took up the commitment products? It was discovered that women who exhibit hyperbolic preferences had a higher tendency to take up the offer. The preferences were delineated through a series of survey questions (such as Options A–E that we asked you earlier).

This highlights that households do value commitment devices. Since these devices can help them to be more financially disciplined, they can overcome their self-control problems.

The commitment devices here were found to have a long-term impact on households' savings. Indeed, it was established that for the groups who were offered the commitment savings plan, there was an increase in savings by 81 percentage points after one year (as compared to those who were not exposed to the commitment devices).

We will now move on to other ways in managing self-control.

Self-Control

Self-control is an issue not only for adults, but also for children. Let us turn to a seminal psychology study by Walter Mischel, Ebbe Ebbesen, and Antonette Raskoff Zeiss, published in the *Journal of Personality and Social Psychology* in 1972. The formal title of the article is "Cognitive and Attentional Mechanisms in Delay of Gratification" but it is now commonly known as the Stanford marshmallow experiment or the marshmallow test.

The marshmallow test was named after young children in the Bing Nursery School of Stanford University who were offered marshmallows as a reward item. In this study, children were told that they could have the marshmallow, but if they waited for 15 minutes, they would be rewarded with a second treat.

The researchers conducted three experiments to examine factors that could impact self-control in the children.

In the first experiment, different groups were provided with different types of distractors while waiting for their delayed rewards:

Group 1: External distractor (playing with toys)
Group 2: Internal distractor (thinking of pleasant thoughts)
Group 3: No distractor

This would allow the researchers to appreciate the significance of distractors in self-control.

The second experiment follows the first experiment with a twist. Here, children were given ideas about what to think about when waiting.

The third experiment is the same as the first and second experiments, except that the reward items were kept out of sight. Unlike the earlier two experiments, children were not able to see that the marshmallows were placed under the tray.

The study unveiled several intriguing findings that can guide us in effectively managing our self-control. The first experiment shows that with distractions, children were able to wait for a longer period of time. This highlights that distractions could be useful for us when managing our money as distractions may increase our self-control.

However, the second experiment shows that only certain distractions, such as happy thoughts, are effective in having longer wait time. With unhappy thoughts, or thoughts related to the rewards directly, the wait time gets shorter. Therefore, it is important to have positive thinking in our lives!

Finally, the third experiment highlights that when the reward is not visibly present, the children are able to wait longer. As the saying "Out of Sight, Out of Mind" goes, when the rewards cannot be seen by the children, they are less tempted and have better self-control.

The same concept applies for us too. There are many possible reasons that can explain why we end up overspending and not saving enough.

While spending on necessities are unavoidable, other forms of spending such as buying luxury goods can be better managed.

To control the temptation of our growing wants, we could rely on different forms of distractions. Instead of visiting shopping malls, go for an outdoor activity such as a hike or a visit to the museum. Imagine the great times and memorable moments that you can share with your family and friends. Sometimes, the best things in life are free.

Save More Tomorrow™

So far, we have highlighted several behavioral biases that we might face when saving for the future. Why subject ourselves to these biases when the biases could work in our favor?

Alongside policymakers, economists have designed several savings plans and tools to help individuals save. Let us focus on one of them: Save More Tomorrow™ .

Pioneered by Richard Thaler and Shlomo Benartzi, the Save More Tomorrow™ program allows individuals to allocate a portion of their increase in salary toward their retirement.

This seeks to help individuals overcome issues with their self-control and relies on the following key concepts that we have discussed so far.

To begin with, the program avoids the present bias problem by asking individuals to commit to saving more in the future. As compared to increasing their savings in the present moment, linking savings to a future increase in salary is more palatable to households who display hyperbolic discounting.

Next, it minimizes loss aversion as the take-home pay never falls. As the planned increases in savings are linked to increases in future pay, individuals do not experience any fall in the amount that they bring home at the current time.

In addition, it relies on inertia as individuals remain in the program unless they choose to opt out. Hence, the status quo bias work toward keeping households in the plan, and thereby encourage savings.

The findings of the program have been presented in a 2004 article in the *Journal of Political Economy* by Thaler and Benartzi, titled Save More Tomorrow™: Using Behavioral Economics to Increase Employee Saving." This article highlights the success of the program in encouraging savings.

Over 40 months, the average savings rate of the participants increased from 3.5 percent to 13.6 percent. On top of that, there was a high take-up rate and low attrition rate. Of those who were presented with the plan, 78 percent of them took up the offer, and out of those who joined the program, 80 percent of them remained in the program through their fourth pay rise.

This implies that we can harness the power of behavioral economics tools to our advantage. As we might not have the willpower to save on our own, we can rely on external help.

Key Takeaways

Savings are key building blocks in the management of our household finances. We have highlighted that many households are not saving enough because they are impatient and lack self-control. Moreover, households are present biased, resulting in time inconsistency.

At this point, should you realize that you are guilty of this, there is no need to dwell in regret. As shared by Sun Tze in the Art of War, "If you know the enemy and know yourself, you need not fear the result of a hundred battles." Now that we have acknowledged our enemy (in not saving sufficiently), what's important is to come up with concrete plans to overcome the challenges and save for the future.

This requires us to be financially disciplined and constantly remind ourselves of the bigger picture when making decisions. We can also learn from the children in the Stanford marshmallow test by relying on distractors in self-control.

Alternatively, we have the option of external help, such as commitment savings devices, or programs, such as Save More Tomorrow™ which overcomes our behavioral biases. By committing toward our long-term goals, we can better manage our household finances and prepare ourselves for retirement.

6

Building a Nest Egg

Let us now consider savings for retirement and highlight why it is crucial to start building a nest egg. Retirement occurs when we leave our job and stop working. In most countries, there is a statutory retirement age, which is the age at which you must retire. This is also the time when you can receive your full retirement benefits.

The retirement age varies in different countries. In 2022, the retirement age for Vietnam stands at 60 years and 6 months for males and 55 years and 8 months for women. In Denmark, the retirement age is 67 years.

Being financially secure throughout our retirement is essential. Without our monthly income from work, we run the risk of running out of money when we retire. Coupled with an increase in medical costs as we age, we might not be able to maintain our standard of living.

Moreover, some of us would like to have a comfortable retirement where we could visit new places and try new experiences. As we might not have the time and capacity to travel during our preretirement days (due to work and family commitments), retirement is most often the best time to fulfill them.

This underscores the importance of building a nest egg for our retirement. However, as mentioned previously, it has been documented that households are not saving enough for retirement.

According to the World Economic Forum in 2015, the retirement savings gap, (which is the difference between what retirees need and how much they have accumulated) stands at US$70 trillion for eight of the world's largest markets.[4]

To overcome these challenges, retirement planning plays a crucial role.

The Role of Retirement Planning

How does financial planning impact retirement security? This question has been explored in an article titled "Baby Boomer Retirement Security: The Roles of Planning, Financial Literacy and Housing Wealth," written by Annamaria Lusardi and Olivia Mitchell in a 2007 *Journal of Monetary Economics* article.

It is determined in the study that differences in savings among households nearing retirement can be explained by their approach to retirement planning.

The study relied on two cohorts of data from the U.S. Health and Retirement Study (HRS) in 1992 and 2004. Conducted by the University of Michigan since 1992, the HRS surveyed more than 26,000 Americans over the age of 50 every two years.

As an indicator for retirement planning, the authors focused on the response to the following question in the HRS:

> *"How much have you thought about retirement? A lot, some, a little, or hardly at all?"*

Table 6.1 presents the survey results of this question, together with the median net worth of the respondents in each category.

Here, we have some interesting findings, which are consistent across both cohorts. First, it shows that individuals are unprepared for retirement. Out of the four choices, the largest percentage falls under "Hardly at all," which highlights that a large proportion of the respondents hardly thought

[4] They include the Netherlands, Australia, Canada, Japan, the United Kingdom, India, China, and the United States.

Table 6.1: Retirement Planning from the U.S. Health and Retirement Study (HRS)

Group	Percentage of Sample	Median Net Worth (2004 dollars)
1992 Cohort		
Hardly at all	32.0	76,910
A little	14.3	126,560
Some	24.8	172,340
A lot	28.9	173,690
2004 Cohort		
Hardly at all	27.9	79,000
A little	17.0	173,400
Some	27.7	189,000
A lot	27.4	199,000

of their retirement. In addition, these respondents possess the least financial assets, suggesting that the degree of retirement planning is linked to the level of savings.

As households are more prepared for retirement, there is an increase in their median net worth. Lusardi and Mitchell further highlighted that there is a bimodal relationship between the amount of effort that is put into financial planning and household net worth. In fact, respondents that indicated having "a little" thought about retirement, had a significantly larger net wealth at retirement as compared to those that indicated "Hardly at all".

Have you thought of retirement?

The fact that the findings are consistent across different cohorts has implications for retirement planning as well. Despite the 2004 cohort (also known as the baby boomers) having more housing equity and stocks in their retirement assets, the composition of household assets did not appear to influence households' decisions.

While Lusardi and Mitchell have documented the relationship between retirement planning and wealth, they went a step further to show that planning affects wealth, and not vice versa. Investigating changes in regional housing prices, they found out that when individuals get richer, retirement planning does not increase.

What drives retirement planning? One possible reason is financial literacy. In the 2004 HRS, the respondents were asked the following financial literacy questions:

1. *"If the chance of getting a disease is 10%, how many people out of 1,000 would be expected to get the disease?"*
2. *"If 5 people all have the winning number in the lottery and the prize is 2 million dollars, how much will each of them get?"*

The first question is known as the percentage calculation problem, while the second question is the lottery division problem. Respondents who answered either the first two questions correctly were then given a third question (which is regarded as the compound interest problem):

3. *"Let's say you have 200 dollars in a savings account. The account earns 10% interest per year. How much would you have in the account at the end of two years?"*

Finally, they were asked the names of the U.S. President and Vice President, which is regarded as the political literacy problem.

The percentage of the respondents who answered the questions correctly were shown in Table 6.2.

While more than 80 percent were able to calculate percentages and identify the U.S. President and Vice President correctly, only 18 percent could calculate the compound interest.

In examining the relationship between retirement planning and financial literacy, it was further established that those with low financial

Table 6.2: Financial Literacy from the U.S. HRS

Problem	Percentage Who Got Correct
Percentage calculation	83.5
Lottery division	55.9
Compound interest	17.8
Political literacy	81.1

literacy (defined as those who answered the problems incorrectly) are less likely to plan for their retirement! This is after considering their demographics, such as education, race, and gender.

Evidently, financial literacy matters for retirement planning. Given that a majority of individuals underestimate the necessary funds for retirement, including healthcare expenses, it is vital for us to plan prudently.

Challenges of Aging Population

Planning for retirement is challenging. This is exacerbated by the fact that the average life expectancy has been steadily rising in recent decades. Driven by a combination of medical advances and structural changes in the economy, we are now living longer than before, which means we will have a longer runway for retirement.

To provide some motivating evidence, Figure 6.1 presents the life expectancy of individuals in the United States, Japan, and Singapore from 2009 to 2019. Clearly, there has been a rise in life expectancy worldwide, including those in developing nations as well.

Since we are living longer, it would be wise to plan for a longer retirement period as compared to our elders. This means that we ought to save more and at a faster rate.

The challenges associated with an aging population could impact retirement savings and these have been examined by James Poterba in the 2014 Richard T. Ely Lecture. Titled "Retirement Security in an Aging

Figure 6.1: Life Expectancy of Different Countries from 2009 to 2019

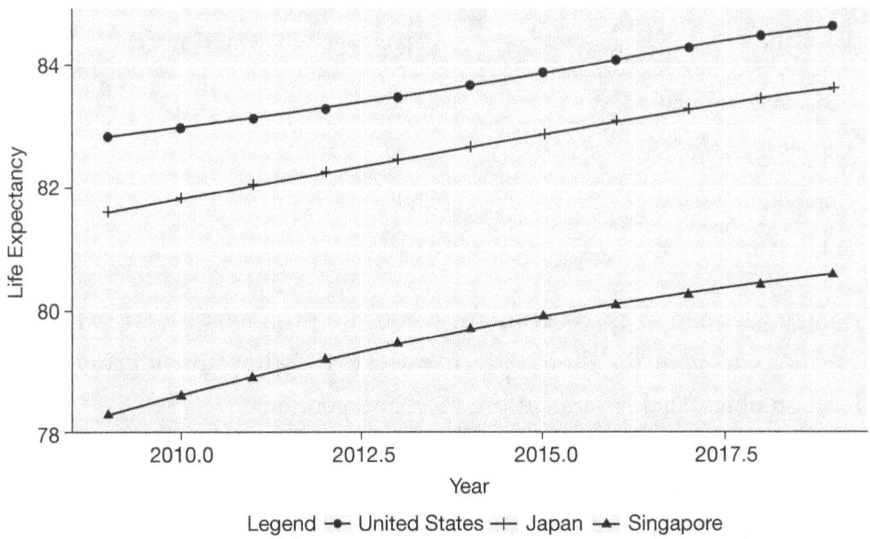

Population," it has been published in the *American Economic Review*. Let us highlight a few key lessons.

The first point relates to the planning period. Poterba emphasized that we should not plan based on the average life expectancy, but rather on the upper tail of our life length.

A quick caveat when planning for retirement: An average life expectancy of 80 years means that the total number of years an average person will live is 80. It does not mean that we should budget for our spending until the age of 80 years old. We need to plan beyond that.

Moreover, the chances that you will live longer gets higher when you age. Consider the case of a 65-year-old American male in 2015. While his remaining life expectancy is 18.6 years, he has a 20 percent chance of living for more than 25 years. For an American woman in the same cohort, her remaining life expectancy is 20.3 years, but 20 percent of them will live till age 93 years old.

This is because there is a difference between one's conditional survival probability and average life expectancy. While the average life expectancy refers to how much an individual can expect to live on average from birth, the conditional survival probability is based on how much more an individual is expected to live, given that an individual has already survived up to a certain point. The conditional survival probability provides additional insights and is preferred for retirement planning.

Additionally, the article points out the potential macroeconomic consequences of an aging population, which could have implications for the rate of return on our savings.

For instance, when a large cohort of the baby boomers reaches retirement, they might draw down their savings. In turn, asset prices may decrease. Furthermore, an aging population could slow down economic growth through a fall in technological change and level of entrepreneurship.

Hence, when one plans for retirement, it is paramount to keep abreast of the changing financial conditions. As one ages, the assumptions and parameters we use in our financial planning could change. This means that we need to constantly update our financial plans.

The Age of Reason

Another reason why we should plan for retirement early is that we tend to make more poor financial choices when we get older. With aging, we will experience considerable cognitive impairment. As a case in point, dementia becomes predominant after age 60.

Together with John Driscoll, Xavier Gabaix, and David Laibson, Sumit explores the role of age and financial decisions in a 2009 research article in the *Brookings Paper on Economic Activity*.

The study, titled "The Age of Reason: Financial Decisions over the Life Cycle and Implications for Regulation," highlights the life-cycle patterns in financial mistakes. By delving into the financial mistakes made by households, it was revealed that there is a U-shaped pattern in the tendency to make mistakes across ages.

While younger individuals make more mistakes, the propensity of them making mistakes decreases when they grow older. This is due to the experiences they gain as they learn over time. However, as they age, their analytical ability reduces, resulting in a higher likelihood to make mistakes.

Hence, there is a trade-off between two age-based effects: rising experience and declining analytical function. It was discovered that the cost-minimizing age was around 53 years. At this age, the most optimal financial decisions are being made.

The article focused on 10 different types of credit transactions made by households. They include credit card balance transfer offers, home equity loans, home equity lines of credit, automobile loans, mortgages, personal credit cards, small business credit cards, credit card late payment fees, credit card overlimit fees, and credit card cash advance fees.

What are some of the mistakes that households make? One of them is the optimal use of credit card balance transfer that we have discussed in Chapter 1 of this book.

As mentioned earlier, when households are offered a new credit card to transfer their account balance with a teaser rate, they should make all new purchases on the old credit card and not the new one. This is because payments on the new card are applied to the transfer balance first and not the new purchase.

Interestingly, when examining the propensity of those who implement the optimal strategy immediately across different age groups, it was observed that there was an inverse U shape. In other words, the younger and older population are more likely to make financial mistakes. With time, they are also less likely to discover the optimal strategy.

Another example will be the interest rates that are paid on home equity loans and lines of credit. It was found that the interest rates are U shaped as well. The younger and older population pay higher APRs that can be 50 basis points more than the middle-aged. Upon further investigation, one of the key reasons was attributed to the misestimation of the value of their homes.

Key Takeaways

We have focused on the importance of retirement planning and challenges that one could face when planning for retirement.

To overcome these challenges, financial planning plays a crucial role. We end off with a quote by Ben Bernanke, former chairperson of the Federal Reserve of the United States:

> *"Smart financial planning—such as budgeting, saving for emergencies, and preparing for retirement—can help households enjoy better lives while weathering financial shocks. Financial education can play a key role in getting to these outcomes."*

Indeed, without adequate financial planning, we could end up spending more than our lifetime income in our working years. As a result, we may be required to prolong our employment into our later years and undergo significant lifestyle adjustment.

We will now move on to the next segment on retirement income support.

7

Retirement Income Support

In most countries, retirement income support comes from the traditional three-legged stool: government provision, private savings, and employer-sponsored retirement plans.

Government provision differs in many ways. Provision from the government includes universal social pensions, such as those in Denmark and Sweden, or social security in the United States.

Universal social pensions are designed to provide all individuals a minimum level of financial security, irrespective of their background. This ensures a basic income floor for everyone. In contrast, social security is based on eligibility criteria and is typically funded by individuals or their employees.

As individuals, it is our duty is to determine the extent of government provision, so that we can make up for the shortfall through our private savings and employer-sponsored plans. If the payout from the government is low (or even zero in some cases), we will have to rely primarily on the other two legs of the stool.

Within this chapter, we will delve into individual retirement savings and employer sponsored retirement plans.

Individual Retirement Account (IRA)

To encourage individuals to save for retirement (on their own), governments worldwide have come up with many incentives. These include having individual retirement accounts (IRAs) with tax advantages.

There are many variants of IRAs with different benefits and costs. Prior to making a commitment to a particular plan, it is important to comprehend the complexities and prerequisites of each plan. This is because as IRAs are earmarked for retirement, there will be penalties when we choose to have early withdrawals from IRAs before retirement. Let us consider two popular types of the IRA: traditional IRA and Roth IRA.

In general, contributions to traditional IRAs are tax deductible. To give an example, if we deposit $5,000 into the IRA, our taxable income will be reduced by $5,000. It will only be taxed when we withdraw the money during our retirement years.

This is beneficial from a taxation point of view. Given that we won't be employed during our retirement years, our taxable income (and as a consequence, our tax bracket) will be lower at that time. This implies that we will pay a lower tax rate. If the taxable amount is low enough, we might not even need to pay taxes!

One thing to note is that the maximum contribution to these schemes varies by country and age. In Singapore, the yearly maximum contribution to a variant of the traditional IRA, which is commonly known as the Supplementary Retirement Scheme (SRS), is S$15,300. With limitations in the contribution rate, we might not be able to rely entirely on traditional IRAs for our retirement savings.

In the United States, another type of IRA is known as the Roth IRA.[5] The key difference between the two types of IRA is that the Roth IRA is funded with after-tax dollars. However, when we withdraw the funds, it is not taxable. In light of this, if we project a higher income in retirement than what we currently have, it is advisable to consider the Roth IRA.

---

[5] Note that the Roth IRA goes by other names in different countries. In the United Kingdom, it is named the Individual Savings Account (ISA).

Regardless of whether we choose traditional or Roth IRAs, we gain from paying lower taxes. While tax subsidies are clearly beneficial to us, economic studies have indicated that individuals are not responsive to these incentives. Let us zoom in on a study by Raj Chetty, John Friedman, Soren Leth-Petersen, Torben Heien Nielsen, and Tore Olsen that was published in *The Quarterly Journal of Economics* in 2014.

Titled "Active vs. Passive Decisions and Crowd-Out in Retirement Savings: Evidence from Denmark," the article explores the savings decisions of the entire population of Denmark based on two types of policies implemented by the government.

The first policy involves a price subsidy by the government, while the second policy involves an automatic contribution of a portion of the individual's salary to his/her retirement account.

Based on 45 million observations, the authors discovered that there are two types of savers: active savers and passive savers. Active savers respond to changes in subsidies and automatic contributions, while passive savers take no action and are invariant to any policy changes.

Based on the observations in Denmark, it was found that 15 percent of individuals are active savers, while the remaining 85 percent of them are passive ones.

This means that only a minority are responsive to incentives given through tax policies. Moreover, it was found that active savers shift their assets from taxable accounts to retirement accounts. In other words, retirement accounts crowd out other forms of private savings.

Taken together, tax subsidies have little impact on the total amount of wealth. The authors estimated that an increase in tax expenditure by 1 Danish Krone only led to an increase in savings by 1 percent!

In comparison, automatic contributions managed to increase wealth to a large extent. As an illustration, it was revealed that when individuals moved to a new firm that contributed more to their retirement account, they ended up saving more. For each additional 1 Danish Krone in the retirement account, their overall savings increased by more than 0.85 Krone.

Unlike government subsidies, there is no crowding out of other forms of savings with automatic contributions. This highlights the role of inertia and behavioral biases in influencing households' choices.

Moreover, the authors established that active savers are primarily financially sophisticated individuals who are older with larger wealth and income. They also have more training in Economics! Consequently, these individuals are more responsive to changes in price subsidies and consciously offset their automatic contributions.

Are you an active or passive saver? It is timely to take advantage of government subsidies, if you have not done so.

Employment Sponsored Retirement Plan

Next, we will discuss employer-sponsored retirement plans. These are retirement plans funded by the employer.

In general, there are two types of employer-sponsored retirement plans: defined benefit and defined contribution plans.

Defined benefit plans are funded by employers and they stipulate the exact amount that each employee receives upon retirement. On the other hand, defined contribution plans are funded by both employees and employers and are dependent on the individual's contributions.

With defined benefit plans, the employer is charged with the responsibility to manage the investments accrued by the retirement plan. By having a set retirement income, individuals can plan for their retirement more confidently. As the retirement income can be guaranteed for life by the employer, this provides stability and certainty.

However, employees lack control over the management of their retirement fund, and there are fewer options for flexible withdrawal available. As a specific example, they are unable to change the frequency of payments.

There also exists the danger that the company gets into a difficult financial situation in which they are unable to pay the promised sum. While some countries, such as the United Kingdom, have pension protection funds to protect the employee when the employer becomes insolvent, the level of protection varies across countries and time.

In comparison, defined contribution plans do not have a guaranteed amount that individuals can get upon retirement. The amount that employees will get is dependent on the contributions of both employers and employees, as well as the performance of their financial portfolio.

In defined contribution plans, employees contribute money directly to the plan and the employer usually makes a matching contribution. Thereafter, employees have to make decisions on how to manage their retirement funds. While this provides them with more flexibility, they now have to take on more responsibility for their own financial decisions.

As defined benefit plans are more expensive and complex to manage, companies have shifted toward defined contribution plans in recent years. Figure 7.1 presents the proportion of people with defined contribution plans in the United States across time.

Figure 7.1: Proportion of People with Defined Contribution Plans in the United States

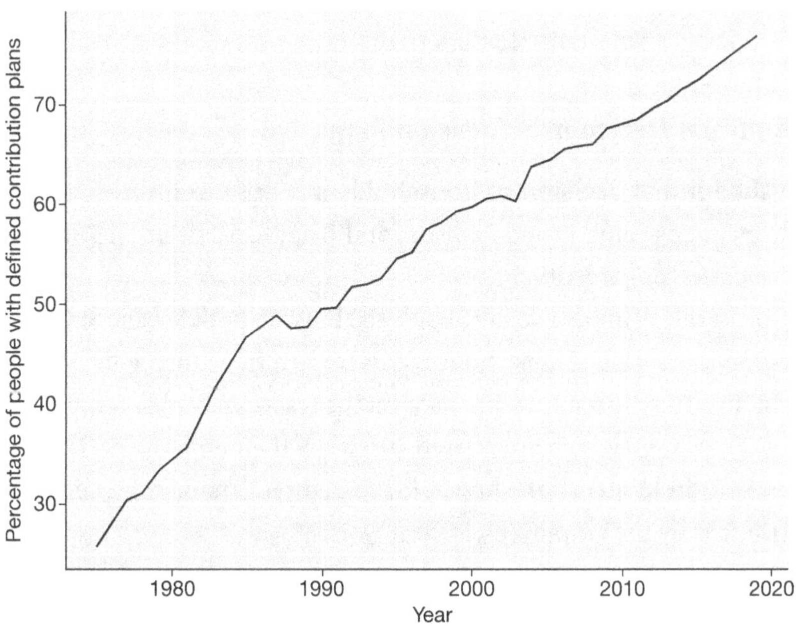

One example of a defined contribution plan is the 401(k) in the United States. Named after a section of the U.S. Internal Revenue Code, the 401(k) is a popular company-sponsored retirement savings plan in which employees contribute directly from their salary into an investment account. The employer would subsequently match a certain percentage or the entirety of the contribution made.

Just like the IRAs, there are tax advantages with the 401(k). With the traditional 401(k), the employee's contributions will reduce the taxable income. Taxes would only be imposed when the contributions are being withdrawn. For the Roth 401(k), contributions are made with after-tax income and withdrawals are tax-free. Likewise, there will be penalties if there are early withdrawals before reaching the stipulated retirement age.

With the 401(k), households are tasked to choose their investments. Ranging from money market accounts to mutual funds and exchange-traded funds, households are required to select funds that best meet their needs. This is not an easy decision, and households tend to make poor decisions in managing their investments.

With many choices to make, they end up making suboptimal decisions while managing their 401(k) plan.[6]

Suboptimal Decisions in Pension Plans

One suboptimal decision of households has been examined in a 2011 study by James Choi, David Laibson, and Brigitte Madrian in *The Review of Economics and Statistics.*

As the title of the article suggests "$100 Bills on the Sidewalk: Suboptimal Investment in 401(k) Plans," households forgo a free lunch when offered.

In this study, the authors focused on the response of older employees at seven companies, which are offered 401(k) by their employers. The policy states that up to a certain threshold, the employers match every dollar contributed by the employees.

[6] In Part V of this book, we will highlight several other mistakes that households make when they handle investment decisions in their 401(k) plan.

With employers matching their contributions, older employees thus have the incentive to contribute to the 401(k). This is due to the fact that employees who are older than 59.5 years old are permitted to have unrestricted access to their 401(k).

In other words, they can put in an extra dollar to their 401(k), and their employer will match it accordingly (so long as it is within the threshold). Thereafter, the employee can withdraw the extra dollar straight away without any penalty. Isn't that a free lunch?

It is worth noting that there is little effort and time needed in withdrawing. Employees can request withdrawals just by calling a toll-free number.

Hence, the optimal strategy for older employees should be to increase their contributions till the match threshold, and then withdraw the contributions after they are made. This will increase their wealth inside the 401(k) plan, without changing their wealth outside the plan.

However, the study documented that many employees do not contribute up to the match threshold. Across the seven firms, between 20 percent and 60 percent of employees did not reach the match threshold.

The authors highlighted that the loss could be significant. They illustrated an example of a 60-year-old employee who does not contribute to the 401(k) plan. Suppose the company matches the contributions up to 6 percent of her salary and that her salary is $52,000, the incremental amount that she stands to gain is $3,120 per year!

She could choose to save this money in the 401(k) or withdraw this amount to spend. Either way, it will be beneficial for her to take advantage of the employer match.

Across the seven firms in the sample, the losses are estimated to be around $160 to $782 per year. This is approximately 0.66 percent to 2.32 percent of their annual salary.

Why do these older employees fail to take full advantage of their 401(k) match? The authors conducted a field experiment with Hewitt Associates and revealed that these employees are less financially sophisticated and more likely to delay other profitable actions as well.

Furthermore, they find that simply telling individuals about the optimal strategy only has a minimal impact. In a randomly selected group, some individuals were informed about the foregone match money and that there is no loss in liquidity. However, there was only a small increase in contribution rate: one-tenth of one percentage point.

Consequently, the authors indicated that providing better information is not sufficient. To encourage savings, formal financial education could be provided.

Financial Education Intervention

The role of financial education on retirement savings has been investigated by Eraj Ghafoori, Edwin Ip, and Jan Kabatek in a 2021 article in the *Journal of Banking and Finance*.

Titled "The Impacts of a Large-Scale Financial Education Intervention on Retirement Saving Behaviors and Portfolio Allocation: Evidence from Pension Fund Data," the research study examined the impact of a nationwide retirement seminar program that is managed by a large Australian pension fund.

The seminars took place across Australia from 2017 to 2018 and involved more than 100 retirement seminars. In each session, the seminars focused on financial literacy and institutional knowledge.

Due to the variation in the timing of the seminars, the authors were able to examine how pre-retiree members of the pension funds responded after attending the seminars.

Indeed, it was shown that seminar participants were more likely to make voluntary pension contributions. It was estimated that seminar attendance resulted in an increase in voluntary contributions by 6 percent. This corresponds to an average of A$15,259.

On top of that, it was observed that those who attended the seminars began to adopt more sophisticated savings strategies that helped lower the risk of their portfolio. They also demonstrated higher engagement in pension management, accessing the online portal for funds more frequently.

This provides evidence that financial education can help to improve one's retirement planning.

Key Takeaways

Retirement income comes in many forms. This includes provision from the government, own savings as well as employer-sponsored retirement plans.

Governments across different countries have implemented a range of incentives to spur individuals into saving more. Nonetheless, we have shown you that many households are not making use of the benefits that are provided by the government or their employers.

For instance, many individuals are found to be passive savers and do not take advantage of the subsidies provided by the government. Moreover, it was discovered that individuals leave their money on the table when it comes to investments in pension plans.

To improve our financial outcomes, we should be proactive in enhancing our understanding of household financial management. This includes attending financial seminars and of course, reading this book to the end!

As such, one key takeaway of this book is also to draw your attention to these commonly made mistakes, so that you can stop missing out on "free money" provided by the government and your employers.

An awareness of different policies intended to aid us in our retirement plans will ultimately be to our benefit. By familiarizing ourselves with these policies, we hope that more of us will become active savers and reoptimize our pension choices when given the opportunity.

The government may have the best intentions in helping us to save for retirement. However, what matters at the end of the day is our willingness to help ourselves.

8

Retirement Savings Puzzle

We now move on from retirement income to retirement savings by looking at changes in households' actual savings after they retire. As it turns out, individuals tend to reduce their savings at a much slower pace than anticipated upon retirement. This is contrary to the predictions of the life cycle hypothesis (which we have discussed in Chapter 4), and this scenario is recognized as the retirement savings puzzle.

In its simplest form, the life cycle hypothesis implies that households seek to keep their consumption at a constant level across time. At retirement, we expect households to reduce their savings steadily to maintain a constant level of spending. Nonetheless, households are not doing so. What is happening here?

Understanding the retirement savings puzzle is important to us. By considering the actual behavior of households when they retire, solving the puzzle can help us in our retirement planning.

In recent years, much research work has been done to find out reasons behind the puzzle. This has been summarized in a 2016 article named "Savings After Retirement: A Survey," published in the *Annual Review of Economics* by Mariacristina De Nardi, Eric French, and John Bailey Jones.

In this study, the authors explain why many elderly households hold a large amount of assets even when they get older.

Primarily, there is a high degree of uncertainty when one gets older. These include uncertain life spans, as well as uncertain medical and long-term spending. Consequently, households are more careful and therefore would save more to prepare for unexpected expenditures, such as medical needs. This is often referred to as having higher precautionary savings.

The next reason is due to the desire of households to have bequests. As people would like to pass on their wealth to their children or other heirs, they would intentionally save more than expected. This could be due to altruistic motives or strategic bequest motives, in which potential bequests are used as rewards for caregivers.

Another reason is related to the type of assets that individuals hold. As one of the main assets of households, housing could potentially shape the savings decisions of individuals.

For instance, it has been shown that retirees reduce their non-housing wealth at a faster rate relative to their housing wealth. One main factor is that homeowners have a preference to stay in their own homes. Besides, liquidating houses have larger transaction costs with high taxes as compared to bequeathing to their loved ones.

Does any of the reasons above resonate with you? If so, this could influence your decisions in your retirement plan. This is because different considerations would require having different financial instruments to reach your personal goals.

If you are primarily concerned about having precautionary savings, you could consider taking up annuities and long-term care insurance.

With annuities, you will receive periodic payments for the rest of your life, which ensures a reliable income stream. With long-term care insurance, you will receive financial support when you have chronic or disabling conditions that require constant supervision. This includes expenses in nursing home care and assisted living services.

However, this comes at a cost. As you are required to pay a lump-sum cost for annuities, you have lesser bequests for your loved ones.

On the other hand, if you have a strong bequest motive, you should have life insurance. With life insurance, your beneficiary will obtain a sum of money when you pass away. Hence, your potential bequests will increase. However, since you are required to pay a premium for life insurance, this will reduce the amount of precautionary savings that you have.

Consequently, there is a trade-off between leaving assets to the next generation and being insured against medical and longevity risks. We will have an in-depth discussion about the role of annuities and insurance in Part VII of the book.

In addition, if you would like to continue staying at your own house (rather than leaving a bequest to someone else), you could choose to take up reverse mortgage loans.

As the name suggests, reverse mortgage loans are "reverse" from traditional mortgages. Instead of homeowners making mortgage payments to lenders, homeworkers receive payment based on the value of the house itself.

In essence, homeworkers are now borrowing based on the value of their house. By giving up equity in the home, they could receive regular monthly payments. This would allow homeowners access to their savings, which are locked in home equity.

But this is not without cost. There will be monthly interest added to the loan, resulting in higher debt and lower equity. As time goes on, the required payment amount increases, while their ownership stake in the house decreases.

Thus, there exists the risk of having the loan balance exceed the actual value of the home. If borrowers are unable to repay the loans, they would lose ownership of their homes.

Despite the risks involved, reverse mortgages can be useful for asset rich-cash poor retirees who are unwilling to sell their houses and require liquidity. While the take-up rate has been low globally, we expect to see a growth in these financial instruments as it increasingly meets the needs of retirees who have locked in a large proportion of their savings in their homes.

Retirement Consumption Puzzle

On a related note, how might consumption be impacted if households do not decumulate their savings quickly? Here, we have the counterpart of the retirement savings puzzle: the retirement consumption puzzle.

Let us now analyze the actual consumption response of retirees. Figure 8.1 plots changes in the household expenditure by age of the household head in the United States (Panel A) and in Singapore (Panel B). In both diagrams, we find that in terms of spending, there is an inverse U-shaped pattern as the household head gets older. This means that people do not smooth their consumption over time.

In addition, it has been documented that there is a one-off drop in consumption when individuals retire. What drives the drop in consumption upon retirement? An appreciation of how retirees actually change their consumption preferences and lifestyle would allow us to set more accurate retirement goals and prepare for our retirement.

This time, we will examine the consumption response of retirees in Italy. Let us turn to a study by Erich Battistin, Agar Brugiavini, Enrico Rettore, and Guglielmo Weber. Published in the *American Economic Review* in 2009, the title of the article is "The Retirement Consumption Puzzle: Evidence from a Regression Discontinuity Approach."

The regression discontinuity approach is a method used by economists to study how different individuals respond near a threshold. In this case, the threshold refers to the pension eligibility age in Italy.

Here, the authors explore the variability in pension eligibility to evaluate the impact of retirement on spending. By assuming that consumption would be the same for individuals around the threshold should they not retire, we can estimate the causal effects of retirement by comparing the observations on both sides of the threshold.

Using data from the Bank of Italy Survey on Household Income and Wealth (SHIW) from 1993 to 2002, the authors concluded that there is a 10 percent fall in nondurable spending when households retire.

Figure 8.1: Household Expenditure by Age

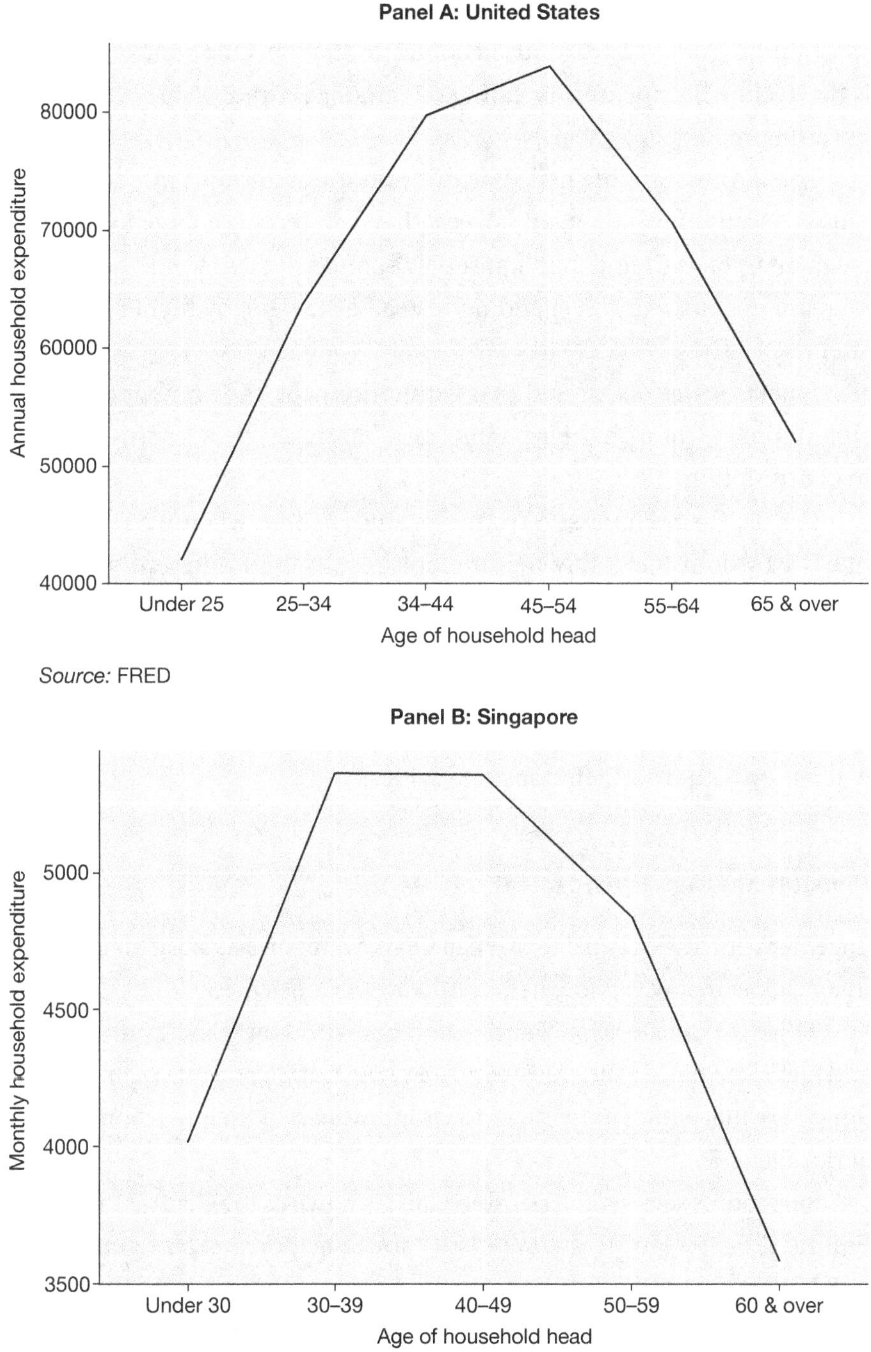

Source: Singapore Statistics

This is driven primarily by a fall in spending on work-related expenditures, such as clothing and transport. Moreover, there is a substitution from market goods to home production. One notable example is the decline in expenses for eating out among retirees as they transition toward home-cooked meals.

The authors established that this is not due to liquidity concerns. This is because for Italian employees, they will receive a large lump-sum payment upon retirement. If liquidity is a concern, there would be a sharp increase in consumption spending instead as they enjoy higher liquidity after they retire.

Finally, it was discovered that with retirement, the number of grown children who live with their parents also decreases, thus leading to a fall in consumption.

For us, the main lesson from this study is that when we retire, our lifestyles would inevitably be different, resulting in different spending habits. Accordingly, it is necessary to consider the lifestyle we desire in our financial planning for retirement and make concerted efforts to realize it.

We have highlighted that upon retirement, households decreased their spending and reduced their savings at a slow rate. So, what do retirees do when they withdraw their pension savings?

Pension Savings Withdrawal

Together with Jessica Pan and Wenlan Qian, Sumit investigates this question in an article that was published in *Management Science* in 2020.

Titled "Age of Decision: Pension Savings Withdrawal and Consumption and Debt Response," the study focused on an administrative regulation in Singapore that allows individuals to withdraw part of their pension savings at the age of 55.

Singapore's savings and pension plan is known as the Central Provident Fund (CPF). By law, it is compulsory for Singaporeans and permanent residents to contribute to the fund, which can be used to meet their retirement, healthcare, and housing needs. In general, employees will contribute 20 percent of their gross monthly salary, while employers will contribute an additional 16 percent of the salary.

The savings are divided into different accounts. While some parts of the savings are earmarked into a retirement-exclusive account (and cannot be withdrawn before retirement), other parts can be withdrawn for authorized reasons, such as housing, education, and medical expenses. Until retirement, no cash withdrawals are allowed.

This study specifically examined the timeframe between April 2010 to March 2012, in which individuals were able to withdraw 10 to 30 percent of their CPF when they turned 55. Their remaining balances would be disbursed to them when they reach age 65.

Through the analysis of monthly transaction data from a commercial bank during this period, the study centered on how individuals' financial decisions are affected when they become eligible to withdraw from their pension (i.e., at age 55).

It was found that individuals do choose to withdraw from the pension fund when presented with the opportunity. For retirees, there was a S$15,000 increase in their bank account balances, translating to an increase of 32 percent relative to the month before they turned 55 years old.

It was further documented that most savings were left unutilized in the bank account. Why would these retirees choose to withdraw and leave money in their bank accounts? By keeping their savings in CPF, they can enjoy a guaranteed interest rate ranging from 2.5 percent to 4 percent. Considering that deposit rates in other savings accounts are below 0.25 percent, it is worth exploring why these individuals would opt to withdraw their savings from the CPF and earn lower yield.

Besides increasing bank deposits, it was revealed that some retirees also pay their credit card debt and increase spending. This is particularly pronounced for low income households. Further evidence suggest that the rise in spending is connected to credit limitations, rather than discretionary expenses. For instance, the increase in spending is more significant for non-durable and non-visible goods when compared to visible goods.

We provided you with an example of what households do when they withdraw from their pension savings. While understanding individuals' actions when they withdraw money from pension funds is crucial, it is important to remember that everyone has different needs. What would you have done differently from the retirees discussed above? Would you opt to withdraw your savings early too?

Key Takeaways

Retirement is a major life change. As highlighted by the retirement savings puzzle and the retirement consumption puzzle, retirees tend to adjust their saving and spending habits after retirement.

Evidently, understanding our individual preferences and requirements when we retire is central to our savings plan. As we prepare to save for retirement, we ought to actively consider the different options that are available to make an informed choice.

In the earlier chapters, we have established the importance of savings and underscored the various challenges that we face. Our starting point is that individuals are not saving enough as they are present biased and are unable to consider the future.

Consequently, visualization techniques and tools help. Just like how imagery and visualization support professional athletes in improving their skills and performance, we should visualize our lives 10 or 20 years down the road. How do you envision your future savings and spending? We will turn to consumption in the next section of the book.

Part III

Spending

9

Weather

In Part III of this book, spending will take center stage. Spending and savings can be seen as opposite sides of the same coin. When individuals decide to spend, they forgo the opportunity to save. This is commonly known as opportunity cost.

In the previous chapters, we have discussed about the role of savings and highlighted that households are not saving enough for retirement. We also examined how households manage their retirement savings.

One fundamental principle behind savings is that we need to spend less than what we earn. Since most of us lack self-control, we prefer to spend now to derive immediate satisfaction.

This is exacerbated by external factors, which influence how we spend our money. When making decisions, we are exposed to a variety of psychological biases, which cause us to make suboptimal decisions.

While standard economic theory suggests that rational individuals make decisions that can maximize their lifetime utility, economic studies have documented that individuals are heavily influenced by current conditions.

To kick off our discussion of spending, we are going to talk about the weather. Indeed, it appears that the weather has the potential to impact our financial decision-making too.

Let us have a look at some case studies now.

Weather and Car Purchases

First and foremost, we are going to understand how weather impacts the purchase of cars. This has been discussed in a 2015 article in *The Quarterly Journal of Economics* by Meghan Busse, Devin Pope, Jaren Pope, and Jorge Silva-Risso.

Titled "The Psychological Effect of Weather on Car Purchases," the article examined how the weather at the time of purchase will impact individuals' decisions to purchase a convertible or four-wheel drive in the United States.

Cars are consumer durables that we use for a long period of time. On average, the life span of a car is around 8 to 12 years. Thus, at the time of purchase, buyers must estimate which vehicle will provide them with the highest benefit throughout the lifetime of the car.

Nonetheless, the article showed that buyers have erroneously purchased vehicles that have a higher perceived benefit at the time of purchase instead of basing the decision on the item's lifetime benefits.

Using transaction-level data for more than 40 million new and used vehicles from dealerships across the United States, it was found that changes in weather at the time of purchase will influence buyers to focus on specific features of the vehicles.

When the weather is warm and sunny at the time of purchase, buyers prefer vehicles that are more suitable for warm weather, such as convertibles. After taking into account seasonal sales patterns, it was estimated that an increase in temperature by 10 degrees Fahrenheit than normal will result in a 2.7 percent increase in the share of convertibles among sold cars. The results are also consistent across different seasons.

On the contrary, when the weather is cold and snowy at the time of purchase, buyers switch to vehicles that are more suitable for cold weather, such as four wheel drive vehicles. It was realized that with a snowstorm of

10 inches, the proportion of vehicles sold that are four-wheel drive increased by about 6 percent over the next two to three weeks.

For an economist, this is surprising! Since weather at the time of purchase will have little impact on the lifetime benefits of owning a vehicle, buyers should not respond to changes in the weather.

This stands in contrast to nondurable products, such as ice cream. It is understandable that one will prefer to have ice cream on a warm and sunny day, but we use cars for a longer period of time which spans different weather conditions.

Besides, buying a car is costly, and it takes up a large proportion of our income. Hence, we will expect individuals to pay more attention to their purchases.

The authors concluded that the findings can be explained by two psychological effects: projection bias and salience.

With projection bias, individuals' forecasts about the future are influenced by the current conditions and beliefs they have at the time of the prediction. Consequently, when it is sunny at the time of purchase, car buyers will predict that the weather will continue to be sunny in the long run.

Salience directs individuals' attention toward particular attributes of a product that stands out. By paying more attention to specific characteristics in different contexts, car buyers will value the features of a vehicle differently. For instance, on a sunny day, the feature of having a convertible will become more attractive as compared to a rainy day.

Recent economic studies have highlighted the importance of salience and consumer choices. Let us delve deeper into it.

Salience and Consumer Choice

In a 2013 article, titled "Salience and Consumer Choice" published in the *Journal of Political Economy*, Pedro Bordalo, Nicola Gennaioli, and Andrei Shleifer show that the context matters in drawing our attention to salient attributes of different goods.

The study highlights many interesting examples that can be accounted for using salience. One example involves choosing a red wine. Consider the following choices in a wine store:

- French Syrah: $20 a bottle
- Australian Shiraz: $10 a bottle

Let's suppose that you prefer French Syrah 50 percent more than Australian Shiraz. Despite your preference for French Syrah, you will end up choosing the Australian Shiraz as it is perceived to be a better bargain. For 1 French Syrah, you can get 2 Australian Shiraz.

Now, instead of visiting the wine store, you visit a restaurant that sells the same wine. This time round, both prices are marked up by $40 and you are provided with the following options:

- French Syrah: $60 a bottle
- Australian Shiraz: $50 a bottle

In this scenario, it is likely that you will order the French Syrah as you think that the French Syrah is worth 50 percent more than the Australian Shiraz. However, as it is only 20 percent more expensive than the Australian Shiraz, you will believe that it is a better deal.

What is happening is that in the wine store, the price difference is more salient than the quality difference. Hence, you will go for the cheaper wine. In comparison, in the restaurant, the quality difference is more salient, encouraging you to purchase the more expensive wine.

This implies that choices are made in context, as we choose goods by comparing them with others. Put differently, the choice set matters. As our attention is drawn to the salient attributes, we will focus on goods with high quality-to-price ratio.

Therefore, it is crucial to note what our options are. In some cases, by introducing irrelevant alternatives, it could even change the reference item and the salient attributes of existing alternatives. Ultimately, this could impact our decisions.

Mood and Credit Card Spending

We now consider the relationship between weather induced mood changes and spending. Weather has the potential to affect our mood as it influences how we feel and what we feel like doing. For instance, cold temperature is often associated with fatigue and sadness. Medical studies have also documented the presence of seasonal affective disorder (SAD), which is a type of depression that is more apparent in winter.

Together with Souphala Chomsisengphet, Stephan Meier, and Xin Zou, Sumit looks into how sunshine-induced mood could impact contemporaneous household credit card spending in the United States. This is examined in a 2020 article, in the *Journal of Banking & Finance* titled "In the Mood to Consume: Effect of Sunshine on Credit Card Spending."

To identify changes in mood, this study analyzed changes in local sunshine. It has been widely documented that sunshine has the ability to induce positive mood in individuals, resulting in more prosocial behavior and even romantic relationships. Among other reasons, this can be linked to the release of serotonin, which is a hormone that regulates our mood, appetite and sleep. On the contrary, a lack of sunshine is related to pessimism and depression.

How do we then measure sunshine? This can be achieved through the measurement of sky cover to quantify how much sunlight we can get. Sky cover refers to the percentage of opaque clouds that cover the sky. Thus, higher sunshine is related to lower sky cover.

As sky cover varies by season, seasonal patterns are accounted for by having another measurement that is known as the abnormal sky cover measurement. In its simplest form, the abnormal sky cover measurement refers to the deviation of daily sky cover for each zip code, as compared to the weekly average sky cover. As such, it shows the surprise change in the sky cover for the week.

Thereafter, the study makes use of administrative data from a large bank in the United States that issues credit cards nationwide to find out how consumption changes with sunshine. Through the analysis of 2 million credit card transactions from more than 125,000 customers in 19,000 zip codes, it was established that sunshine matters.

It was observed that an increase in the same day local abnormal sunshine by 1 unit led to a 0.3 percent rise in credit card expenditure. This is economically significant. For an average individual, this translates to an increase in spending of US$0.41 when the abnormal sunshine grew by 1 unit. Taking into account the size of the sample (125,000 customers), this signifies a US$51,000 boost in consumption!

Moreover, those with lower self-control are deemed to be more prone to the sunshine effect. It was shown that individuals with higher credit card debt as well as lower credit scores tend to be affected more by their mood.

What do individuals spend on when they are in good mood? It turns out that they spend more on durable goods, and not entertainment goods. When households are in a good mood, they become overly optimistic of the future.

So next time, when you are in a good mood, stop and think before you spend! Do you really need to buy the product? We will discuss more about credit card spending in Chapter 14 of this book.

Air Quality and Health Insurance

Next, we will discuss about air quality and its relation to spending. Changes in the quality of air, such as air pollution, have proven to be detrimental to one's health. With air pollution, individuals could experience symptoms, such as shortness of breath or watery eyes, almost immediately.

In the long run, this could result in respiratory issues, such as asthma attacks, and cardiovascular events, such as heart attacks.

Air quality can have significant impact on household behavior in different ways. While one could become more conscious toward their health and the environment, they could also change their lifestyle and purchase goods and services on impulse.

With that in mind, let us turn to a study by Tom Chang, Wei Huang, and Yongxiang Wang, titled "Something in the Air: Pollution and the Demand for Health Insurance." Published in *The Review of Economic Studies* in 2018, the research shed light on how changes in daily air pollution could impact the number of insurance contracts sold in China.

Changes in air quality are determined through the Air Quality Index (AQI), which is based on the level of PM2.5 in the air.

PM2.5 refers to fine particles with diameters less than 2.5 micrometers. While exposure to a small amount of PM2.5 poses little risk, high levels of PM2.5 could lead to serious aggravation of heart or lung diseases.

How do you think changes in air pollution could influence households' decisions to take up health-insurance? As the PM2.5 is rather stable over time, we should not expect individuals to react to short-term fluctuations in its value. This is because insurance involves long-term considerations. Moreover, the health insurance in question do not include preexisting conditions and have a 180-day waiting period before coverage commences.

Nonetheless, just like how daily weather impacts consumer durables, and daily sunshine impacts credit card spending, we find that daily air quality also impacts the purchase of insurance in China!

It was estimated that with an increase in daily AQI by one standard deviation, the number of insurance contracts sold on that day increased by 7.2 percent.

On the other hand, when the air quality improves thereafter, the study showed that more individuals end up canceling their contracts!

What is particularly interesting in this setting is that households can cancel their health insurance without any penalty within a 10-day cooling-off period. This provision is mandated by the Chinese government to protect the interests of consumers.

It was observed that during the cooling-off period, when there is a decrease in daily AQI by one standard deviation, the return probability increased by 4 percent!

In other words, when pollution is high, individuals are found to purchase health insurance. But once the pollution decreases during the cooling-off period, they cancel it!

Just like the previous study examining the psychological impact of weather on car buying decisions, the results of this study can be attributed to projection bias and salience too.

With projection bias, individuals will value health insurance more when there is high pollution that causes them to feel unwell. During that period, this led to a surge in the demand for insurance. However, once the pollution decreases and they no longer feel sick, the projection bias disappears. Subsequently, they end up canceling the insurance.

Salience in this situation refers to the risks of contracting pollution-related diseases being more salient when air pollution is high. Consequently, there is a higher demand for health insurance when air pollution is high, and a higher cancellation rate when air pollution is low.

Key Takeaways

We have shown you that our consumption patterns are driven by external factors, such as the weather. This could result in us overspending or purchasing goods and services that do not meet our needs.

What should we do to overcome these issues? It is time to follow the old adages "sleep on it" or "never go grocery shopping on an empty stomach."

To "sleep on it", we should devote more time and free our minds from distractions before making a decision.

As shown by studies of households changing their decisions during the cooling-off period, we should prioritize purchases that give us the opportunity to revert our decision (whenever possible).

This includes relying on "free returns" policies by retailers, or "free cancellation" policies for services. This provides us with time to deliberate and detract from our psychological biases.

10

Peer Effects

Social influence is another force that drives our spending habits. As Aristotle once said, "Man is by nature a social animal". Our attitudes, beliefs and behavior are most often influenced by others, including social comparison among peers.

Indeed, our peers and our social network play an important role in influencing our behavior. For instance, earlier studies have highlighted that the academic scores of college students are deemed to be heavily impacted by their roommates.

It is hence not surprising that our peers affect our spending behavior too. In general, economic studies have documented two types of behavior.

On one hand, we have individuals trying to "keep up with the Joneses" by comparing themselves with their peers. In trying to not fall behind their peers, they will attempt to match up with material possessions.

Besides, some would indulge in conspicuous consumption to signify their wealth and status. As a result, they end up buying expensive cars and clothes beyond their means.

On the other hand, there are also positive peer effects. By comparing with their peers, some individuals start to spend less and save more when they see that their peers are doing so.

In this chapter, we will examine the roles of peer influence in our financial decisions.

Peers' Income and Financial Distress

We first show that relative income differences among peers have the ability to cause financial distress. When an individual witnesses a growth in income relative to their peers and proceeds to spend more, it is possible that their peers will also respond by increasing their spending. This could potentially result in lower savings and higher borrowing for the peers.

Together with Vyacheslav Mikhed and Barry Scholnick, Sumit addressed this topic in an article in *The Review of Financial Studies* in 2020.

The article, titled, "Peers' Income and Financial Distress: Evidence from Lottery Winners and Neighbouring Bankruptcies," examines how the lottery winnings of an individual affects borrowings and bankruptcies of her neighbors in Canada.

Income shocks from lottery wins are a good way to understand peer effects because they eliminate the difficulty of distinguishing cause from effect. In this context, we are able to identify the lottery winner that enjoyed an increase in income.

Based on the random amount that is won in the lottery, we will know how much more the winner gains relative to his/her neighbors. As the income of the neighbors did not change, changes in their spending habits are most likely related to the lottery winners.

Indeed, peer effects matter. The analysis indicated that with an increase in the lottery prize of one individual in a small neighborhood, there would be more subsequent bankruptcies from other individuals in the same neighborhood.

More precisely, it was estimated that with a lottery win that is equivalent to the median annual income in the sample (S$29,229), the bankruptcies of neighbors within three years after the win is 6.59 percent higher than the average bankruptcy rate.

Financial insolvencies of neighbors can be attributed to changes in conspicuous consumption. Bankrupt neighbors spent more on visible assets (such as cars), as compared to less visible assets (such as furniture).

There are also changes in risk-taking behavior for neighbors of lottery winners. At the time of bankruptcy filing, the magnitude of the lottery win increases the value of risky assets (such as equities) and decreases the value of non-risky assets (such as pension savings) held by these individuals.

In terms of borrowing, it was found that the increase in debt for bankruptcy filers was driven through more secured debt (which is backed by collateral), and not unsecured debt. This provides suggestive evidence that lenders are cognizant of the higher risk that they are bearing and seek to mitigate their losses by issuing secured debts, which are less risky for them.

Finally, it was illustrated using credit bureau data that all individuals in lottery-winning neighborhoods increased their borrowing in areas with larger lottery wins as compared to smaller ones. This further supports the role of relative income in peer effects.

Thy Neighbor's Misfortune

We have seen how an increase in income of a lottery winner resulted in her peers being in financial distress. In the event that an individual falls into financial distress, how will their peers respond?

Sumit takes on this question with Wenlan Qian and Xin Zou in an article named "Thy Neighbour's Misfortune: Peer Effect on Consumption," published in the *American Economic Journal: Economic Policy* in 2021.

Through an examination of individuals' consumption response to same-building neighbors declaring bankruptcy in Singapore, the article aims to uncover insights into peer effects with negative shocks.

There are many strict laws that govern bankruptcy in Singapore. With the supervision of the government, individuals need to pay back their debt after bankruptcy. They are only deemed to be discharged from bankruptcy after they repay their debts (in full) or make a settlement offer, which is accepted by a majority of their creditors.

For an extended period of time, bankrupt individuals are not allowed to consume anything beyond subsidence needs. As an illustration, they cannot purchase any luxury goods or go traveling overseas. They also cannot purchase a vehicle, or even take taxis to travel around. In fact, they can only commute by public transport.

In addition, personal bankruptcy is public information. Singapore government publishes the notification of bankruptcy through the *Government Gazette*, so individuals will know that their neighbors have experienced bankruptcy.

With stringent laws and high social stigma, individuals in Singapore will avoid filing for bankruptcy, unless they are left with no other choices.

Nonetheless, the bankruptcy law in Singapore does offer some form of protection for individuals who declare bankruptcy.

For example, for those staying in public housing, their houses are protected from being seized and liquidated. Hence, individuals can still interact and maintain ties with their neighbors.

In Singapore, more than 80 percent of the resident population stays in public housing. Known as the Housing Development Board (HDB) flats, it is catered to Singaporean citizens and permanent residents, and is heavily subsidized. One of the key objectives of HDB in Singapore is to promote a cohesive community. HDB flats are located in estates with many shared amenities, such as schools and supermarkets.

As HDB flats are mainly located in buildings, there are also ample opportunities for individuals to interact. These include common corridors, lift lobbies, or open spaces on the ground floor.

To examine how bankrupt individuals and their peers change their spending behavior, this study relied on the credit card and debit card spending data from a leading Singapore bank with a market share of more than 80 percent.

First, it was observed that individuals who encounter bankruptcy experienced a 78 percent decrease in spending. The substantial decrease in consumption is not surprising and can be attributed to the decline in personal liquidity and the constraints imposed by bankruptcy laws.

What about their neighbors? It would be of interest to examine whether neighbors in the same building change their behavior when their neighbors are in financial distress.

The study demonstrated peer effects at work. It was estimated that relative to the period of 12 to 2 months before an individual declared bankruptcy, their neighbors in the same building decreased their total debit and credit card spending by 3.4 percent.

In comparison, there are no changes in consumption for individuals who are in immediately adjacent buildings.

Put together, it was found that a 10 percent fall in card consumption by the bankrupt individual results in a fall in card consumption of 0.44 percent for one peer. With an average of 65 households in each HDB building, it means that the total consumption impact is around 28 percent.

Thus, there is a significant social multiplier, which is 2.8 times the magnitude of the initial financial distress by the bankrupt individual.

Crowdsourcing

Given that peer effects have the potential to influence our spending, can we use them to change our spending behavior?

This has been examined in a recent study by Francesco D'Acunto, Alberto Rossi, and Michael Weber. Titled "Crowdsourcing Financial Information to Change Spending Behavior," the study relied on a FinTech app to examine how individuals in the United States change their spending behavior when provided with information about their peers.

The free-to-use FinTech app is called Status. Users sign up for the app on their own and provide Status with personal information, such as demographic characteristics, credit scores, and salary.

In order to help users improve their saving decisions, Status provides them with information on the national average spending, as well as their peers' spending. Their peers' spending is calculated through the average (seasonally adjusted) monthly expenditure of other consumers with similar characteristics as the users.

With the information on the users' past and present transactions from their accounts that are directly linked to Status, Status can then compare the progress of the users' monthly expenditure with that of their peers. They are then presented to the users through easy-to-understand graphics.

Having information of others do matter! The authors revealed that when users are provided with information on their peers' spending, they do respond by reverting to the mean.

Relative to their peers, users who overspend reduced their average spending by $237, while users who underspend increased their average spending by $71. The impact is larger for users who are further away from the spending average.

This suggests that individuals are learning from the crowdsourced information provided by Status, and they seek to converge to the mean. It is noteworthy that at no point in time, Status mentioned that the average expenditure of the peers is optimal. Users automatically followed "wisdom of the crowds."

It was discovered that overspenders cut their spending by a larger extent as compared to underspenders, who increased their spending. The cut in spending is most pronounced for the low-income users. Hence, it is likely that users do face pressure when they are being compared with their peers.

Upon further investigation, the fall in spending is attributed to discretionary spending, such as food and drinks, clothes, and entertainment. On the other hand, nondiscretionary spending, such as groceries and utility bills, remained unchanged.

Consequently, this study shows that FinTech apps have the potential to transmit financial literacy and provide financial information to households. This serves as a cost-effective and salient way for individuals to learn from others.

By providing individuals with crowdsourced information about others, they will be able to learn from their peers' spending choices, impacting their own spending.

Savings More in Groups

We have provided you with several examples of peer effects influencing consumption. Do peer effects directly influence how much we save too? Can they help us overcome the self-control problems that we have highlighted earlier?

As changes in savings indirectly impact our consumption expenditure, it will be interesting to see if we can target savings through social influence as well.

The role of peer influence and savings have been examined by Felipe Kast, Stephan Meier, and Dina Pomeranz in an article in the *Journal of Development Economics* in 2018.

Titled "Saving More in Groups: Field Experimental Evidence from Chile," the authors conducted randomized trials among 2,687 microcredit clients in Chile.

The field experiment was conducted with clients of a microcredit association in Chile who often met in groups. They were given the opportunity to have a formal savings account and were randomly assigned to one of the following three groups:

1. Control Group
   - The first group is the control group in which individuals were offered a basic account with an interest rate of 0.3 percent.
2. Savings Group
   - The second group is the savings group in which individuals were offered the basic account and given the choice to set and openly announce their savings goals.
   - Based on the deposit slips that the participants brought to the meeting, the goals would be monitored publicly in the weekly meetings.
   - Participants who met their goals would be given a nonmonetary recognition in the form of a sticker in a booklet. With enough stickers, they will receive a diploma as an award. There are no financial rewards.

3. High-Interest Group
   - The third group is the high-interest group. As compared to the basic account in the other two groups, they are given a high interest rate of 5 percent.
   - It was explicitly mentioned that it is the "Most Profitable Interest in the Market," and that participants were taught about the importance of interest rate returns.

Guess which group managed to save the most? It's the savings group! Individuals in the savings group deposited 3.7 times more frequently than the control group and that their average saving balances are double that of the control group. The increase in savings for the savings group corresponds to 32 percent of their monthly savings.

In comparison, the high-interest group experienced a smaller increase in savings relative to the control group. The findings suggest that nonfinancial incentives in groups play a more significant role in influencing individuals to save.

In a follow-up interview, it was observed that the increase in savings by the savings group corresponds to the amount of precautionary savings that they would like to have. These include unexpected visits to doctors or payments for food and electricity when there are fluctuations in short-term income.

What drives the increase in savings for the savings group? Is it due to peer pressure? To have a better understanding of the drivers behind the increase in savings, the author conducted another experiment: a Feedback Message Experiment. This time, the authors focus on 871 participants in the savings group with cell phones

It was found that having a real-life savings buddy who consistently monitors their behavior yielded comparable results to those who are simply informed of their own accomplishments and the achievements of others through text messages.

Hence, peer pressure (through a savings buddy) does not influence the behavior of households when it comes to savings. Rather, social influence offers a mutual service by holding each other accountable and reminding them of their goals. We will save more just by seeing how much more our peers are saving.

Key Takeaways

Social influences shape our thoughts and behavior, including how we spend and save. This is particularly pertinent in today's society where social media influence is prevalent. However, it is unclear whether social influence is our friend or foe. Whether peer effects can positively or negatively impact us depends on the situation.

While managing our finances, it is important to consider the role of peer effects and be wary of them in our daily lives. Nonetheless, we can also use them to our advantage to reach our financial goals.

As motivational speaker Jim Rohn once said, "You are the average of the five people you spend the most time with." Therefore, it is crucial that you make wise choices regarding the people you surround yourself with.

11

Digital Payments

We will now discuss about the mode of payment. There has been an increase in the use of digital and contactless payments globally. This has been partially accelerated by the coronavirus pandemic as households avoid handling cash to reduce the spread of the virus and rely on online shopping to maintain social distancing.

Based on estimates from the World Bank, in countries such as Australia, Canada, and Japan, the percentage of people above the age of 15 who have made or received a digital payment in 2021 was above 95 percent.

Since individuals in many countries are turning to alternative ways to make their purchases instead of using cash, it is timely to understand the impact of using digital payments on us. Popular forms of digital payments include the use of debit and credit cards, mobile payments, as well as mobile wallets.

Both debit and credit cards are payment cards that individuals can use to pay for their spending. The key difference between debit cards and credit cards is that our debit cards are linked directly to our bank account, and the funds will be deducted in real time.

In comparison, credit cards allow us to pay later. Hence, credit cards serve another function: borrowing. As the use of credit cards plays a huge role in how we finance our purchases, we will devote one chapter on credit cards in the next part on borrowing. In this chapter, we will focus primarily on its role as a cashless form of payment.

Mobile payments relate to the use of spending using our mobile phone. For example, we could make contactless payments using our phone by tapping near a point-of-sale (POS) terminal. Popular mobile payment services include Apply Pay and Google Pay.

Similarly, there are also mobile wallet applications, which allow us to make payments through stored value. For instance, we can buy a cup of Starbucks coffee using the value that we have stored in the Starbucks mobile app.

This is not to be confused with mobile money, which is a privately owned service that allows individuals to send and receive money using their mobile phones. In the case of mobile money, we do not require a bank account. Only a mobile number is necessary!

A leading mobile money operator in Africa is M-PESA. Operated by Vodafone and Safaricom, the largest mobile network operator in Kenya, M-PESA is estimated to have more than 50 million customers in 2022.

Digital and contactless payments provide multiple benefits. Without the need for cash, households enjoy greater convenience in a safer setting as they no longer have to store, transport, and count large amounts of paper bills and coins. This saves time, resulting in a fall in transaction costs. Moreover, data is encrypted, providing more security to customers.

In what follows, we will discuss the impact of different digital payments in Mexico, India, and Singapore.

Debit Cards in Mexico

Digital payments have the potential to benefit individuals that have restricted access to financial resources. This is commonly known as the underserved population. By providing individuals access to affordable financial services, it can reach out to those who did not have opportunities to access financial services previously.

Furthermore, digital payments in the form of debit cards can reduce transaction costs as it will become more convenient for individuals to make purchases. Cardholders can also access their money easily through a network of ATMs. This will lower the monitoring cost of checking their balances, which will increase their trust in banks.

With a fall in transaction costs and monitoring costs, it has been shown that individuals in developing countries are able to spend less and save more when debit cards are being introduced to them.

Let us delve into a study by Pierre Bachas, Paul Gertler, Sean Higgins, and Enrique Seira that is published in *The Journal of Finance* in 2021. The study, titled, "How Debit Cards Enable the Poor to Save More," revolved around a natural experiment in Mexico, in which debit cards that are linked to current savings accounts were given to recipients of the Mexican conditional cash transfer program Oportunidades.

Oportunidades is one of the largest conditional transfer programs globally. Every two months, the program gives cash to poor families who meet the requirement of sending their children to school and having preventive health checkups.

For most beneficiaries, the transfer benefits were deposited directly into their savings account at Bansefi, a government bank that is formed to support financial inclusion among the underserved population.

Prior to the issuance of debit cards in 2009, it was discovered that most recipients would withdraw the transfers physically at the nearest Bansefi branch. On average, 99.5 percent of the transfers were withdrawn. After the debit cards were being introduced, it was found that the beneficiaries started to save. In two years, they built up savings that were close to 2 percent of their annual salary.

The increase in savings did not result from beneficiaries redirecting other sources of savings to their bank accounts. It was established that the increase in savings is financed by a fall in current consumption.

Why does having debit cards make formal savings more attractive? The authors documented that with debit cards, savings can be easily accessed when needed. Consequently, the transaction costs of accessing the account have been reduced.

Nonetheless, the increase in savings takes time. It was observed that most beneficiaries made use of the card to monitor the account balances first. This highlights the importance of trust in digital payments.

Hence, digital payments provide opportunities for the unbanked and underbanked households to access financial services that they did not have previously. As the introduction of digital payments reduces transaction costs and monitoring costs, it has the potential to transform the lives of many.

QR Code Payment in Singapore

Another benefit of digital payment is that it can stimulate business creation, leading to economic growth and more choices for consumers.

Together with Wenlan Qian, Yuan Ren, Hsien-Tien Tsai, and Bernard Yeung, Sumit examined how mobile payment technology managed to influence business growth in Singapore.

In a research study named "The Real Impact of FinTech: Evidence from Mobile Payment Technology," it was shown that the introduction of Quick Respond (QR) code payment technology by the largest bank in Singapore managed to reshape business activities.

The study relied on two key initiatives that happened in 2017. In April 2017, DBS, Singapore's leading bank, introduced QR code payments to its customers. In July 2017, mobile interbank fund transfer was introduced to allow funds transfer between different banks using mobile phones.

This led to an increase in the adoption of mobile payments in Singapore. In fact, the number of customers who used mobile payments for the first time increased by more than 300 percent after the first year.

How do firms respond?

The QR code payment is a form of new mobile technology that allows consumers to make financial transactions by scanning QR codes on their mobile phones. As its launch primarily benefits industries with retail customers, the study compared changes of business-to-consumer industries with those of business-to-business industries.

Using administrative business registry data of all the firms in Singapore, it was found that there was an increase in monthly business creation among business-to-consumer industries by 8.9 percent relative to business-to-business industries after the introduction of QR code payments. This is equivalent to an increase of 156 firms.

The increase in business creation is attributed to small firms. As mobile payment technology provides cost savings benefits to merchants, the relative impact is felt more by companies who are smaller in scale.

Besides, stronger business creation is found in high cash-cost industries, showing that industries with a higher cost of cash handling benefit the most from digital payments.

What about consumers?

It was observed that consumers who switch from cash usage to mobile payment end up withdrawing a lesser amount of cash from ATMs. This eventually relates to the closure of ATM machines by the bank.

In addition, consumers end up spending 4.2 percent more per month! It is worth noting that the increase in spending is not only due to spending using mobile payments. There is also an increase in credit card spending. With an increase in spending, this could further benefit merchants by boosting sales growth. Consumers also benefit by having more variety and enjoying more goods and services.

Notwithstanding, there remains one unanswered question. Are consumers spending too much when there are digital payments?

Demonetization in India

It is possible that digital payments can also lead to overconsumption if left unchecked. Since cash is more salient than digital payments, individuals might end up overspending instead!

This is related to the psychology of using cash. With mental accounting, households might treat cash and mobile wallets differently. With loss aversion, households feel the pain of cash being taken away relative to the use of contactless payments.

Also known as the cashless effect in the behavioral science literature, it has been proven that when payments are more tangible, spending money is more psychologically painful. Consequently, when digital payments are more convenient and less noticeable, individuals may end up spending more.

We now address this concern through a recent article that Sumit coauthored with Pulak Ghosh, Jing Li, and Tianyue Ruan. This article is titled "Digital Payments Induce Over-Spending: Evidence from the 2016 Demonetization in India" and shed light on how households in India changed their spending due to demonetization in India.

On November 8, 2016, the Indian government unexpectedly announced that all 500 rupees and 1,000 rupees banknotes of the Mahatma Gandhi Series were not legal tender overnight, effectively removing 86 percent of the existing currency in circulation.

The stated objective of demonetization was to remove fake paper notes, weed out black money, and reduce corruption. Nonetheless, new notes were not made available immediately. Instead, they were introduced gradually, causing a shortage of cash in the economy. Thus, individuals had no choice but to rely on digital payments.

The study relied on transaction level data from a large supermarket chain in India. Following demonetization, the percentage of payment in cash fell by 20 percentage points in November 2016.

Since cash-reliant individuals were affected to a larger extent as they were compelled to switch to digital payments, the study focused on an individual level measure of forced adoption. This is based on the amount of cash payments before the demonetization.

It was estimated that for each 10-percentage point increase in cash dependence before demonetization, the use of digital payments grew by 3.38 percent, and monthly spending increased by 3 percent.

Additionally, individuals with lower spending habits were observed to exhibit a greater shift toward digital payments and a larger spending response compared to individuals with higher spending habits.

We would like to highlight that the growth in spending is persistent across time, even when the demonetized notes were being replenished. As a result, the increase in digital payments induced by the reduction in cash availability led to an increase in spending.

This is due to nonfood and durable spending, as compared to food and nondurable consumption. In addition, households who were compelled to use digital payments rather than cash ended up purchasing more expensive goods in several narrowly defined categories.

The study further showed that the change in spending is attributed to the diminished saliency of digital payments. For instance, the study compared the changes in the offline supermarket with an online grocery store. It was subsequently found that while the switch to digital payments is stronger in the online grocery panel, the spending is much muted. This suggests that salience plays a key role in consumer spending as cash is more salient in the offline supermarket than the online grocery store.

Key Takeaways

Innovation in payments has transformed the banking sector and will continue to do so. In the near future, there will be further improvements in cross-border payments and central banks could even start offering digital currencies.

While this is expected to further improve financial inclusion and help central banks better manage the economy, we must be careful not to be overly carried away by the new freedom that we have.

We have underscored the proliferation of digital payments, and how it has impacted different economies. By looking at case studies from Mexico, India, and Singapore, we find that digital payments can encourage savings and spur economic growth at the same time.

With an increase in convenience and efficiency, digital payments are here to stay. In fact, some places have shifted toward a cashless system, such that they only accept digital payments.

However, there is a danger of overspending associated with the dwindling salience of physical money. Amid the new payment landscape, it is more important (than ever) for individuals to keep track of their spending and consume responsibly.

And this can be done easily with digital payments. Through mobile apps from banks, we can download and track our expenditures over time. This allows us to track our spending behavior and identify whether we have overspent our budget. Keeping to our budget will ensure that we are not spending beyond our means.

Finally, digital payments carry significant downside risks, if not managed carefully. We will discuss about the technology-related risks in the next chapter.

12

Online Privacy and Fraud

Without a doubt, technology has made our lives much easier and more comfortable. From online shopping to food delivery, digital services have transformed our lives and provided us with great convenience. As discussed in the previous chapter, digital payments have also reduced transaction costs, time spent, and resources.

Nonetheless, this is not without risk. With more data being available online, there is the potential misuse and abuse of data.

As we rely more on digital services in our financial transactions, we need to be aware of the potential dangers posed in the digital era. In this chapter, we are going to address two main threats: online privacy and fraud.

Online Privacy

Recently, there has been a huge increase in digital data as more of us turn to the digital economy in managing our financial transactions. As companies accumulate a significant amount of confidential consumer data, there is a threat of cybersecurity breaches.

For users of digital services, cybersecurity breaches can result in data leakages, posing privacy concerns. There have been several incidents of massive data breaches in recent years. Yahoo's data breach in 2013 exposed the real names, e-mail addresses, dates of birth, and telephone numbers of all its 3 billion users. eBay's data breach in 2014 revealed the passcodes as well as the personal information of 145 million users.

Hence, there is a trade-off between convenience and privacy. How much do individuals value convenience relative to privacy?

Together with Pulak Ghosh, Tianyue Ruan, and Yunqi Zhang, Sumit addressed this question in a recent study titled "Privacy versus Convenience: Customer Response to Data Breaches of Their Information". The study investigated how customers respond to privacy leakers in different unexpected data breaches in India.

In all, data breaches for three different Indian firms in different industries were being examined. We will only focus on the first data breach that involved a leading online food delivery platform.

The aggregator platform allows individuals to order food across different restaurants and have their food delivered to them. Customers can choose to pay using cash or digital payments.

In May 2017, it was reported that there was a data breach involving 17 million users. While no payment information was leaked, users' names, e-mail addresses, and passwords were revealed.

Upon examining the receipts from the platform, it was found that there was a fall in overall usage after the announcement of the data breach. Moreover, this was driven by a fall in food orders using digital payments rather than cash.

This suggests that consumers are more concerned about payment security (rather than their private information). Despite the fact that no payment information was revealed, digital payments fell by 6 to 10.6 percent as compared to cash payments during the first month.

However, the fall in spending was short term. By the third month of the data breach, the difference between digital and cash payments disappeared. Evidently, consumers seem to value convenience over the cost of privacy leakages.

In fact, the data breaches do not seem to deter new customers from using the platform. In terms of observable characteristics, new customers were similar to the existing ones.

The study showed similar results in the other two data breaches. In the second data breach, user information of an online grocery store was leaked in 2018 due to Facebook's third-party login function. In the third data breach, more than 3.2 million debit cards from major Indian banks were compromised.

While users did respond in the short run, they did not change their behavior significantly and continued their lives as per normal thereafter.

Cyber Fraud

We will now turn to cyber fraud, which occurs when criminals illegally obtain an individual's personal and financial information stored online.

Upon acquiring the personal data of the victims, these criminals would then attempt to access the victim's bank accounts and payment cards. As long as the criminals are able to utilize the victim's banking account services, they can make payments or obtain cash illegally. In some cases, all the financial assets of a victim could be stolen within seconds!

How does cyber fraud work?

To obtain personal data from individuals, fraudsters will directly contact their potential victims. This could be in the form of phishing e-mails, vishing, and smishing. Vishing (phishing through voices) makes use of fraudulent phone calls, while smishing (phishing through SMS) is implemented through text messages.

Once the fraudster catches the attention of the victim, they will then ask for confidential information. This is often done by pretending to be a person of higher authority, such as police officers and tax authorities.

Other common lies include suggestions that the victim has won a lottery or that their bank accounts have been compromised.

In doing so, they will ask for highly confidential information involving their bank details as well as personal information, such as date of birth and address.

This will provide them with sufficient information to do banking transactions through the victim's accounts. Occasionally, voices would be recorded and used as one of the biometric identifiers to overcome security measures.

Another type of technology-enabled fraud occurs when the victims unknowingly access fraudulent websites.

In this situation when the victim keys in their personal credit card details to purchase products on fraudulent e-commerce websites, the fraudster would have all the necessary information to purchase products using the victim's card illegally.

Besides purchasing products or withdrawing money illegally, fraudsters might also take over the entire account, so that the original owner can no longer access it. The list of cyber fraud goes on and on, and the possibilities seem limitless. With each passing moment, cyber fraud is constantly evolving as technology advances and criminals become more sophisticated. What is important for us is to stay informed and take measures to protect ourselves proactively.

Behavioral Biases and Scams

Individuals fall for scams as fraudsters seek to elicit an emotional response. Fraudsters rely on the behavioral biases of households, so that they provide emotive responses, rather than cognitive ones.

According to the Bounded Rationality theory developed by Herbert Simon, the 1978 recipient of the Nobel Memorial Prize in Economic Sciences, individuals are unable to make decisions rationally due to cognitive ability, time constraint, and imperfect information.

We recognize that fraudsters seek to exploit all three factors, engineering individuals to fall for their scams.

Firstly, research has documented that individuals with lower cognitive ability are more susceptible to scams. For instance, the elderly is specifically targeted by scammers as they are less familiar with technology, making them vulnerable to fraud.

Individuals with lower cognitive ability are also more likely to have regret aversion bias, which is making decisions to avoid regretting their decision in the future. This is also associated with the fear of missing out (FOMO) whereby these individuals fear that they will miss the "opportunity" that is presented to them.

The second factor is time constraint. This is related to the principle of scarcity. By showing that the offer is only limited for a short period of time or that households would be penalized if they do not comply immediately, time pressure is put on them.

Consequently, establishing a sense of urgency makes it more difficult for households to think clearly and make a sound decision.

Finally, we have imperfect information. Scammers usually show that they have information about their victims, validating the narrative of the message. While this information could be obtained from social media or the dark web, it inevitably increases the credibility of the message.

On top of that, scammers often include information about real-world events and claim to be from reputable organizations, making the message appear more reliable and trustworthy.

Protecting Our Personal Data

After understanding how technology fraud works, we hope that you have a better appreciation of the need to protect your own personal data.

It is most crucial that we do not send personal data to strangers, especially those that we cannot verify. This will reduce the likelihood that our information is being misused by scammers.

To prevent falling prey to fraudulent websites or mobile apps, one way is to refer to the official channels as far as possible. Therefore, we should exercise caution and refrain from taking shortcuts or relying on QR codes that we cannot authenticate.

In addition, we should be particularly wary of time-sensitive offers and avoid taking part in online promotions from unknown companies that ask for our personal details. When in doubt, it is wise to consult someone else first. By openly discussing our concerns with a trusted party, we can make a more informed judgment. As the Chinese proverb goes, "An outsider can see things more clearly and objectively than those involved."

Finally, it is of utmost importance to have a secure password. Passwords are like the keys to one's home in the virtual world. It is crucial not to disclose it to anyone.

Short and simple passwords are also highly discouraged. With an easy-to-guess password, it is akin to hiding the keys under the doormat. How fast it would take for a computer to crack a password depends on the number of characters, as well as the type of characters.

For a password with less than seven characters, hackers are able to guess the code almost instantly. In contrast, the following lists how long it will take to crack a password for passwords with 10 characters:

- Lowercase letters only: one hour
- At least one uppercase letter: one month
- At least one uppercase letter and one number: seven months
- At least one uppercase letter, one number, and one symbol: five years

Evidently, it is advisable to have long passwords with a combination of different types of characters.

On top of that, unique passwords and security settings for separate accounts are recommended, so that criminals will not be able to access all the accounts once one account is compromised.

Nonetheless, economic research has documented that households tend to use the same passwords for almost all their accounts. Besides finding it difficult to remember so many passwords, another reason is due to the endowment effect in behavioral economics. As passwords are personal, they grow an attachment to them and tend to use these passwords more often. Hence, households take the easy alternative of recycling passwords.

How is it possible to remember so many passwords?

We recognize that it is challenging to remember so many passwords. To overcome the challenge of recalling multiple passwords, password managers that provide strong encryption could be used instead. Password managers are programs that help to store, generate, and manage passwords for the user. This will reduce the need to memorize so many passwords.

Key Takeaways

We have discussed about online privacy and fraud in this chapter. These are particularly pertinent as we rely more on digital platforms in our financial decisions.

In an age of misinformation and online fraud, digital literacy is of paramount importance when managing our finances. This is an essential part of the household financial management toolkit. While managing our finances online, we must proactively learn how to safeguard our personal information and passwords, and develop the skills to identify potential scammers.

When faced with new e-mails, text messages, phone calls, or websites, always learn to verify first. Do not rush. Take time to consider and verify the authenticity of the recipient before proceeding.

As we equip ourselves with the necessary skills and knowledge, we can better detect fraud, and not fall prey to scammers. After all, fraud prevention is ultimately an individual's responsibility.

Part IV

Borrowing

13

Credit Markets

In Part IV, we will address the topic of borrowing. It is common for most of us to require financial borrowing at some point in our lives. This is done through the credit markets when lenders lend us a sum of money. In return, we will pay them interest on top of the amount that is being borrowed.

The credit market is integral to the functioning of the economy. In fact, one of the primary objectives of finance is to channel credit into its most productive use. When firms borrow more and increase their investments, they create more jobs, leading to an increase in economic growth. Similarly, when individuals borrow more and increase their consumption, their standard of living increases.

Borrowing has the potential to improve one's financial situation. For instance, it can help us pay for assets that we may not be able to afford right away. As most of us do not have the full amount needed to purchase houses and cars, we take up housing loans and car loans to finance our purchases. This will help us to build wealth and increase our quality of life.

Moreover, study loans allow students to access higher education if they are financially constrained, increasing their employment opportunities and prospects. Loans can also help individuals tide over in the short run. These include handling emergencies, such as medical bills, repairs, or a sudden loss of income.

Nonetheless, it is important to borrow responsibly. We have seen that individuals are present biased and exhibit hyperbolic discounting. Consequently, some individuals could have the tendency to consume more today, and often at the expense of tomorrow.

In addition, they could be overly optimistic about their ability to repay these loans. If they borrow more to finance more purchases, they could eventually end up in debt that they are unable to repay.

We will first provide an overview of borrowing in this chapter, before discussing about other types of borrowing, such as credit cards, overdrafts and payday loans, in the next few chapters. We will also have an in-depth discussion about home loans (mortgages) in Chapter 23 of this book.

When we borrow, it is important to obtain the appropriate loan that best suits our needs since different loans serve different purposes. To develop a better understanding of the types of loans, it is necessary to gain some insights on how credit markets work.

Asymmetric Information

In credit markets, financial intermediaries provide loans to borrowers after weighing their credit risk and determining their viability of repayment. Based on the individuals' circumstances, credit would then be given for a certain amount at a provided interest rate.

As interest rates reflect the risk of borrowing, different individuals with different credit risks would be offered different interest rates. The less creditworthy you are, the higher the interest rate. If the individual is deemed too risky, financial intermediaries might not be able to lend them as well.

This is due to asymmetric information in credit markets. As the borrower has more information than the lender, the lender does not know whether the borrower would be able to repay their loans.

There are two possible causes of asymmetric information: adverse selection and moral hazard.

In the case of adverse selection, high-risk borrowers will have a higher tendency to borrow. Therefore, before granting loans, financial intermediaries spend a lot of time collecting information about these borrowers before determining whether they are worthy of getting credit.

The other problem financial intermediaries face is moral hazard. If the bank gives credit, borrowers may have incentives to behave badly, splurge the money, and even default.

The combination of adverse selection and moral hazard results in financial intermediaries studying and monitoring customers on a regular basis in order to avoid delinquency defaults and bankruptcies.

Credit Scores and Collateral

One important indicator of how likely a customer can pay back is the credit score. Through credit reports produced by credit reporting companies (known as credit bureaus), lenders will decide on the type of loan that will be offered to a customer.

The type of credit scores varies across countries. In the United States, the FICO credit scores are often used as a measure of risk for borrowers. Ranging between 300 and 850, the higher the score, the more creditworthy the borrower is.

The credit scores are determined by specific factors, such as payment history, utilization of credit, credit age, credit mix, and credit inquiries. For instance, on-time payments could increase the scores, while late or missed payments could decrease the scores.

Consider the purchase of a $305,000 single-family home with a 20 percent down payment. Based on calculations from Forbes, the interest rates (based on APR) that are offered on a 30-year mortgage of $244,000 (i.e., 80 percent loan) are shown in Table 13.1.

It is evident that the higher the FICO Score, the lower the interest rate. The interest rate differences could be substantial. Across the lifetime of the loan, those with FICO Scores in the highest bracket (760–850) pay lesser total interest payments of $85,000 as compared to those in the lowest bracket (620–639).

Table 13.1: FICO Score and Interest Rate

FICO Score	APR	Total Interest Paid
760–850	4.147%	$182,840
700–759	4.369%	$194,261
680–699	4.546%	$203,476
660–679	4.76%	$214,745
640–659	5.19%	$237,797
620–639	5.736%	$267,829

Source: Forbes

Hence, it is paramount to have a good credit score. We should actively engage in activities that could increase our credit scores. These include paying on time, every time, as well as reducing debt balances.

Besides the credit score, another critical element that impacts interest rate is the amount of down payment. The higher the down payment, the less risky the loan is, and consequently, the lower the interest rate.

This is related to the role of collateral, which is something that we pledge as a form of security when taking loans.

In general, there are two types of loans: secured loans and unsecured loans. With secured loans, the loan is backed by a collateral—such as a home or a car. A home mortgage is an example of a secured loan.

As the financial intermediaries will have a claim on the asset if the borrowers are unable to repay the loans, the risk borne by the lenders will be reduced. Therefore, the interest rate will be lower as compared to unsecured loans.

Table 13.2 presents the average interest rates of different types of loans in the United States as of December 2021. Since credit card loans are unsecured in nature, they require higher interest rates than auto loans and mortgages.

Treasury bonds, in contrast, have the lowest interest rate. This is because as government securities, treasury bonds are deemed to be less

Table 13.2: Per Annum Interest Rates Across Loans in the United States as of December 2021

Credit Card	48-Month Auto Loan	30-Year Mortgage	30-Year Treasury Bond
14.51%	4.58%	3.10%	1.85%

Source: FRED

risky than debt payable by us. In fact, government securities are considered to be among the safest, as they have the backing of the government that issued them.

We need to be mindful of the different types of loans and interest rates that are being charged. Given the choices available to us, we ought to optimize our decisions by choosing across different types of loans with the lowest interest rates.

FinTech Lending

Apart from choosing the loan types, we must also decide on the lenders. Beyond traditional banks, there are also modern financial intermediaries such as FinTech lenders. There has been an increase in FinTech lenders that rely entirely on technology to process loans in recent years. In the United States, FinTech lenders are growing at a rapid pace and have gained double-digit market share in the mortgage market.

In fact, since 2018, the largest mortgage originator in the United States is a FinTech lender, Rocket Mortgage. By relying on electronic documentation, Rocket Mortgage collects information about the borrower and makes approval decisions in as little as eight minutes.

Recent studies have suggested how innovations by FinTech lenders have resulted in cost savings and increased convenience for borrowers. Let us have a closer look at an article by Andreas Fuster, Matthew Plosser, Philipp Schnabl, and James Vickery in *The Review of Financial Studies* in 2019.

The research article, titled "The Role of Technology in Mortgage Lending," demonstrates that FinTech lenders process mortgage applications faster than other firms. On average, it is estimated that FinTech lenders process mortgage applications about 20 percent faster.

It is noteworthy that the speed does not reduce the quality of the loans as faster processing does not result in riskier loans. In fact, the default rates on FinTech mortgages are lower than that for traditional lenders.

In addition, FinTech lenders are found to be more responsive to changes in demand shocks. As an illustration, when the application volume doubles, FinTech lenders require 7.5 days to process applications, whereas traditional lenders typically take 13.5 days.

Consequently, FinTech lenders could be attractive to borrowers who prefer speed and convenience as compared to traditional intermediaries that provide personal interaction with bankers or mortgage brokers.

Besides traditional credit scores, advancements in technology and the prevalence of big data have allowed financial intermediaries and service providers to use alternative sources of data to learn more about their customers.

In doing so, there will be a reduction of the asymmetric information problem, allowing financial intermediaries to expand their product offerings to individuals who did not have access to credit previously. One example relates to social footprints.

Together with Shashwat Alok, Pulak Ghosh, and Sudip Gupta, Sumit explores how social footprints that are obtained from an individual's mobile phone, can be used as an alternative to traditional credit bureau scores.

The research article is named "Financial Inclusion and Alternate Credit Scoring: Role of Big Data and Machine Learning in FinTech" and relies on the universe of loan applications from a large FinTech lender in India between 2016 and 2018.

In order to apply for a loan, the potential borrower allows the lender to use its digital presence to evaluate the creditworthiness. This includes detailed information, such as the applications that are being installed, social connections, phone calls made, and the type of mobile operating system.

Through machine learning-based techniques, it was found that alternative credit scoring through mobile and social footprints can be good predictors of default and can be used as a good proxy for unobservable aspects of individual behavior.

This implies that alternative data for credit decisions do matter. This is particularly beneficial for borrowers with lower levels of income and education, as well as those who are financially excluded from the traditional financial system.

Over-Indebtedness

Although there are more opportunities to borrow now, it is vital to exercise caution and avoid falling into a state of over-indebtedness. Over-indebtedness occurs when one accumulates more debt than their current income. Therefore, he or she will have difficulty in repaying the amount being owned.

Failure to repay debts could have dire consequences for us, as we could slip into a cycle of debt. Since we do not have sufficient funds to pay off current debt, we could end up borrowing more. This leads to higher interest costs. Eventually, we could end up defaulting on our debts and declare ourselves to be bankrupt.

With bankruptcies, it will impact our future borrowing as lenders are more unwilling to lend to those who have defaulted previously. In addition, there are many other restrictions that will be imposed on us.

Therefore, it is of utmost importance to evaluate and question whether borrowing is truly necessary. Do we really need to borrow now or is it simply a matter of self-control? If it is the latter, is there anything we can do about it?

We will turn to a study authored by John Gathergood in the *Journal of Economic Psychology* in 2012, titled "Self-Control, Financial Literacy and Consumer Over-Indebtedness." As the title suggests, households with a lack of self-control and financial literacy are most likely to have difficulties paying their debt.

Through a consumer-credit-focused DebtTrack survey in the United Kingdom, the author examined the self-control of individuals through the following survey question:

- "I am impulsive and tend to buy things even when I can't really afford them".

Respondents will indicate whether they "Agree Strongly," "Tend to Agree," "Neither Agree nor Disagree," "Tend to Disagree," "Disagree Strongly," or "Don't Know."

Out of 1,234 respondents, 14 of them indicated "Agree Strongly," while 100 of them indicated "Tend to Agree." It was observed that these individuals who reported having self-control issues also experience over-indebtedness. In particular, they stated that they are in higher financial distress and have higher delinquency rates for repayments. Furthermore, they also make use of quick-access credit products, such as in-store credit cards or mail-order catalogs.

Similarly, respondents who have lower financial literacy (based on their responses to questions on compounding interest) are discovered to experience over-indebtedness too.

Key Takeaways

We have discussed about how credit markets work, and how we can borrow. While borrowing has many benefits and can improve our well-being, borrowing money is a huge responsibility.

Before committing to a loan, we should assess our ability to repay the borrowed funds. Specifically, it is crucial for us to have a comprehensive understanding of our financial circumstances and establish a plan for repaying the loan prior to borrowing.

It is imperative that we only borrow how much we can repay. Furthermore, we need to take into account possible uncertainties, such as changes in interest rates or future income flows.

14

Credit Cards

We will now direct our attention to one important segment of borrowing: credit cards. Credit cards are popular forms of digital payments. Table 14.1 shows the worldwide take-up rates of credit cards in 2021. In many countries, a large proportion owns credit cards, highlighting the importance of credit cards in the economy.

As a form of digital payment, our points of discussion in Chapter 11 of this book apply to credit cards too. Even so, credit cards differ from other digital payments in many ways.

Unlike the other forms of digital payments, using a credit card is effectively a form of borrowing. In fact, that is what the term "credit" in credit cards means. The bank that issues the credit card is offering us credit up to the limit that is being agreed upon.

In comparison, when we use a debit card or mobile wallet, money is directly deducted from our bank account. Hence, the use of credit cards allows us to buy now and pay later. This will increase our purchasing power and is particularly helpful when we are liquidity constrained.

At the end of each month, we can decide whether to make the minimum payment or the full balance for purchases. If we do not pay off the full balance of the credit card statement, interest will be charged.

Credit card users can be segmented into two groups: transactors and revolvers. Transactors refer to individuals who pay off their credit card bills. From Table 14.1, we see that the majority of credit card users are

Table 14.1: Credit Card Usage as of 2021

Country	Percentage of Population (Above the Age of 15) Who Used a Credit Card	Percentage of Credit Card Users Who Pay Off Credit Balance in Full
Canada	83	79
China	38	90
Japan	70	96
New Zealand	57	81
Spain	57	87
Singapore	42	95
Thailand	23	85
United States	67	75

Source: World Bank

transactors. They benefit from all the convenience and perks provided by their credit card company and do not need to pay interest fees, as they have managed to pay off all their credit card "transactions."

However, there is still a significant number of users who do not pay off their bills in full. These individuals are known as revolvers. A revolver only pays off the minimum payment and carries on the remaining charges to the following month. Since revolvers are allowed to carry the credit balance over to the next month, they will be charged an interest.

Revolving debt has been growing globally. In 2021, the revolving credit card debt in the United States exceeded US$1 trillion.

As credit cards are unsecured debt, the interest rate for a credit card is much higher than other forms of interest rates, such as mortgages or auto loans. This has been discussed in the previous chapter.

Consequently, we expect individuals to avoid owning credit card debt if they have access to cheaper alternatives. Moreover, they should pay off their debts if they have the means. Nonetheless, economic studies have shown otherwise. This is widely known as the credit card debt puzzle or the co-holding puzzle.

The Credit Card Debt Puzzle

It has been documented that in many countries, such as the United States, Denmark, and the United Kingdom, many individuals simultaneously hold high-interest credit card debt and low-interest assets that could be used to pay off these balances.

This was initially highlighted by David Gross and Nicholas Souleles in an article titled "Do Liquidity Constraints and Interest Rates Matter for Consumer Behavior? Evidence from Credit Card Data" and published in *The Quarterly Journal of Economics* in 2002.

By relying on a proprietary dataset of anonymous issuers of bank cards in the United States, the analysis indicated that among those with credit card debt, 95 percent of them have positive net worth and that most of them hold assets in checking and savings accounts, which can be converted to cash easily. This scenario presents a puzzle because the interest rates on the savings account are considerably lower compared to the credit card loan, indicating that individuals would be better served by directing their efforts toward paying off their credit card debt.

The credit card debt puzzle remains even after setting aside one month's worth of household income for transaction purchases. For example, one-third of credit card borrowers have more liquid assets than credit card debt.

According to the authors, the credit card debt puzzle persists across different demographics and financial wealth. This includes high-income and high-education households as well as those with significant debt. Hence, this might not entirely be an issue of financial illiteracy.

Furthermore, 70 percent of the respondents with credit card debt have positive housing equity. From a financial standpoint, this is clearly not optimal. Instead of relying on credit card debt with high-interest rates, it will be more prudent for them to use lower-cost home equity loans.

The question remains. Why do individuals choose to hold both high-cost revolving credit card debt and liquid assets with low yields simultaneously?

One possible reason is that individuals prioritize liquidity and maintain liquid assets to pay for cash-only spending. Irina Telyukova provides evidence for this explanation in her article, "Households Need for Liquidity and the Credit Card Debt Puzzle."

Published in the *Review of Economic Studies* in 2013, the article showed that there is a significant part of households' monthly spending that cannot be paid by credit card and can only be paid by cash. Hence, individuals will prefer to have money in their bank accounts for transaction purposes.

In addition, due to the unpredictability of some expenditures, households would like to have liquid assets for precautionary reasons. This implies that revolving debt offers a safeguarding or insurance benefit. As individuals have limited sources of credit, they would like to build a cash buffer to prepare for future expenses.

Another explanation is attributed to self-control, and is examined by Carol Bertaut, Michael Haliassos, and Michael Reiter in a 2009 article in the *Review of Finance*.

Titled "Credit Card Debt Puzzles and Debt Revolvers for Self Control," each household can be conceptualized as being composed of two entities: the "accountant" and the "shopper." It could be interpreted as two different people (say husband and wife) or two selves (that compete).

The accountant is deemed to be rational, while the shopper is impatient and not financially sophisticated. As the rational party, the accountant is charged with the responsibility for managing the household assets and debt, including how much debt to repay. Thereafter, the shopper will choose how much to spend based on the unused credit line that is decided by the accountant.

As the accountant is aware that the compulsive shopper will spend more when given the opportunity, the accountant will choose not to pay off the credit card debt in full. Hence, the shopper will have lesser to spend. Consequently, self-control can explain the credit card debt puzzle.

If you are holding any credit card debt now, do any of the above reasons sound familiar to you? Do you think this is the best decision for you? It is perhaps time to look at your own financial portfolio and determine if you can be better off by paying down your debt earlier.

Recent studies have further highlighted how households make mistakes in their choice and use of credit cards. Let us look at some of them now.

Annual Fees

To start with, we examine the role of annual fees and interest rates. Annual fees are fees that are charged by card issuers and are a fixed amount that we need to pay per year. In recent years, some card issuers have moved away from annual fees and offered consumers with different options.

For instance, some banks allow consumers to choose between a card with annual fees (but with a lower interest rate), and another card without any annual fees (but with a higher interest rate). When faced with this situation, what will you choose?

Ultimately, the optimal strategy depends on whether you expect to borrow using the credit card. If you expect to borrow a sufficiently large amount, you should select the card with an annual fee. If you do not expect to borrow (much), you ought to choose the card without an annual fee.

Together with Souphala Chomsisengphet, Chulin Liu, and Nicholas Souleles, Sumit explores individuals' choices across these two types of credit card options in *The Review of Corporate Finance Studies* in 2015.

In the research article titled "Do Consumers Choose the Right Credit Contracts?" it is shown that on average, consumers chose the correct contract.

Based on a proprietary dataset from a large bank in the United States, the study revolved around 150,000 accounts. It was estimated that 56 percent of the accounts chose to pay annual fees. By paying an average annual fee of $20, they would have their interest rates reduced by 3 percentage points. In comparison, the remaining 44 percent do not pay an annual fee and have a higher interest rate of around 15.2 percent.

The analysis indicated that individuals who pay annual fees borrow more. For those who pay annual fees, more than 31 percent of them have a debt of more than $1,200 monthly. Thus, they made the optimal choice as their cost savings from interest rates are higher than the annual fee.

On the contrary, 24 percent of them paid the annual fee but did not borrow. While the mistakes are small as they are bounded in magnitude by the size of the annual fee itself, it is likely that this group of respondents overestimated the probability that they would borrow.

Of those who do not pay annual fees, more than 50 percent of them do not borrow, suggesting that the majority of the credit card holders chose the right contract.

Despite this, 12 percent of them could have experienced greater benefits by paying the fees, as their interest savings would have exceeded the annual fee. For this small group of respondents, they had underestimated the probability that they would borrow. This is similar across both wealthy and non-wealthy individuals.

Overall, the article shows that most of the errors do not appear to be particularly costly. This is because as the dollar magnitude of the potential error increases, there is a lower chance of choosing the suboptimal contract. Besides, those who made larger errors in their choice tend to switch to the optimal contract subsequently.

Additional Credit Card Fees

In addition to interest payments and annual fees, additional credit card fees occur when we do not pay the minimum sum by the due date or exceed our credit limit. Most of the time, these are mistakes that we make and could be linked to forgetfulness.

Do individuals learn from these mistakes over time? Together with John Driscoll, Xavier Gabaix, and David Laibson, Sumit delves into this question in a research article titled “Learning in the Credit Card Market.”

By relying on a proprietary dataset from a large bank in the United States, the study examined four million monthly credit card statements.

It then focused on three important types of fees that are imposed by the bank: the late fee, over-limit fee, and cash advance fee.

Late fees are incurred when the individual does not make the minimum sum payment by the due date. In contrast, over-limit fees are imposed when an individual exceeds the given credit limit for the month. For late fees and over-limit fees, the bank imposed a direct one-time fee of $30 or $35 per month.

Moreover, there are indirect late fees and over-limit fees as the bank will introduce penalty pricing by raising the interest rates to more than 24 percent when the borrower is recalcitrant. In the case of late fees, this happens when within a year, the individual is late by more than 60 days once, or by more than 30 days twice.

Cash advance fees are incurred when we use our credit card to withdraw cash or make a cash-like transaction. The fees amount to 3 percent of the amount that is being advanced. While cash advances do not lead to penalty pricing, the interest rates that are being charged are much higher than that of typical credit card borrowing.

Upon examining the direct late fees, over-limit fees, and cash advance fees, it was estimated that on average, new credit card accounts pay $14 worth of additional credit card fees per month. This is on top of the other types of credit card related payments (such as interest or annual fees).

Nonetheless, across the first four years of the account's life, the additional fees fell by 75 percent. The decline in fees can be attributed to learning. As cardholders learn about the fees over time, they become more cautious in their usage of credit cards.

For instance, when a cardholder pays the additional credit card fees in the previous month, it reduces fee payment in the current month by 40 percent.

While there is evidence of learning taking place, a strong recency effect is observed. The learning effect of additional credit card fees depreciates over time. According to the findings, cardholders forget at a rate of 10 to 20 percent per month.

This is akin to how a driver will respond after getting a speeding ticket. The driver might drive slower for a while, before reverting to the previous speed again.

Regulation

We have highlighted the various types of fees that are being charged by credit card companies. For consumers who are not financially sophisticated, they could be vulnerable to their behavioral biases, such as present bias and inattention, resulting in higher costs.

To protect consumers in the credit card markets, regulators have implemented various policies. One example is the Credit Card Accountability Responsibility and Disclosure (CARD) Act that was introduced by the U.S. Senate in 2009. As this act seeks to help households make better choices, it strives to increase the transparency of credit card companies.

Sumit sought to discover the effectiveness of this initiative with Souphala Chomsisengphet, Neale Mahoney, and Johannes Stroebel in a 2015 article titled "Regulating Consumer Financial Products: Evidence from Credit Cards," which was published in *The Quarterly Journal of Economics.*

It was evident from the research that regulations to reduce borrowing costs were highly effective. By comparing the impact on consumer credit cards (covered by the CARD Act) together with small business credit cards (which are not covered by the CARD Act), the estimates show that the CARD Act reduced borrowing costs by 1.7 percent of the average daily balances.

The savings are more pronounced for individuals with low credit scores. For borrowers with a FICO score below 660, over-limit fees fell by 3.3 percentage points, while late fees fell by 1.5 percentage points.

Overall, the fee reductions of the CARD Act are estimated to save U.S. consumers US$12.6 billion per year! As such, it is possible to help households increase their financial well-being if the correct initiatives are being introduced.

On top of that, the CARD Act required companies to disclose the cost savings that individuals could have when they pay their balances in 36 months, as compared to making minimum payments. The objective is to nudge consumers to pay a larger fraction of their balance each time.

This had an impact on repayments. On a base of 5.7 percent, the number of cardholders who repaid their balance increased by 0.5 percentage points, which reduces the amount of interest payable.

Accordingly, there is evidence to support the notion that behavioral interventions, such as nudges, have the potential to bring about improvements in household welfare!

Besides relying on government policies and regulations, is there anything we could do as private individuals?

Reminders for Late Payment Fees

One simple way is to proactively set up reminders. Just like how we use alarm clocks to wake us up, we can use reminders to alert us of our credit card bill repayments and the amount that we can save by paying early.

Several studies have highlighted how nudge-based interventions can help to manage late payments. We look at a study by Paolina Medina published in *The Review of Financial Studies* in 2021. Titled "Side Effects of Nudging: Evidence from a Randomized Intervention in the Credit Card Market," the article examines how nudging could impact the repayment of credit card bills.

Through a financial management platform in Brazil, the author designed a field experiment in which certain cardholders receive reminders about their future credit card payments that are due.

With smartphone push notifications, these cardholders received reminders at different stages of the credit card billing cycle. One example is as follows: "Your credit card due date is approaching. Pay today and avoid late-payment fees (R$40 on average)! Ignore if you already paid."

What do you think happened here? The author observed that those who received reminders effectively reduced the cost of late fees paid by 14 percent. Sometimes all we need is a gentle reminder!

However, the author finds that there is an indirect effect. Reminders for credit card payments end up increasing overdraft fees in the checking accounts by 9 percent. This is attributed to the role of salience. When one receives more attention, consumers will overweight its importance.

While we will turn to overdrafts in the next chapter, the key point here is that there could be spillover effects. For households with a history of using overdrafts, total fees actually increased by 5 percent overall. In comparison, the rest of the households enjoyed a fall in total fees by 15 percent. Accordingly, there is a need to manage our finances holistically. There might not be a one size fit all approach when it comes to bill repayments.

Key Takeaways

In this chapter, we have shed light on several common mistakes made by individuals in the credit card market. For instance, the credit card debt puzzle shows that individuals are holding on to unsecured credit card debt with high interest while holding on to assets that pay low interest.

This highlights the importance of having a comprehensive understanding of the household balance sheet. As indicated in Chapter 4 of this book, when making financial plans, it is helpful to have a thorough understanding of our finances.

We cannot stress the importance of financial planning enough. By comparing the interest payments across different assets and liabilities in our balance sheet, we will be able to choose loans with the lowest borrowing rate and direct our savings to the highest returns holistically.

In addition, we have discussed about the additional fees paid by individuals in the credit card market. Most of the time, they are a result of neglect or ignorance. Now that we are all aware of these fees, it is time to take some action. For a start, set a reminder!

15

Overdrafts

An overdraft occurs when we make withdrawals from our bank account without having sufficient funds. This could include withdrawals from ATMs, debit card transactions, or cheques that are being issued.

Inevitably, overdrafts entail financial costs. As our account balances end up being below zero, we are effectively borrowing from the bank. This gives rise to interest payable on the overdraft. Moreover, an overdraft fee or non-sufficient fund (NSF) administrative fee will be incurred. In the United States, it is typically around US$20 to US$35.

Nonetheless, having an overdraft account is not necessarily a bad thing. Overdrafts could save us from embarrassing moments when we are out of funds and would like to make payments at supermarkets or restaurants. As a financial backup, it allows us to deal with unexpected expenses of emergencies.

In addition, there are usually no charges involved for having an overdraft account unless we trigger it by withdrawing more than what we have in our bank account. We pay interest only for the amount that is being used.

Hence, overdrafts provide us with a form of security in response to future uncertainty. This has the potential to give us more confidence to spend, and reduce precautionary savings.

Perceived Precautionary Savings

Let us first examine recent work by Francesco D'Acunto, Thomas Rauter, Christoph Scheuch, and Michael Weber. In an article titled "Perceived Precautionary Savings Motive: Evidence from FinTech," the authors find that the provision of overdraft facilities to first-time borrowers indeed led to an increase in spending and a fall in savings.

As households with more liquid assets respond more than others, the authors termed this behavior as "perceived precautionary savings." Households perceive that they need to save for precautionary reasons even when they have access to liquid assets that can be converted into cash easily.

To examine how the introduction of overdrafts could impact households' decisions, the authors worked with a leading FinTech bank in Europe. As a fully digital bank with more than 1 million customers across Europe, the digital bank provides fast and convenient services. As a case in point, individuals can open a bank account through mobile apps in less than 10 minutes.

The company does not offer any credit facilities, such as the issuance of credit cards until February 2015. As such, the authors are able to examine how new borrowers would respond to the initiation of overdraft facilities.

In February 2015, the company began to introduce a mobile credit line to users with sufficiently high credit scores. Assessing their personal characteristics, they would be issued a maximum overdraft amount ranging from 500 to 5,000 Euros.

Using the mobile app, users can activate the credit line within a minute. The annual interest rate of the used overdraft is around 10 percentage points.

As compared to users who did not activate their overdraft facilities, those who activated the facilities spent more by 4.5 percentage points of their income inflows. Evidently, individuals spend more and save less when credit is being made available to them.

The changes in spending behavior are observed to be persistent across time. This is especially the case for individuals with high ratios of liquid deposits to income inflows. In fact, individuals with the highest liquidity spend more when they have more credit.

While liquid users increase their spending permanently, 90 percent of them do not ever rely on the use of a credit line. In this case, why do they not spend in the first place? This is because of precautionary motives. Individuals would like to have a safety net before they are willing to spend.

The authors showed that changes in liquidity are not related to individuals' personal preferences or beliefs. For instance, households with different liquidity have similar risk aversion and patience.

It should be noted that the attention here is directed toward new borrowers, not the ones who are already in existence. For existing borrowers, they have already enjoyed the insurance effect of the facility.

Limited and Varying Consumer Attention

While overdrafts provide an additional form of security, it has been demonstrated that some individuals end up with overdrafts due to their limited attention.

As we can only process a limited amount of information at any point in time, we might be unaware of how much we have in our bank account. Consequently, we end up paying overdraft fees and interest rates unknowingly.

If the individual has access to other sources of spending, this cost can be avoided. Furthermore, the fees might seem disproportional as the additional transaction cost may, in fact, be higher than the cost of the product. As an illustration, when we purchase a cup of coffee worth \$4 using an account without sufficient balance, we could end up paying a \$35 overdraft fee.

The role of limited information has been highlighted in a 2014 article by Victor Stango and Jonathan Zinman in *The Review of Financial Studies*.

Titled "Limited and Varying Consumer Attention: Evidence from Shocks to the Salience of Bank Overdraft Fees," it shows that households have limited attention. Thus, when households are provided with information on overdraft-related content, there is a lower propensity for them to incur an overdraft fee in the survey month.

This finding is determined by examining thousands of individual's checking accounts who provided transaction records to a market research company in the United States.

Given this context, participants of the panel voluntarily enrolled themselves with the market research company in exchange for payment.

Besides providing the market research company with information about their checking accounts, participants took part in online surveys periodically. The content of the surveys varied across different periods.

In general, the surveys asked questions related to their banking and financial needs. This includes the type of bank accounts that are held by the participants, usage of credit card and debit card, as well as their attitudes toward borrowing and savings.

There are also several surveys that focused on questions related to overdrafts.

Questions in this type of survey include the following:

- *Do you have overdraft protection for your checking account?*
- *Do you think that having overdraft protection makes you more or less likely to overdraw your account?*
- *In the past six months, about how many times have you overdrawn your checking account?*
- *What types of purchases or payments have caused your overdrafts?*

By leveraging on overdraft-related surveys, we can examine the role of information and attention in managing overdrafts.

It was found that during the month with an overdraft-related survey, on a base of 30 percent, the likelihood that individuals incur an overdraft fee decreased by 3.7 percentage points.

Besides, when the respondents took multiple overdraft-related surveys, they built a "stock" of attention. While the stock of attention falls over time, it continues to reduce overdrafts for up to two years.

The more overdraft-focused the survey is (i.e., the more overdraft-related questions there are in the survey), the larger the impact on the respondents' decisions in reducing their usage of overdrafts.

Conversely, surveys not related to overdrafts, such as those pertaining to auto loans or gift cards, do not influence the rate at which overdrafts are taken up. This indicates that by providing overdraft-related information to individuals, concerns related to limited attention will be reduced.

To avoid overdrafts, it was shown that individuals manage their spending transactions (rather than increasing inflows). For instance, they make lesser low-balance transactions using their debit cards, to reduce the possibility of having negative bank balances.

They also cancel automatic recurring withdrawals and switch to manual payments. This will provide them with more control over their spending.

While it was identified that individuals with low income, low education, and low financial literacy are more likely to incur overdraft fees, exposure to overdraft-related surveys caused them to be responsive, as they cut back their spending at a larger rate.

Underestimation of Overdraft Costs

On top of limited attention, there is also evidence that individuals underestimate overdraft costs.

This has been highlighted in a 2018 study by Sule Alan, Mehmet Cemalcilar, Dean Karlan, and Jonathan Zinman in *The Journal of Finance*.

In their article titled "Unshrouding: Evidence from Bank Overdrafts in Turkey," the authors proved how the take-up rate of overdrafts responds directly to a randomized direct marketing experiment in Turkey.

Through Yapi Kredi, one of the largest banks in Turkey, the authors provided different messages to different groups of bank customers. Broadly speaking, there are two main groups.

The first group includes those that were informed of the overdrafts, with discounts. In this setting, there are also several variations, such as highlighting debit card discounts or auto-bill discounts among others.

Customers in the second group were merely informed of the presence of overdrafts.

Which group do you think will have a higher take-up rate of overdrafts? You may be surprised to find that the answer is the second group.

It was discovered that when a large discount on overdraft interest rates was being announced, it led to a decrease in the usage of overdrafts instead. In comparison, when the availability of overdrafts was being announced, without any mention of prices, the usage of overdrafts increased.

Why does a fall in prices lead to a lower usage? While this may sound counterintuitive, the authors relate this to a combination of limited attention and underestimation of overdraft costs.

By merely highlighting prices, the emphasis reminds individuals that overdrafts are costly (even though the objective is to tell them that prices have been reduced!)

Amongst the first group, the drop in demand for overdrafts is even more pronounced when overdrafts are bundled with a discount on debit cards or auto-debit transactions.

Intuitively, this can be explained from the idea that including overdrafts with transactions (that could directly activate overdrafts) seeks to remind customers to avoid such transactions instead.

For the second group, they perceived the overdraft costs to be lower. Subsequently, they respond by having more overdrafts relative to the first group (which is offered a lower price).

This underscores the importance of financial education and consumer attention in managing overdrafts. One possible way is through mobile applications.

Mobile Apps and Financial Decision-Making

We will move on to a 2023 study by Bruce Carlin, Arna Olafsson, and Michaela Pagel in the *Review of Finance*.

The article, titled "Mobile Apps and Financial Decision Making," shows that by using financial decision-making apps, individuals pay lesser fees that are related to NSF in Iceland.

In Iceland, when an individual ends up exceeding the overdraft limits when they make purchases, there will be an NSF charge. Furthermore, the purchase will be denied. This is clearly a mistake. You incur a cost, without getting the goods or services!

The authors rely on individual, transaction-level data from a financial aggregator in Iceland. As a financial aggregation platform, it links all the financial accounts of the individual in one place. Consequently, users can view all their spending and income transactions at once.

In November 2014, the financial aggregator introduced a mobile application. While users were only able to access the financial aggregation platform through an internet browser previously, they could now have access to their finances on the go. This led to a sharp increase in the usage of the application.

The study focused on how the launch of the mobile application impacted NSF fees. As the mobile application provided comprehensive information of household finances, it is intriguing to determine how the application impacted their financial choices.

By comparing individuals who used the platform before the introduction of the mobile app with those who have not accessed the platform prior to the introduction, a sharp fall in NSF fees was found.

With a 24-month window, it was estimated that there was a 38.4 percent fall in NSF fees. This suggests that by providing information through the aggregation platform, individuals are less likely to make mistakes.

It is noteworthy to highlight that the platform only provides financial information. Individuals are unable to rely on the app to make decisions, such as paying bills. Moreover, there are no nudge-based interventions or reminders.

Put together, the findings imply that simply providing information through technology has the potential to improve one's financial well-being. As the financial aggregator help us gather information more efficiently, we can make better decisions.

Key Takeaways

In this chapter, we have deliberated on the role of overdrafts. We find that overdrafts are being valued by households. As a case in point, households perceive overdrafts as a form of precautionary savings and have more confidence in spending.

However, we would like to caution that some individuals end up with overdrafts as they have limited attention and they underestimate overdraft costs.

As suggested in the previous topic on credit cards, it is useful for individuals to include the role of overdrafts in their balance sheet and set reminders.

Given that information becomes easier to access in the digital era, we can make use of different methods to capture our attention pertaining to matters of financial management.

16

Payday Loans

In the final chapter on borrowings, we will discuss about payday loans. Payday loans are short-term borrowings with extremely high-interest rates. For instance, the annual percentage rate of an average payday loan in countries, such as the Philippines and the United States, ranges from 390 percent to 780 percent.

With such high-interest rates, payday loans are highly controversial. In the United States, 14 out of 50 states as well as the District of Columbia have effectively banned payday loans.

The high-interest rate is primarily due to the loan being unsecured with little credit check and very fast approval. Most of the time, the lender does not examine the credit history, as long as the borrower has a job and will receive their income soon.

Payday loans are usually for small amounts to help individuals tide them through to the next payday. Due to unexpected expenditures, some individuals might require urgent need of cash before their next payday.

Without easy access to credit, small-scale personal emergencies could escalate to late fees, utility suspensions, repossessions, or even evictions. Hence, payday loans help individuals bridge their financial shortfalls in the short run and prevent personal emergencies to spiral out of control.

How do payday loans work? As the name suggests, payday loans are based on the next paycheck. When we would like to take up a payday loan, we will bring our most recent paycheck to the lender to obtain approval, promising that we will repay them on our next payday.

In return for instant cash, we will write a personal check for the amount that is borrowed as well as the interest payments. The check will be postdated to the next payday, which is usually 10 to 14 days after. Alternatively, we can authorize our bank to draw the relevant amount to the payday lender on our next payday.

When taking up payday loans, it is important that we have the financial means to repay the loan by the next payday. If we are unable to repay the loan, refinancing might be required.

In refinancing the loan, we will roll over the previous loan amount and interest rates, incurring additional finance charges. This will result in a higher repayment in the future.

Why do individuals take up payday loans? One possible explanation is that they are unable to borrow from traditional means, such as banks or credit cards, as they do not meet the requirements.

When faced with a sudden income loss or unexpected expenses, they turn to payday lenders for convenience. Borrowing through payday lenders is fast and easy, allowing individuals to meet their short-term needs.

Payday Loans Versus Credit Cards

Nonetheless, studies have documented that individuals make the mistake of turning to payday loans even when there are cheaper alternatives available. This includes the use of credit cards.

In Chapter 13, we have highlighted that credit cards have much higher interest rates than other types of secured loans, such as home loans and auto loans. In 2021, the average interest rate for credit cards in the United States stands at 14.51 percent per annum.

But this is still much cheaper than payday loans. In fact, the credit card interest rate is almost 30 times lower than that of payday loans! Rationally, we should expect individuals to use credit cards instead of payday loans, if possible. Unfortunately, it does not appear as such.

Households' choices between payday loans and credit cards have been examined in a study that Sumit coauthored with Paige Marta Skiba and Jeremy Tobacman.

This is done by combining loan records from a large payday lender to a financial institution in the United States that offers checking accounts, credit cards, mortgages, and auto-financing.

Published in the *American Economic Review* in 2009 and titled "Payday Loans and Credit Cards: New Liquidity and Credit Scoring Puzzles?" the article highlights three key findings.

Firstly, it was observed that consumers do not prioritize the use of their lowest-cost credit option. In the matched sample, two-thirds of households who take pay loans have at least $1,000 of credit card liquidity on the day that they take their first pay loan. As a benchmark, the average payday loan is around $300. Hence, they have the opportunity to use their credit cards to borrow instead of opting for payday loans.

For a two-week payday loan of $300, it is estimated that if individuals use their credit cards instead of a payday loan, they will save around $52. As most people in the matched sample have credit card liquidity higher than the typical payday loan, they will be much better off using their credit card instead.

It is important to note that these individuals also have other sources of liquidity they can rely on. If they had managed to access cheaper funds, the actual interest saved could even be larger.

Next, it was indicated that in the months prior to the take-up of payday loans, the credit card liquidity of borrowers fell steadily. This suggests that individuals do not use payday loans in response to a single negative shock.

Rather, individuals resort to payday lending after months of consideration. Thus, it is likely that the basis of payday lending can be ascribed to ongoing negative events in the lives of these individuals or overall mismanagement of finances.

Despite the initial use of their credit card, they rely on payday lending after some time. Consequently, individuals are aware of the benefits of credit cards but stop short of utilizing all the credit that is available to them.

Finally, the study revealed that when individuals take out a payday loan, the likelihood that there will be delinquency on the credit card doubles. Cardholders are more likely to fall behind on required monthly payments after they take a payday loan.

Hence, there is a correlation between payday lending and default probability. Households with payday loans have a higher propensity to default on their credit card. Therein lies the question: does payday lending improve or worsen one's well-being?

A priori, it is unclear. On one hand, payday lending could result in more defaults as it allows individuals without self-control to bite off more than what they can chew. Coupled with a high interest rate, borrowers are most likely to end up with a cycle of debt as they take on another loan to cover the previous loan. This is unsustainable.

On the other hand, individuals who took payday lending are already in a bad shape financially. So, it is no surprise that more of them default. What is of interest is to understand whether payday lending could reduce the number of people who would otherwise default.

Currently, there is no consensus on the impact of payday loans on the economy. While some studies have documented that payday loans are beneficial as they reduce insolvencies, others have suggested that access to payday loans may reduce welfare. Therefore, the effect of payday loans on individuals' well-being depends on their specific circumstances.

Natural Disasters and Foreclosures

We will first examine a 2011 article in the *Journal of Financial Economics* by Adair Morse. Titled "Payday Lenders: Heroes or Villains?," it was found that payday lenders can be a hero in times of need.

Morse discovered that when there are natural disasters, having payday loans mitigate foreclosures for the state of California in the United States.

Foreclosures occur when a borrower is unable to make their mortgage payment, resulting in the lender to repossess the house. This is most undesirable for homeowners as they will be asked to move.

To pin down the role of foreclosures driven by external shocks, the authors centered on foreclosures that are induced by natural disasters between 1996 and 2002 in California. As natural disasters are random and unexpected, they come as a surprise to homeowners.

Natural disasters include incidents, such as earthquakes, floods, landslides, as well as storms and wildfires. During this time period, there were a total of 1,568 incidents, with the average zip code incurring property damage of US$12.6 million.

Consequently, homeowners faced a negative financial shock from the damage to their houses. On top of that, they could lose their income when there is a natural disaster and may not be able to repay their home loans.

It was estimated that for every 1,000 homes, natural disasters increased foreclosures by 4.5 units in the year that follows the event. With payday lenders, the increase is mitigated by 1 to 1.3 units. Hence, payday lenders were able to help homeowners that are hit by natural disasters to overcome borrowing constraints.

There is also a fall in shoplifting when there is payday lending. However, payday lending does not influence more serious crimes, such as vehicle thefts and burglaries. This shows that payday lending can also reduce individuals' need to resort to small property crimes when they are in financial distress.

It is important to note that the focus of this study is on payday lending in terms of an unexpected financial distress. Therefore, in terms of managing short-term emergencies, payday lending could be a hero as it prevents small debts from spiraling out of control.

On the other hand, it is also possible that some individuals have a lack of self-control and rely on payday loans to make up for the shortfall in cash. By creating the opportunity to overspend, payday lenders could become villains rather than heroes.

Low-Income Households

We now turn our attention to low-income households. It is of interest to understand the impact of payday loans on low-income households. As these individuals have reduced access to traditional means of borrowing, payday lending could potentially play a significant role in alleviating economic hardship (or not).

This has been examined in a 2011 article in *The Quarterly Journal of Economics* by Brian Melzer. In the article titled "The Real Costs of Credit Access: Evidence from the Payday Lending Market," it was demonstrated that poor households that have access to payday loans in the United States tend to be worse off.

To understand how access to payday loan makes a difference, Melzer relied on geographic differences in the availability of payday loans in different states. As mentioned earlier, payday lending is banned in some states in the United States, such as New York and Pennsylvania.

The primary area of focus in this study were borrowers in the states where payday lending is banned. Given the absence of payday lending in their home states, these borrowers must travel to a neighboring state that allows payday lending in order to obtain a loan. For example, someone in Pennsylvania will need to travel to nearby Ohio or West Virginia.

As households from states that have outlawed payday lending venture across the border in search of loans, it is expected that there will be a greater number of payday lenders situated at the border compared to those in distant locations.

Indeed, Melzer demonstrates that in payday-lending states, there are 20 percent more payday stores in zip codes that are nearer to payday-prohibiting states. Therefore, the distance to the border can be used as a good measurement for loan access.

By examining the impact on loan access to low-income households, it was shown that those with access to payday loans end up finding it more difficult to pay important bills, such as mortgages, rents, and utilities.

For households with US$15,000 to US$50,000 in annual income, it was revealed that the incidence of households not paying bills increased by 25 percent.

Besides, these households displayed a tendency to delay essential expenditures, such as medical care, dental care, and prescription drugs.

One possible reason relates to the high interest on payday loans. As borrowers need to pay off high-interest payments, they have less money to pay for essential bills. Thus, the debt service burden could outweigh the benefits of the payday loan.

Now, let us look at how payday loans impact different households across time.

Time Dynamics

This time, we will consider a study in the United Kingdom. After the United States, the United Kingdom has the world's second largest payday-lending market.

In a 2018 article in *The Review of Financial Studies*, John Gathergood, Benedict Guttman-Kenney, and Stefan Hunt leveraged on a unique dataset that included 99 percent of loans that were approved in the United Kingdom from 2012 to 2013.

Titled "How Do Payday Loans Affect Borrowers? Evidence from the UK Market," the article aims to gain insights into how payday loans shape households' decision-making over a period of two years.

It was found that borrowers do not move away from other forms of credit after getting a payday loan. In fact, they end up applying for more credit within six months after obtaining the payday loan.

For instance, they applied for more personal loans and credit cards. This resulted in an increase in the total debt for non-payday credit.

However, one crucial question remains. Do borrowers default more? The answer is dependent on the time period.

It was documented that while delinquencies fell during the first few months, they subsequently increased. Hence, while payday loans are able to help individuals over the short term, they are unable to help individuals over a longer period.

After the first few months, there was a persistent increase in the total amount of debt and the delinquency of non-payday loans. It was estimated that 6 to 12 months after getting the payday loan, the likelihood of missing a payment on a non-payday loan increased by 31 percentage points (with a baseline of 67.4 percent).

Furthermore, there is evidence that there is an increase in default on non-payday loans. For instance, there is a 20 percent increase in the ratio between the sum of default balances on non-payday loans and all loans.

This suggest that when individuals take up payday loans, it puts stress on current loan commitments. Consequently, borrowers end up defaulting on other debts.

Notwithstanding the above, the authors showed that not all individuals end up in a worse shape financially. For individuals with good credit scores, they do not suffer from higher debt and delinquencies. This suggests that payday loans have benefited them in tiding over in the short term.

How do we help individuals make better decisions? It turns out that information disclosure, which prompts borrowers to adopt a broader mindset, has a positive impact.

Information Disclosure

We will now examine a 2011 research article titled "Information Disclosure, Cognitive Biases and Payday Borrowing," published in *The Journal of Finance.*

The authors, Marianne Bertrand and Adair Morse, conducted a randomized field trial in one of the largest payday lending companies in the United States to study the role of information disclosure.

In this study, different information was provided to potential borrowers in different stores and days across two weeks. This includes 77 stores in 11 states.

The different information treatments are as follows:

Treatment 1: APR Information

- In Treatment 1, potential borrowers are given information on the average interest rate of payday loans relative to other types of loans that they are familiar with. This includes car loans, credit cards, and subprime mortgages.
- A summary of the information is presented in Table 16.1.
- This reinforces the understanding that payday loans have the highest interest rates.

Table 16.1: Annual Interest Rates on Different Types of Loans

Type of Loan	Median Annual Interest
Payday loan	443%
Car loan	18%
Credit card	16%
Subprime mortgages	10%

Treatment 2: Dollars Information

- In Treatment 2, potential borrowers are provided with the accumulated fees for having a $300 payday loan that is outstanding for a different length of time.
- A summary of the information is presented in Table 16.2.
- The study also compares the total fees for payday loans with that of credit cards.

Table 16.2: Total Fees Payable Based on Repayment Period

Repayment Period	Total Fees Payable
Two weeks	$45
One month	$90
Two months	$180
Three months	$279

Treatment 3: Refinancing Information

- In Treatment 3, potential borrowers are informed about the typical repayment profile for payday borrowers. This includes the time to repay a given loan.
- A summary of the information is presented in Table 16.3.

Table 16.3: Frequency Table (Out of 10 Typical People)

Number of People	Decisions
2.5	Will pay it back without renewing
2	Will renew one or two times
1.5	Will renew three or four times
4	Will renew five or more times

It was found that the provision of information impacted payday borrowing. After receiving the information treatments, potential borrowers end up borrowing lesser than the control group (which did not receive any information).

While all three treatment groups reported a fall in borrowing, the largest fall in borrowing is in Treatment 2. In providing potential borrowers with information on the accumulated fees, borrowing fell by $55. This corresponds to a fall of 23 percent as compared to the control.

In contrast, the fall in spending for Treatment 1 and Treatment 3 is $38 (16 percent) and $28 (12 percent), respectively. Consequently, this shows that information disclosure impacts individuals' decisions to take out a payday loan as it allows them to think more broadly about the fees involved.

This suggests that borrowers are not fully aware of the high interest rate that they need to pay for payday loans (relative to other types of borrowing). They are also unaware of the consequences of having payday loans.

Key Takeaways

So far, we have focused on three types of loans: credit cards, overdrafts, and payday loans.

We hope that by sharing different case studies of borrowing across different domains, you are now equipped with the relevant knowledge to make a more informed decision when it comes to borrowing.

As we face different interest rates from different types of loans, it is important to choose our loans carefully.

This is because, for the same individual, the interest rate charged by lenders is dependent on the risk of the loan. The higher the likelihood that we will be able to repay the loan, the lower the interest rate.

As payday loans are unsecured personal loans that do not require credit standing, there is a greater risk for the lender. Hence, the interest rate is significantly higher than all other types of loans and should be used only as a last resort.

Before taking payday loans, check if there are any other alternatives that provide a lower interest rate. To gain access to loans with lower interest rates, it is also essential for us to build up our credit score and allay the lender's concerns about our inability to pay them back.

Remember, the more creditworthy we are, the lower the interest rate will be. It is thus important to have a track record to show that we can properly manage our debts. Make it a priority to pay your bills on time! Building trust with the lender can go a long way.

Part V

Investing

17

Stock Market Participation

Based on the content of the book thus far, we have covered savings, borrowing and spending. How do we then grow our assets? We will now proceed to examine investing in Part V of this book. Particularly, we will focus on investments in the stock market. Here, we elucidate how households might benefit from owning equities and uncover common pitfalls that households are susceptible to.

Stock markets play a major role in the economy. Through the stock market, companies can raise funds directly from households, giving individuals like you and me the opportunity to partake in a company's future performance. Thereafter, individuals can trade directly with one another in the stock market itself.

By owning a stock in a company, you are now a shareholder. Effectively, this means that you own a certain proportion of the company, entitling you to partake in the benefits that result from the company's future growth and potential performance.

For instance, when you are a shareholder of Apple, you stand to gain when Apple makes profits through their iPhone and iPad sales. When Apple goes up in value in the stock market, you can sell them at a higher price, enjoying capital gains. Furthermore, you will also receive distributions of the company's earnings in the form of dividends.

To initiate the process of learning about stock market investments, we could first familiarize ourselves with stock market indexes.

Most countries have their own domestic stock market that allows individuals access to trade in companies that are listed in the specific market. For instance, we have the New York Stock Exchange in the United States, the Tokyo Stock Exchange in Japan, as well as the London Stock Exchange in the United Kingdom.

The market index across different stock markets is usually used as a benchmark to assess performance. Generally, they are designed to track the performance of selected companies based on common characteristics.

In the United States alone, there are more than 5,000 indexes. Allow us to highlight three widely followed indexes. We first have the Standard and Poor's 500 Index. Commonly known as S&P 500, it is a market-weighted index that includes 500 top companies in the United States. Market weighted indicates that the stock's value is proportionate to the market capitalization, which reflects the overall market value of the company's equity.

Next, there is the Dow Jones Industrial Average (DJIA). Unlike the S&P 500, DJIA is a price-weighted index that covers only 30 companies. Since the index is price weighted, a $1 increase in a $10 stock has the identical impact on the index as a $1 increase in a $100 stock, although the percentage change for the former is larger.

We also have the Nasdaq Composite Index, a technology-focused index. This index includes a wide range of publicly traded companies listed on the Nasdaq stock exchange and is weighted based on market capitalization. As such, each index is unique in its on way, and conveys different information.

It is essential to recognize that the stock market is highly volatile in the short run. Prices go up and down all the time. Hence, it is vital for us to appreciate the risks involved in the stock market and avoid treating it as a gamble. To navigate the stock market effectively, we must formulate a plan to manage our portfolio during market volatility and maintain a long term perspective.

Investing in the stock market is a long game. Despite the short-term fluctuations, the stock market has outperformed the returns of many

Table 17.1: Stock Market Returns in Different Countries

Economy	Benchmark Index	5-Year Returns (2016–2020)	15-Year Returns (2006–2020)
China	CSI300	6.82%	9.79%
Germany	DAX	6.96%	6.06%
Hong Kong	HSI	6.71%	3.72%
Malaysia	FBM KLCI	−0.49%	3.92%
India	Sensex	13.94%	11.04%
Indonesia	IDX Composite	5.31%	11.05%
Singapore	STI	1.58%	1.10%
USA	S&P 500	14.12%	7.44%
Vietnam	VN Index	15.15%	N/A
Thailand	SET	2.18%	4.37%

Source: Yahoo Finance

other asset classes over time. The historical returns of selected stock market indexes in their respective economies are presented in Table 17.1.

Consider the Vietnam Stock Market, if you have invested in the VN Index (or Ho Chi Minh Stock Index) between 2016 and 2020, you would have enjoyed a high return of 15.15 percent! In comparison, the bank deposit rate in Vietnam during this time period stands at 4 percent.

The high returns offered by equities have the potential to increase our lifetime income, especially when we consider the impact of compounding. Recall the Rule of 72 that we have discussed in Chapter 1 earlier. As a mathematical formula, it estimates the time taken for an investment to double its value. For instance, based on the formula, it will take six years to double the investments when the returns are 12 percent.

Thus, households are advised to invest in equity markets to enhance their income over their lifetime. Traditional economic models lend credence to this notion. This includes theoretical work from Robert Merton, the 1997 recipient of the Nobel Memorial Prize in Economic Sciences, which proved mathematically that individuals ought to hold some fraction of their financial portfolio in stocks throughout their lifetime.

Furthermore, with globalization, we can invest not just in our own countries, but also internationally. For example, if you are a Singapore investor, you can invest not only in the Singapore stock market but also in other countries such as China, India, and the United States. This provides us with many different opportunities to grow our portfolio.

Nonetheless, many households do not hold equities. Figure 17.1 shows the stock market participation rate in the United States from 2010 to 2021. It is clear that the stock market participation rate is relatively constant, hovering around 54 percent over time.

Figure 17.1: Stock Market Participation in the United States

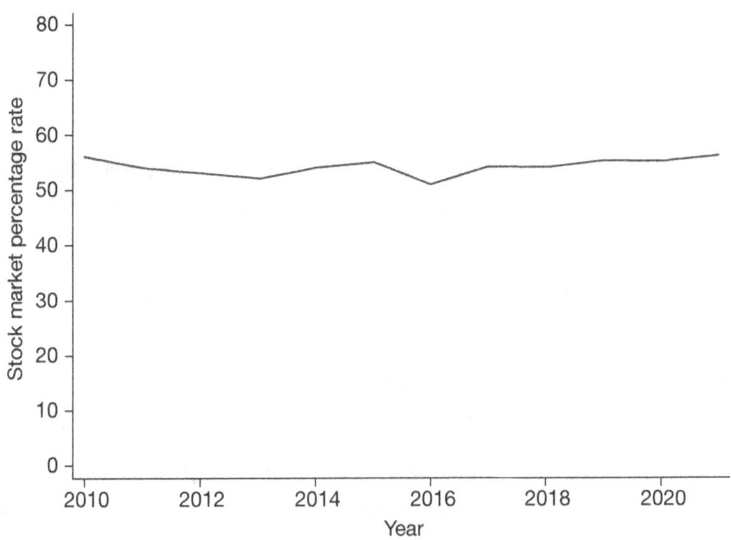

Source: Gallop Polls

Similar numbers have been found in other developed countries, such as Japan, Australia, and Singapore. However, in less developed countries such as Vietnam, the stock market participation rate is lower, standing below 10 percent.

Why do households not participate in the stock market, when economic theories suggest that it will be better off for them to invest? This phenomenon is widely recognized as the stock market participation puzzle.

Researchers have proposed many possible reasons for the limited stock market participation. We highlight three of them: Lack of Trust, Loss Aversion, and Ambiguity Aversion.

Trusting the Stock Market

The role of trust in the stock market has been examined by Luigi Guiso, Paola Sapienza, and Luigi Zingales in a 2008 article in *The Journal of Finance*. In their article titled "Trusting the Stock Market," the authors show that trust matters.

What do we mean by trust? In this article, the authors define trust as the possibility of individuals being cheated. Intuitively, only when you trust the fairness of the stock market and the reliability of the data that is given to you, will you then be willing to put your money in the stock market.

In Fall 2003, the authors seek to investigate the importance of trust among 1,943 Dutch households in the Dutch National Bank (DNB) Household Survey. Following a similar question in the World Values Survey, respondents are asked the following question:

> *"Generally speaking, would you say that most people can be trusted or that you have to be very careful in dealing with people?"*

Respondents have three options: (1) Most people can be trusted, (2) One has to be very careful with other people, and (3) I don't know.

What is your answer? If your answer is (1), you are similar to 37.7 percent of the respondents in the 2003 DNB Household Survey.

By comparing the response of this question to the households' portfolio in the survey, the authors show that individuals in the 2003 DNB Household Survey who are less trusting (i.e., one that indicated that one has to be very careful with other people) are less likely to buy stocks.

The authors further show that this relationship holds worldwide. For instance, they established a positive correlation between trust[7] and stock market participation of the wealthy globally.

On one hand, we have countries such as Greece and Spain with low trust ratings and low stock market participation. On the other hand, we have countries such as Sweden and Denmark with high trust ratings and high stock market participation rate. Consequently, trust matters.

Loss Aversion

Next, we turn to another explanation as to why households do not participate in equity markets: loss aversion.

Loss aversion refers to a cognitive bias where individuals display a preference for avoiding losses rather than obtaining gains of equal value. For example, think of the joy you might feel if you had received $1,000 today. Now, compare this with the pain of losing $1,000. Which is larger? If the pain of losing $1,000 is larger than that of gaining $1,000, you are experiencing loss aversion.

This is supported by the prospect theory developed by Daniel Kahneman and Amos Tversky in 1979, whereby individuals value gains and losses differently.

We illustrate this concept in Figure 17.2. Starting from the reference point where the value and outcome are both zero, we observe that higher outcome (gains) are valued differently from lower outcome (losses). This is because as individuals are fearful of losses, the disutility associated with losses is greater than the utility associated with gains of the same magnitude.

As a benchmark, consider the 45-degree line which reflects the case of a sure gain or sure loss. While individuals prefer a sure gain situation over the riskier prospect, they become more willing to take risks as

[7] The same question from the World Values Survey was used.

Figure 17.2: Prospect Theory

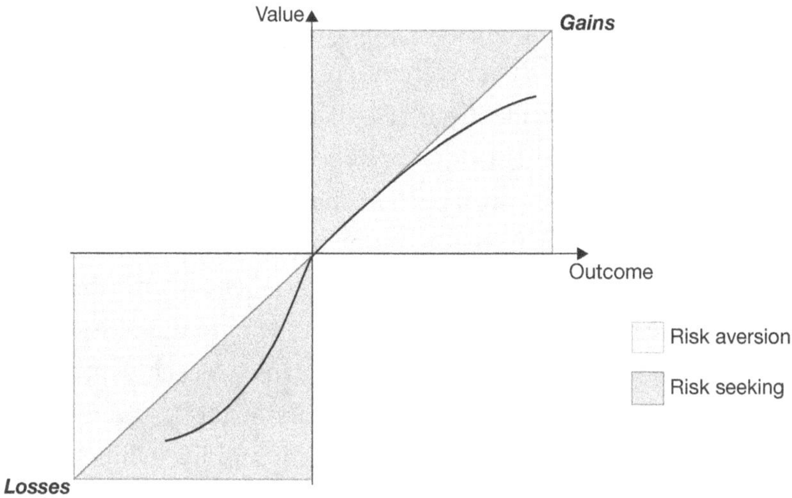

compared to a sure loss scenario. Due to the asymmetric valuation for gains and losses, individuals end up being risk averse in the gain frame and risk loving in the loss frame.

Consequently, this suggests that households are reluctant to allocate their assets to the stock market as they place a relatively lower value on potential gains as compared to potential losses.

Loss aversion does not only affect one's inclination to invest in the stock market. In fact, those that invest in the stock market also tend to make other mistakes due to loss aversion. One example is that investors end up selling their winners and holding on to losers in their financial portfolio. This is known as the disposition effect.

Consider a stock that has gone down in value (due to deteriorating fundamentals). Even though the stock price is expected to deteriorate further, investors hold on to them as they are unwilling to record a loss. On the other hand, they prematurely sell their assets that have made financial gains even though the fundamentals are strong and have the potential to go further up in value.

Ambiguity Aversion

We will now move on from loss aversion to ambiguity aversion. To do so, we will need to distinguish between the concepts of risk and ambiguity.

When economists talk about risk, it relates to cases in which the probability of the future outcomes are known. As an illustration, when you flip a fair coin, there is a 50 percent chance of getting heads and a 50 percent chance of getting tails. Hence, the probability is known.

In comparison, ambiguity aversion occurs when the probability of the future outcome is unknown. To illustrate, let's refer to the classic Ellsberg urn problem (Figure 17.3). Consider two urns. In each urn, there are 10 balls with two different colors (say black and white).

The first urn holds exactly five black balls and five white balls. The second urn also holds black and white balls, but the mix is unknown. In other words, you do not know how many black and white balls there are in the second urn.

One ball will be drawn at random from the urn that you choose. You will win if a black ball is chosen.

Figure 17.3: Ellsberg Urn

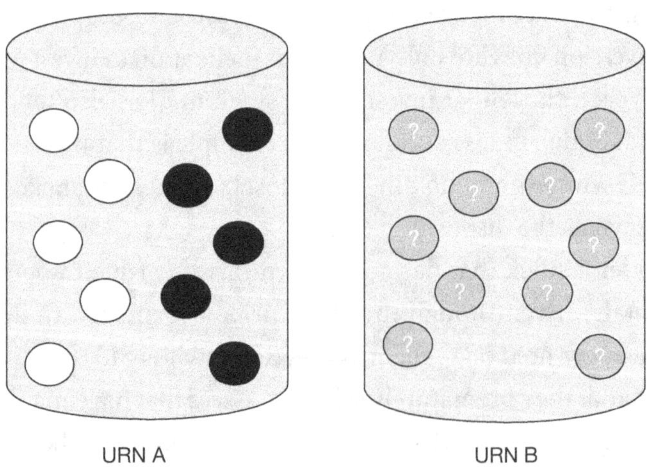

Which urn will you choose? Or will you be indifferent? If you chose the first urn, you are experiencing ambiguity aversion. As the probability of the second urn is unknown, you tend to prefer the first urn.

We will now look into a 2016 *Journal of Financial Economics* article by Stephen Dimmock, Roy Kouwenberg, Olivia Mitchell, and Kim Peijnenburg, titled "Ambiguity aversion and household portfolio choice puzzles: Empirical evidence".

In this research study, the authors asked a variant of the Ellsberg urn problem to more than 3,000 respondents in the American Life Panel. They observed that a majority of the respondents (52 percent) experience ambiguity aversion.

When the authors examine the relationship between ambiguity aversion and households' portfolios of the American Life Panel, it was found that an increase in ambiguity aversion relates to a decrease in the probability of stock market participation, and the fraction of wealth that is being allocated to the stock market. Conversely, individuals with a stronger aversion to ambiguity tend to exhibit higher levels of stock ownership in the company where they are employed.

How Should You Invest in the Market?

Given the inherent challenges in stock market participation, it is useful to recognize means of overcoming them. One option is to employ passive investment strategies instead of active ones.

Passive investment refers to a strategy of following an established stock index, such as the indexes discussed in Table 17.1. In contrast, active investment involves choosing specific stocks actively based on market trends and research, with the hope to outperform the benchmark.

Investing in a diversified passive index fund and holding it for the long term may be the most suitable option for the average individual investor. With passive investments, we do not need to monitor our investments day-to-day, which would allay concerns of loss aversion and ambiguity aversion. Also, as passive investments are more transparent, individuals would be more trusting.

Nonetheless, for those interested in actively managing their investments, there's the opportunity to utilize FinTech, which has reduced the traditional barriers of entry that discourage participation in active investing. As FinTech apps require a lower minimum sum of investment, and are easy to use, it makes investing more accessible.

Moreover, FinTech has democratized the use of financial service advisors. This include robo-advisors, which are digital applications that run algorithms and custom-make investment portfolios based on information supplied by their clients. Through the use of digital advisory platforms, artificial intelligence is able to recommend investment portfolios based on individuals' preferences and risk appetites.

Key Takeaways

If you have not invested in the stock market, this could be a result of your personal concerns such as lack of trust, loss aversion, or ambiguity aversion. This is relatable. However, by missing out on equity markets, you are missing out on the benefits of equity returns that can help you reach your retirement goals at a faster rate.

To overcome these challenges, you could consider leveraging on passive strategies and enlist the help of experts that you can trust. You are encouraged to seek advice from a professional investment advisor or even robo-advisors that can recommend portfolios based on your preferences.

18

Diversification

One of the fundamental principles behind investing is diversification. As the common adage goes "Do not put all your eggs in one basket," we would like to remind readers not to concentrate all your resources on a single asset class.

This includes purely holding cash or putting all our money into our savings account. Recall our discussion on inflation. With an increase in the inflation rate, it could potentially erode the purchasing power of our bank deposits as inflation rate outstrips the nominal interest rate.

Particularly, when there is hyperinflation (defined as an increase in inflation rate by more than 50 percent per month), the real value of our bank deposits could even potentially be wiped out overnight.

Countries that have experienced hyperinflation in recent years include Argentina (which recorded an inflation rate of 58 percent in May 2022) and Turkey (which faced an inflation rate near 85 percent in October 2022).

However, not all assets perform badly during inflation. One notable example is real estate, which has been shown to act as a good hedge against inflation due to its tendency for both asset value and rental income to rise alongside inflation. Other examples include commodities such as precious metals and oil, which have historically increased in value with inflation.

As such, it is crucial for us not to be overly reliant on one particular asset. Spreading our investments across different assets, sectors and even geographic regions help to reduce the impact of an individual investment's poor performance on our entire financial portfolio.

To gauge the adequacy of our diversification, we can employ techniques from stress testing and scenario testing. For instance, what happens when the company you are working at suddenly declares bankrupt? What happens when all travel comes to a halt (just like what we experienced in the coronavirus pandemic)?

It is time to scrutinize our household balance sheet again. In order to reduce the likelihood that we will be impacted by an adverse scenario, it is prudent to ensure that our income streams are not highly correlated. This includes income from our day job!

Consider the case of the Enron scandal in 2001. As one of the largest American energy companies, Enron enjoyed high growth in its profits from 1990 to 2000. This resulted in a corresponding increase in stock prices. Employees who were given share options benefited as they converted their employee stock options into shares.

But good things come to an end. Due to an accounting scandal, Enron went bankrupt in 2001. Many executives who owned Enron stocks were subjected to a dual blow. Besides losing their jobs overnight, they lost a large proportion of their savings and assets overnight. In fact, it is estimated that Enron employees lost $850 million on Enron stocks that were held in their retirement accounts.

Evidently, overweighing our financial portfolio with a single investment (including our own company stock) significantly increase our exposure to risk. Taking a diversified approach is the best step forward.

We will now zoom in on how diversification could help us reduce risk in the stock market. Diversification is a cornerstone behind Modern Portfolio Theory in finance. Pioneered by Harry Markowitz, 1990 winner of the Nobel Memorial Prize in Economic Sciences, it has been proven that changes in the number of stocks that we own could reduce the total risk in our financial portfolio.

Consider Figure 18.1, it suggests that the total portfolio risk decreases with the number of stocks in the portfolio. This is driven by the specific risk of the stock, such as firm- and industry-specific events. As an example, during the COVID-19 pandemic, not all firms were equally affected. While the tourism industry suffered a downturn, pharmaceutical companies witnessed a rise in their stock prices.

The more uncorrelated the returns of the firms are, the higher the benefits of diversification.

However, we would like to highlight that the total risk in our financial portfolio can never be driven to zero. This is known as undiversifiable systematic risk (market risk) and cannot be avoided as long as we are vested in the equity markets. For instance, this could be driven by changes in interest rate or geopolitical events. All stocks are affected by it.

Despite the importance of diversification, economic studies have documented that households do not diversify their portfolio enough. Let us review some case studies.

Figure 18.1: Diversification

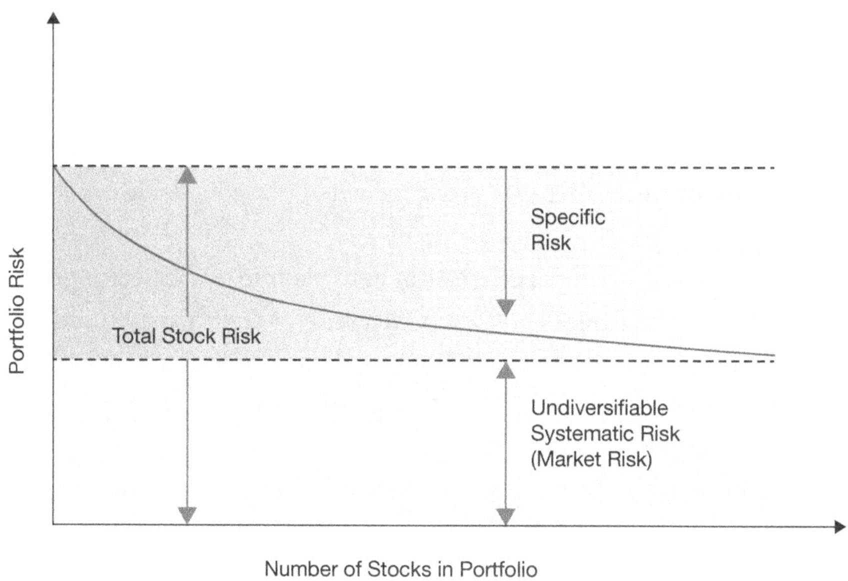

Naive Diversification Strategies

At the outset, there is evidence that individuals have very naïve notions about diversification. When faced with different choices in their financial decisions, individuals may turn to simple rules. One such example is the 1/N heuristic, in which households divide their assets equally among N different options.

We will examine the 1/N heuristic in a 2001 study in the *American Economic Review* by Shlomo Benartzi and Richard Thaler. Titled "Naïve Diversification Strategies in Defined Contribution Saving Plan," the research article sheds light on how individuals in the United States allocate their portfolios in their defined contribution savings plan.

In Chapter 7, we have highlighted that the defined contribution savings plan is a common workplace retirement plan in which both employee and employer contribute to the account.

To understand how the availability of options influence asset allocation, different groups of individuals in this study were provided with different pairs of funds to choose from. For instance, one group could be given a choice between a stock fund and a bond fund. In comparison, another group could be given a choice between a balanced fund (half stocks and half bonds) and a bond fund.

Consistent with the 1/N diversification heuristic, it was discovered that the pair of funds that was being provided played a deciding role in the allocation of assets.

In the study, the authors offered different plans to two different groups of employees: TWA pilots and the University of California employees. TWA pilots were offered five stock funds and one bond fund. On the other hand, the University of California employees were offered one stock fund and four bond funds.

As compared to the national average of 57 percent, it was found that the TWA pilots invested 75 percent in stocks, while the University of California employees invested 34 percent in stocks.

A discerning reader might be concerned that pilots and university employees might have different preferences. For instance, pilots could be more willing to take risks.

To overcome this concern, the authors conducted an extra experiment wherein the university employees were given the opportunity to make an asset-allocation decision under two specific conditions. The first condition relates to the investment options available in their own plan, while the second condition involves the funds provided in the TWA plan.

The analysis showed that when presented with their own plan which is dominated by bond funds, the employees leaned toward an asset allocation heavily focused on bonds. Conversely, when presented with a mostly stock mix resembling the TWA plan, they chose to primarily invest in stocks.

This points to the fact that individuals generally allocate their contributions evenly among the available investment options, rather than thoughtfully considering their desired asset allocation. In other words, our asset allocation is significantly influenced by the specific type of funds we are exposed to.

Now, take some time to think through how you design your financial portfolio. Do you use the 1/N heuristic to manage your portfolio too? While there may be no issue with this approach, it is timely to review your portfolio and see if you can better balance your risk and return.

Familiarity Bias

Another factor that contributes to households' inadequate diversification is familiarity bias. The occurrence of familiarity bias arises from individuals' inclination to prioritize familiarity and avoid the unknown.

One example of familiarity bias occurs when company employees tend to invest almost exclusively in the stock of the firm that they work. An additional example relates to how investors lean toward overweighting stocks of companies whose brands they recognize and have substantial information about.

Equity home bias, or the tendency to invest in domestic stocks, is a closely related concept. As households are more familiar with companies in their home country, they end up focusing on domestic stocks. But when they do so, they are unable to reap the benefits from international diversification.

Through international diversification, one can invest across different countries, reducing the impact of specific country risks and geopolitical concerns. At the same time, it could potentially improve investment returns as one achieves a more balanced financial portfolio.

Nonetheless, it has been widely documented that individuals in most countries tend to invest in domestic equities as compared to international markets. As an illustration, households in Australia invest 66 percent of their assets in domestic markets even though the weight of the Australia stock market as a percentage of global equities is only 2 percent.

What drives the home equity bias? In what follows, we highlight two possible reasons.

The first reason relates to information immobility. While there are fewer restrictions on international capital flows now, investors still have difficulties obtaining accurate information about foreign firms or economic conditions.

The role of information and portfolio choices has been examined in a 2009 *The Journal of Finance* article by Stijn Van Nieuwerburgh and Laura Veldkamp. Titled "Information Immobility and the Home Bias Puzzle," the study provides a theoretical model that underpins how information advantages influence households' preferences to invest in their home country.

While individuals can acquire information from both domestic and foreign markets, they know more about their home country at the outset, and hence have a prior information advantage in their domestic markets. As a result, it is more costly for them to learn about investing in foreign assets relative to assets in their home country.

To maximize their time and efforts, individuals will therefore focus on their comparative advantage in home assets, and devote resources in learning about investments in the domestic market. Thus, they do not invest in foreign assets.

In addition, home bias can be explained through the familiarity of source preferences. This occurs when individuals prefer sources that they are more familiar with when taking risks.

In a recent study "Experimental Evidence of Source Preference: Familiarity and Home Bias" by Chew Soo Hong, Li King King, and Jacob Sagi, the importance of the underlying sources of uncertainty is being discussed.

To unpack how the familiarity of risks influences households' financial decisions, the authors asked respondents how much they are willing to bet based on the value of the trailing digit of closing prices of a company one trading day after the experiment was conducted. The respondents would guess whether the trailing digit would be odd or even.

Theoretically, the trailing digit of the prices in the next period would be random. Knowing the stock does not help us in anyway. Nonetheless, individuals have demonstrated that they are willing to bet more on stocks that they are more familiar with.

For instance, respondents in Shanghai (Hong Kong) are more willing to bet on the trailing digit of the Shanghai Stock Exchange Index (Hang Seng Index), despite being offered bets with better payoffs in the Dow Jones Industrial Average.

Key Takeaways

We have discussed about the importance of diversification, and how we can benefit from it. The more uncorrelated our income streams or return on assets are, the more we can benefit from diversification. However, it has been documented that individuals are not doing enough.

While some turn to naïve diversification strategies, others stick to things that they are familiar with. As a result, households miss out the gains from portfolio optimization or international diversification.

Now that we are aware of the benefits and challenges involved in diversification, it is timely to review our portfolio and see if we can better balance our risks and returns.

We can also proactively find ways to overcome the inherent challenges we face, such as being conscious of the familiarity bias, and improving our knowledge gap in unfamiliar territories, such as foreign assets.

To reduce home equity bias, one way is to focus on products with lower information cost. For example, instead of buying stocks directly from foreign markets, we could purchase mutual funds or exchange-traded-funds that are centered on the foreign markets that we are interested in.

19

Portfolio Inertia and Overtrading

In this chapter, we will discuss two extreme cases in which different households manage their financial portfolios. On one hand, we have portfolio inertia. This occurs when there is inaction on the part of individuals as they stick to the status quo. On the other hand, some individuals exhibit overtrading as they trade excessively in search of higher returns. Both cases are not ideal, as substantial losses could be incurred.

We first explore the case of portfolio inertia.

Portfolio Inertia

There have been many examples of sluggish household behavior in risky asset markets. We turn to one economic study, "When Nudges Are Forever: Inertia in the Swedish Premium Pension Plan" by Henrik Cronqvist, Richard Thaler, and Frank Yu.

In this article, the authors studied how households in Sweden responded to the different nudges in the Swedish Premium Pension Plan. When the plan was first established in 2000, Swedish households were given the option to stick to the default plan or form their own portfolios by selecting their own funds.

To attract households to select their plans, individual funds advertised aggressively, nudging households to select their funds. In the end, two-thirds of the participants elected to choose their own portfolio, suggesting that the nudging from advertising worked.

Nonetheless, after the fund was selected, there was extreme inertia as respondents did not switch across different funds. This is puzzling as several extreme events had occurred during that period.

Firstly, the Swedish government allowed the default fund in 2010 to employ financial leverage at the fund management's discretion. This implies that the risk level of the default fund had increased as the fund managers were able to borrow money to buy more stocks.

We would think that changes in the risk profile of the default fund would cause people to move toward less risky funds (which is similar to the initial risk level of the default fund). But there were no significant changes.

Moreover, there was a scandal in 2017 involving Allra, which is one of the fund companies in the pension system. The possible fraudulent practices of Allra were broadcasted in the Swedish newspapers, with the Swedish Pensions Agency launching a fraud investigation. At this point, the agency stopped new investors to switch to Allra's funds while allowing existing investors to move out of Allra's funds.

Against this background, we would expect to see existing investors moving their funds out of Allra. Again, nothing happened. This provides evidence of portfolio inertia at work.

With the benefit of hindsight now, how would you have reacted? Would you do nothing as well? It is timely to reflect on our past financial decisions in which we had stuck to the status quo. Could we have done better? After all, an inaction is also an action. Not making a decision is also a decision.

Why do individuals not respond? One possible reason is the lack of financial knowledge—that is where this book comes into play. Another potential explanation stems from the endowment effect, a phenomenon widely acknowledged in the field of behavioral economics.

Endowment Effect

To begin our discussion of the endowment effect, let us start with a story from Richard Thaler, the 2017 recipient of the Nobel Memorial Prize in Economic Sciences. In one incident, Thaler mentioned that he has a wine-loving friend[8] who managed to purchase some wine at a low price ($10) previously. Eventually, the market value of the wine increased such that it was worth more than $100.

While Thaler's friend is unwilling to purchase or sell the wine at the market price, he still drinks the wine occasionally! From an economist's standpoint, this is not logical. If he is willing to drink wine that is currently worth more than $100, the benefits from drinking the wine must be worth more than $100. Nonetheless, why will he not be willing to purchase the wine at the current market price?

Thaler sees this as an example of the endowment effect—in which individuals assign a higher value to products that they already owned.

Together with Daniel Kahneman and Jack Knetsch, Thaler conducted a series of experiments that are discussed in the article "Experimental Tests of the Endowment Effect and the Coase Theorem." Published in the *Journal of Political Economy* in 1990, it provides evidence of endowment effects at work.

We will highlight one experiment that involves the trading of mugs. During the fall of 1985, the authors conducted an experiment with 44 undergraduates at Cornell University. Half of them were given coffee mugs with the Cornell insignia. Thereafter, they were asked how much they are willing to sell the mugs to those non-mug owners. The experiments were conducted in four rounds.

It was found that the mug owners (sellers) value the mugs at a rate of $5.25. The valuation is much higher than how much the non-mug owners (buyers) are willing to pay. For instance, the median reservation price for

[8] The wine-loving friend is Professor Richard Rosett, an American economist who served as the dean of the University of Chicago Booth School of Business from 1974 to 1982.

the buyers was $2.75 in one round, and $2.25 in the other three rounds. As a result, there were only a limited number of trades conducted.

How does the endowment effect apply to you? With the endowment effect, you will end up overvaluing the current assets that you are holding. Consequently, you may hold on to your current assets, instead of selling them when a good offer arises. This leads to portfolio inertia, as you are establishing an emotional connection with your financial portfolio.

Evidence from India's IPO Lotteries

We now shift our attention to an example of the endowment effect in a 2018 study in *The Review of Economic Studies* by Santosh Anagol, Vimal Balasubramaniam, and Tarun Ramadorai.

As the title of the research article suggests "Endowment Effects in the Field: Evidence from India's IPO Lotteries," the research delves into how endowment effects influence individuals' decisions to sell the stocks that they are allocated during Initial Public Offerings (IPO) in India.

In India, IPO shares are randomly allocated to applicants through lotteries due to regulation. While lottery winners are allocated the shares at the IPO issue price, lottery losers receive cash back that is equal to the IPO issue price as well.

When the stock begins to trade in the stock market, both winners and losers of the lottery can then trade with one another at the agreed market price. Since both lottery winners and losers are similar in terms of information sets and background, the valuation of the stocks for both groups ought to be the same, and they should hold identical holdings of the stocks over time.

However, the authors did not find convergence in the behavior of both groups. Instead, they found that at the end of the month after listing, 62.4 percent of the IPO winners hold the stock, while only 1 percent of the losers hold the stock.

The disparity between the two groups persisted even 24 months later. Relative to the IPO losers, 35 percent of the winners are more likely to hold the stocks at that point in time. This provides evidence of the endowment effect in the stock market.

Overtrading

At this point, we would like to caution our readers not to swing to the other extreme. We now move on from portfolio inertia to the other end of the spectrum—overtrading.

Excessive trading has also been shown to be harmful. Let us examine a 2000 *The Journal of Finance* article by Brad Barber and Terrance Odean named "Trading Is Hazardous to Your Wealth: The Common Stock Investment Performance of Individual Investors." This study focused on the financial performance of 66,465 households with accounts at a U.S. discount broker from 1991 to 1996.

Based on their monthly turnover (which is the ratio of the market value of shares purchased in the previous month against the current month), the authors divided individuals into five quintiles.

The top quintiles (that trade most often) have an average monthly turnover of more than 20 percent. This indicates that they turn their portfolios over more than two times each year!

Nonetheless, it was established that these individuals earned an annual return of 11.4 percent, which is much lower than the market returns of 17.9 percent. In comparison, the average household enjoyed an annual return of 16.4 percent.

Why does overtrading result in weaker financial performance? One reason is attributed to transaction costs. By failing to account for various costs, such as bid-ask spreads and commissions, individuals that trade more tend to be worse off. Furthermore, overtrading has been linked to overconfidence.

As individuals place a high degree of confidence in their own capabilities and skills, they overestimate their understanding of financial markets. Consequently, they make mistakes, such as having under-diversified portfolios and do not consider risk management in their decisions.

Overconfidence

Overconfidence of investors have been documented in several economic studies. We now take a closer look at a 2009 research article that is published in *The Journal of Finance* by Mark Grinblatt and Matti Keloharju.

The study, titled "Sensation Seeking, Overconfidence, and Trading Activity" combined several data sources in Finland to unpack determinants of households' trading activities. In this study, overconfidence and a penchant for sensation-seeking were identified as factors contributing to households' tendency to overtrade.

To measure overconfidence, the authors relied on a standard psychological assessment that is given to all Finnish males when they are being inducted into mandatory military service. Based on the psychological measurement, it was realized that overconfident investors have a tendency to trade more.

In addition, sensational seeking (which is found to have a low correlation with overconfidence) plays a role too. Sensation-seeking is a stable personality trait that is widely examined in the psychology literature. It is a trait that is related to individuals' desire for new and intense experiences.

To account for sensation-seeking behavior, the authors make use of the number of automobile speeding convictions that are being imposed on the investor. Through their findings, it was established that an increase in sensation-seeking behavior (through speeding convictions) is associated with investors' overtrading behavior.

Expectations of Returns

At this point, it is time to appreciate how individuals form their expectations of future stock market returns.

Let us turn to a 2014 study by Robin Greenwood and Andrei Shleifer. Published in *The Review of Financial Studies*, the title of the article is "Expectations of Returns and Expected Returns."

To obtain data on investor expectations, the authors relied on the following datasets:

- The Gallup Investor Survey
- The Graham–Harvey Chief Financial Officer Surveys
- The American Association of Individual Investors Survey
- The Investor Intelligence Survey of Investment Newsletter
- Robert Shiller's Investor Survey
- The Survey Research Center at the University of Michigan

The authors found that there are strong levels of correlation between these six different measures of expectations, suggesting that they are widely shared beliefs about market returns in the future. We highly encourage you to review these data sources to find out what the expectations of others are.

Besides, the authors revealed that the expectations of stock mark returns are extrapolative in nature. In particular, they are highly correlated with the past stock markets and the current level of the stock market. In other words, if the past market performance is high, households will expect them to be high in the future as well.

While extrapolation is an intuitive way of forming expectations, we would like to highlight to the readers that extrapolation can be unreliable, as past performance is not indicative of future results. The economy goes in cycles, moving from economic expansions to contractions.

As a simple exercise in forecasting, extrapolation might give us a false sense of security, leaving us to be overly confident of our predictions. This could give us an illusion of knowledge or control.

Key Takeaways

In this chapter, we have discussed about two extreme cases of trading: portfolio inertia and overtrading. Neither is desirable and we need to strike a balance between these two cases.

Portfolio inertia could be attributed to the endowment effect when we value our stock holdings even more. How do we then overcome portfolio inertia and the endowment effect?

Here, it will be useful to have periodic reviews with your financial advisors and evaluate your decisions from a fresh perspective each time. Start from a clean slate and ask yourself whether what you are currently doing is the optimal strategy.

On the other hand, overtrading occurs due to overconfidence and extrapolation of returns. Consequently, one would like to time the market, resulting in poor financial performance. After all, as the saying goes "It is not about timing the market, but time in the market".

To manage these issues, it will be useful to understand what our own personality traits are so that we will not fall prey to making rash decisions that could be detrimental in the long run.

Moreover, it is imperative to note the limitations behind our forecasts, and not be overly reliant on them. Self-awareness is the way forward.

20

Mental Accounting

We will now proceed to talk about mental accounting in investments. In Chapter 2, we have discussed about how mental accounting influences households' decisions in consumption. As individuals categorize their budgets and expenditure into different buckets, they seek to increase their well-being in separate categories (rather than holistically). Nonetheless, this is suboptimal as money is fungible.

It appears that mental accounting also influences households' investment decisions. In this chapter, we explore three instances where individuals apply mental accounting in their investment decisions: portfolio selection, dividends, and socially responsible investments.

Portfolio Choice

We first show that households adopt mental accounting in their asset allocation.

This is examined in a 2009 *American Economic Review* study by James Choi, David Laibson, and Brigitte Madrian. Titled "Mental Accounting in Portfolio Choice: Evidence from a Flypaper Effect," the article sheds light on how individuals in a large U.S. firm make investment decisions in their 401(k) retirement funds.

In this company, the process of contributing to the retirement funds is as follows.

The first step involves the employees being directly responsible for the amount of money contributed to their retirement funds. They will also decide on the type of assets they would like to allocate their investments into. Thereafter, the company will make a matching contribution that is proportional to the employee's contribution (subject to a threshold).

However, the company made changes to its matching contribution policy. Before March 2003, the firm's directed matching contribution went directly into the firm's stock. While the employees are allowed to adjust the balances after the firm has made the contributions, it is seldom practiced. Hence, the firm's contributions are usually on the firm's stock.

After the change in policy was made, employees were required to decide on the allocation of assets for the firm's matching contribution as well. This is on top of their individual contributions.

This provided a natural experiment for the researchers to find out the actual preferences of the employees when managing their portfolio. In other words, would employees continue including the firm stock from the firm's contribution?

It turns out that the answer is no.

Before March 2003, employees allocated 23 percent of their own contribution flows to the firm's stock. After including the firm's contribution, which is directed primarily into the firm's stock itself, the total allocation to the firm's stock by the employees was estimated to be 56 percent.

In comparison, after March 2003, the total allocation to the firm's stock by the employees was at 23 percent. This is equivalent to the employees' own contribution flows previously.

Therefore, an increase in the firm's stock by the employers before March 2003 managed to increase the employees' total holdings of the firm's stock by a full dollar! The authors regard this as a flypaper effect since "money sticks where it hits."

Why did individuals not reduce the firm's stock holdings initially? The authors hypothesized that it is related to mental accounting. Before March 2003, employees only consider their own contribution flows and neglect the fact that the firm's contributions were being assigned to the firm's stocks. Hence, they have a separate mental account that focuses on their own contributions, while ignoring the match flow allocation.

However, after March 2003, they were required to consider their entire portfolio and not just their own contribution flows. This made both accounts salient. Consequently, the proportion in which individuals allocate their *own contribution* investments to the firm's stocks before March 2003 is equivalent to the proportion in which individuals allocate their *total* investments to the firm's stocks after March 2003.

This suggests that employees would like to allocate 23 percent of their assets to the firm's stocks in their portfolios which are salient.

Do you practice mental accounting in managing your portfolios as well? As discussed in the introductory chapters, it is useful to prepare your personal balance sheet, and update it regularly, so that you can have a better understanding of your entire portfolio. This will reduce the likelihood of mental accounting in managing your finances.

Next, we move on to dividends.

The Dividend Disconnect

How do we calculate our returns from financial assets? In general, it is attributed to two sources. The first component is due to the change in the price of the asset. This relates to the capital gain of the asset in which we make a profit when we sell an asset at a higher price than our purchase price. The second component is the cash flows, such as dividends from stocks or coupons from bonds.

As money is fungible, individuals ought to treat both components the same and the choice between these two streams of income should not matter.

Notwithstanding, living off dividends as an income stream is a popular retail investment advice. For instance, in a Forbes article "How to make $500,000 last forever" on November 2, 2016, Brett Owens, a frequent contributor, wrote the following "The only dependable way to retire and stay retired is to boost your payouts so that you never have to touch your capital."

To fix ideas for capital gains and dividends, consider the following two stocks at the same price (say $5).

For the first stock (stock A), you receive a $1 dividend (and the stock price remained unchanged). For the second stock (stock B), you do not receive any dividend (but the stock price increased by $1).

Which do you prefer? Assuming that there are no taxes or trading costs, you should be indifferent between these two cases. Nonetheless, mental accounting might shape your decisions with regard to dividends and price changes as you treat them differently.

If you are concerned primarily about your dividends, you would prefer stock A (even though they perform the same). On the other hand, if you are only focusing on the price changes, you would prefer stock B. This is not a true reflection of the stock's performance as we should focus on the total returns (involving both price changes and dividends). As mentioned in Chapter 2, a dollar is a dollar after all.

Consider a 2019 study by Samuel Hartzmark and David Solomon that is published in *The Journal of Finance*. Titled "The Dividend Disconnect," the research article demonstrated that stocks were indeed traded as if dividends and capital gains were disconnected.

In their analysis, the authors determined that instead of combining price changes and dividends together, individuals tracked them separately.

First and foremost, it was shown that prices are more saliently regarded as tools for stock performance. It was further revealed that the trading of stocks was driven by changes in price, rather than total returns. It appears that individuals do not consider dividends when evaluating stocks!

The authors termed it as the "Free Dividend Fallacy," as investors have the misconception that dividends are free money! Rather than thinking that dividends are a shift of money from the stock price to dividends, many treat dividends as additional money.

What do individuals do with the money? The study reported that investors do not reinvest in the companies that pay them. Rather, they invest in other stocks! For instance, it was found that when companies pay dividends, it drove up the demand for other non-dividend-paying shares.

Another issue with the mental separation of dividends and price appreciation is that individuals hold on to dividend-paying stocks for a longer period of time, even though the share prices of the company are falling. Hence, you could end up with negative returns (even though you are still enjoying dividends).

Furthermore, there is evidence that individuals reach for income by turning to dividend-paying stocks when interest rates are low.

One implication of this is that prices of dividend-paying stocks were driven up because investors simultaneously turned to them. In turn, these stocks ended up having lower returns. It was estimated that the dividend-stock returns were 2 to 4 percent lower relative to normal times.

Changes in monetary policy and reaching for income have been documented in recent work as well.

In a research study, "Monetary Policy and Reaching for Income" authored by Kent Daniel, Lorenzo Garlappi, and Kairong Xiao and published in *The Journal of Finance* in 2021, the authors examined households' preferences for current income.

The study relied on data from individual portfolio holdings and mutual fund flows which shows that when interest rates are lowered, a higher demand for income-generating assets occurs. This includes high-dividend stocks and high-yield bonds.

Mental accounting can explain this behavior too. As investors follow the rule-of-thumb of "living off income," they have the tendency to move toward high dividend stocks and high yield assets when interest rates fall. This plugs the gap between individuals' current incomes and consumption levels.

Socially Responsible Investing

There is also evidence of mental accounting in dealing with socially responsible investments, which pay attention to both financial returns and social good.

In recent years, there has been an increasing interest in socially responsible investments. According to Morningstar, flows into sustainable funds doubled from 2020 to 2021 (to US$51.1 billion).

In addition, the number of sustainable funds available to U.S. investors based on Morningstar's sustainable funds universe has also increased fivefold. This corresponds to a huge increase in the investments of risky assets that are related to sustainable funds.

However, as mentioned in Chapter 17, the stock market participation rate in the United States remained constant during this time period. Why is this so? To investigate the relationship between socially responsible investing and stock market participation, Yeow Hwee conducted an experiment with Yiting Chen, titled "Socially Responsible Investing and Narrow Framing."

The study seeks to investigate how changes in social preferences impact households' decisions to rebalance their portfolio. Through an incentivized experiment, subjects were provided with payoffs of different risk-free and risky assets, before being told to make investment decisions.

To indicate prosocial behavior, donations to two charitable organizations, World Wildlife Fund for Nature (WWF) Singapore and Red Cross Singapore were included.

More precisely, three different assets were being introduced in the study. Asset A is a risk-free asset with a fixed interest rate. Asset B is a risky asset with different possible outcomes. Asset C differs from Asset B through the following treatment groups (Control, Self, Red Cross, WWF).

Relative to the Control group, the Self group enjoyed higher returns for themselves. For the Red Cross and WWF group, on top of the individual returns allocated to the control group, donations are being given to Red Cross Singapore and the World Wildlife Fund for Nature (WWF) Singapore respectively.

Comparison of the different treatment groups in Asset C will tell us how much different individuals are willing to invest in assets which are socially desirable.

If subjects are non-altruistic, there would be no difference in their investments that donate to charity (Red Cross and WWF) relative to the Control group. This implies that they do not value the additional returns given to the charitable organization.

In comparison, if subjects are completely altruistic, there would be no difference in their investments that donate to charity (Red Cross and WWF) and investments kept for themselves (Self).

So how do individuals respond? The results show that while payments for oneself increase both new investments and portfolio rebalancing across different risky assets, payments for charities solely induce rebalancing.

It was found that additional payments lead to an increase in investments in the risky asset with different treatment groups (Asset C). Nonetheless, the total amount of investments into Asset C differs across different treatment groups.

Relative to the Control group, the respondents allocate an additional 6 percent of their assets into Asset C when given the opportunity to donate to the charity organizations, Red Cross and WWF. This is lower than the additional 21 percent for the Self-treatment group. Hence, we find that individuals are prosocial, but they are not completely altruistic.

We now focus on total investments into risky assets (Assets B and C). Here, we find that for payments to oneself, there is an increase in investment toward both risky assets (Assets B and C).

However, the total amount of investments into risky assets (Assets B and C) remained unchanged when given the opportunity to donate to the charity organizations, Red Cross and WWF.

The findings of the experiment indicate that the availability of sustainable funds does not lead to new investments into risky assets. Rather, individuals rebalance their portfolios across risky assets when given the opportunity to invest in sustainable funds. This is consistent with the empirical observation that there is no increase in stock market participation rate despite the growth in socially responsible investing.

Why is this so? Through a theoretical model, it was shown that this is a result of mental accounting at work! As individuals only consider social responsibility in the account for risky investments, they do not increase their investments into risky assets despite the growth in socially responsible investments.

Key Takeaways

We have presented many cases of mental accounting in investments. To overcome the mental accounting bias, it is important for us to realize that money is perfectly fungible.

This requires a mindset shift. As some of us might have the tendency to compartmentalize our thinking, we could face difficulties achieving this goal.

To help ourselves, we could leverage on existing technology and toolkits. For instance, by relying on apps or spreadsheets that provide us with a unified budget and a holistic view of our financial position, it is less likely that we would neglect the relationship between our different investment accounts.

As discussed in the introductory chapters, proper financial planning and strategies are the ways forward to overcome our behavioral biases. Don't lose the entire forest for a singular tree. There are times when we need to take a step back and reevaluate, so that we can make progress toward our long-term financial goals.

21

Interpreting Investment Performance

In this final chapter on investing, we would like to draw your attention to some common pitfalls for individuals when they evaluate their financial portfolios.

Recall our earlier discussion on inflation? To maintain our purchasing power, we should consider real values instead of nominal ones. Nonetheless, many individuals only look at nominal prices.

The misunderstanding toward nominal prices is also a frequent occurrence when making investment decisions. This is commonly known as the nominal price illusion.

Nominal Price Illusion

Before we start, we would like to highlight that the level of a stock price is arbitrary. What matters is the percentage of ownership as it determines our share of the company's assets, profits and voting rights.

In reality, nominal share price can simply be influenced by changes in the number of shares. This includes having share splits and bonus shares.

Stock splits increase the number of shares in a company without impacting the total value of all shares. For example, when there is a 2-for-1 split, it means that each investor will now have double the number of shares they had previously. One main objective of stock splits is to decrease the prices of stocks, so that it can be more accessible for retail investors.

Consider the case in which a company is valued at $100 million. If there are 100 million shares, each share will be worth $1. With a 2-for-1 split, it means that there will now be 200 million shares and that each share will be worth $0.50.

Theoretically, the value of our shareholdings should not be affected by the nominal price. It does not matter whether we purchase 10 shares out of 100 million shares (at $1 each) or 20 shares out of 200 million shares (at $0.50 each). The valuation and our percentage of ownership remains unchanged.

Stock splits have been adopted by companies frequently. In 2022, Alphabet, Google's parent company implemented a 20-for-1 stock split. This means that each existing share of the company will be split into 20 new shares. After the split, the share price fell from around $2,200 to $113.

In the United States, other companies that have recently undergone stock splits include Apple, Amazon, and Tesla. Table 21.1 presents the historical stock prices of Apple right before and after the stock split. It can be seen that Apple has gone through several rounds of stock splits, with a corresponding change in stock prices. This seeks to increase the liquidity of the share, and to signal to investors that the stock has done well.

To see how nominal price has the ability to influence households' financial decisions, let us turn to a 2009 study in the *Journal of Financial Economics* by Clifton Green and Byoung-Hyoun Hwang. In their research paper titled "Price-Based Return Co-Movement," the authors show that

Table 21.1: Stock Prices of Apple Before and After Split

Year	Split	Price Before Split	Price After Split
August 28, 2020	4-for-1 basis	500	125
June 9, 2014	7-for-1 basis	656	94
February 28, 2005	2-for-1 basis	90	45
June 21, 2000	2-for-1 basis	111	56
June 16, 1987	2-for-1 basis	79	40

stocks with similar prices move together, suggesting that stock market participants group stocks based on prices.

Furthermore, the co-movement changes when there are stock splits. In fact, stocks that undergo splits increased their co-movement with low-priced stocks and reduced their co-movement with high-priced stocks. This is because stock splits caused a decrease in stock prices, making them resemble low-priced stocks rather than high-priced stocks.

To reconcile the findings, several explanations were provided.

One possible reason is that investors consider prices to be a proxy for firm size. As the change in co-movement is larger for bigger companies, it suggests that investors have mistakenly equated price with size.

Another possible reason is attributed to individuals' beliefs in the upside potential of individual stocks. In this study, the authors observed that changes in co-movement are larger during periods of high investor sentiment, highlighting the importance of psychological heuristics.

This is in line with the idea that as compared to high-priced stocks, individuals overestimate the potential for low-priced stocks to grow. For instance, many think that it is easier for a $3 stock to move up to $6, rather than for a $30 stock to reach $60.

This finding is supported by another 2016 study in the *Journal of Financial Economics* by Justin Birru and Baolian Wang. Titled "Nominal Price Illusion," the authors made use of skewness to study the expectations of the upside potential of stocks.

Skewness is a measurement of asymmetric returns. By utilizing options markets to gauge investor skewness expectations, it was demonstrated that individuals tend to overestimate the skewness of low-priced stocks, primarily due to an excessive emphasis on the stock price itself.

Moreover, following stock splits, investor expectations of future skewness increase. Hence, the nominal price illusion influences investors to mistakenly believe that lower-priced stocks have more room to grow.

The over-estimation in low-priced stocks could be costly. Through the construction of a zero-cost option portfolio strategy, it was documented that profits could be made by exploiting investors' mistaken belief.

Non-Proportional Thinking

Next, we move from prices to returns. When it comes to stock returns, do you think of dollar changes or percentage changes?

Rationally, we ought to direct our attention to the percentage changes. As mentioned earlier, the nominal share price is an arbitrary number (based on the number of shares that are being issued.)

Consider the shares of two companies. The share of company A is trading at $5, while the share of company B is trading at $20. An increase in the price of $1 for company A is different from an increase in the price of $1 for company B. For company A, the share has increased by a whopping 20 percent. In comparison, the share has increased by 5 percent for company B.

It is essential for us to be able to distinguish between dollar changes and percentage changes. To grow our wealth, what matters is the percentage change to our individual portfolio.

Nonetheless, in our daily lives, we are exposed to dollar price changes most of the time through media outlets. This includes newspapers, such as *The Wall Street Journal*, and television networks, such as *CNBC*.

Economic studies have also provided evidence of non-proportional thinking among individuals. Non-proportional thinking means that when faced with new information, individuals think in terms of changes in nominal dollar terms rather than percentage terms.

We now analyze a 2021 study in *The Journal of Finance* by Kelly Shue and Richard Townsend. Their article is aptly titled "Can The Market Multiply and Divide? Non-Proportional Thinking in Financial Markets," and explores how nonproportional thinking results in lower-priced stocks being more volatile than higher-priced stocks.

This is because when individuals think in terms of nominal dollar changes, a $1 change in the price of a stock results in lower-priced stocks being more volatile than higher-priced stocks.

Indeed, they found that when share price doubles in the United States between 1926 and 2016, volatility falls by 20 to 30 percent. This result is consistent during periods of share splits and reverse splits. With share splits, the price fall and volatility is increased. In contrast, with reverse splits (when shares are being combined), prices go up and volatility is reduced.

Through the use of textual analysis, the authors further noticed that lower-priced stocks are more responsive to firm-specific news. They also experience more extreme returns on days with earnings announcements.

What causes non-proportional thinking? This is related to a well-known bias in the psychology literature. Known as "denominator neglect" or "ratio bias," individuals tend to focus on numerators when they compare ratios. For instance, previous work has proven that individuals perceive 10 out of 100 as a larger number than 1 out of 10.

As we process information automatically, we tend to shift our attention on numbers that are more accessible. Thus, we end up being overly influenced by price levels and dollar changes. This includes the evaluation of stock market performances.

Price Versus Returns

Why do individuals focus too much on prices and not returns? One key reason is because we are exposed to prices most of the time, and total returns are seldom displayed.

In fact, most reported measurements of market performance only present changes in prices and do not account for dividends. This includes major stock market indices globally, including the S&P 500 Index.

By ignoring dividends, an index may under-report its actual performance. When dividends are issued, the prices of the shares (ex-dividend) will fall. Therefore, if the index does not include the reinvestments of dividends, it will underperform the actual returns.

This is discussed in a 2022 article in *The Review of Financial Studies* by Samuel Hartzmark and David Solomon. As the title of the article "Reconsidering Returns" suggests, we need to recalibrate how we think of returns. For example, we could display returns by default (instead of prices).

The study shows that displaying prices (and not returns) creates confusion amongst individuals, including newspaper journalists. This is deduced from the tone of *The New York Times* articles based on the previous day's market performance.

It was revealed that on days that dividends were higher, newspaper coverage was more negative. One main reason is due to the mechanical larger fall in stock prices. Thus, there is suggestive evidence that the journalists concentrate on the returns in S&P 500 Index, and not total returns.

We now delve into mutual funds. Mutual funds are investment vehicles that are professionally managed. To calculate the price per share of the fund, investors rely on the Net Asset Value (NAV), which is determined through the difference between the fund's assets and liabilities. Changes in NAV are key indicators of a fund's performance, and they are presented on major websites and financial news.

Nonetheless, NAV does not reflect the total returns to the mutual funds. For example, changes in NAV do not account for changes in dividends, as well as other forms of distributions (such as realized capital gains) from the funds.

How do investors respond to changes in NAV? After controlling for many different measurements of fund performance, Hartzmark and Solomon show that funds that have larger percentage changes in NAV than the S&P 500 receive an additional 0.54% per month in fund flows over the following year. This implies that investors are influenced by NAV and not the total returns.

Consequently, the display of information plays a central role in influencing our perceptions of the fund's performance. To effectively manage our finances, it is important to have a comprehensive understanding of different performance indicators and their role in establishing a basis for comparison.

Key Takeaways

Throughout the previous chapters, we have highlighted that households would be better off if they participated in the stock market. They are also able to diversify their risks.

However, we have provided evidence that individuals might not be as well equipped to make investment decisions on their own due to behavioral biases. In this chapter, we have further identified several pitfalls that individuals might fall prey to when evaluating their financial performance.

Therefore, if you would like to leverage on investments in your financial portfolio, it is important to first invest in yourselves. While you take time to learn about investing, you also need to understand your own strengths and limitations as well as what you know, and what you do not know.

In the words of Benjamin Graham, one of world's most influential investor, "the investor's chief problem—and even his worst enemy—is likely to be himself."

Part VI

Housing

22

Buying and Selling Houses

We now move on from investments in the stock market to the real estate market. This includes purchasing properties for our own stay and for investment purposes. For most of us, buying a house would be the most expensive purchase made in our lifetime.

Globally, residential real estate makes up the largest proportion of households' wealth. According to the Organization for Economic Cooperation and Development (OECD), the average percentage of wealth in housing across all OECD countries was around 50 percent in 2015.

Hence, making financial decisions in the housing market is of utmost importance! Nonetheless, navigating the real estate market is not an easy task. Buying and selling houses are fraught with many challenges that could result in individuals making financial mistakes.

One reason is that buying a home is highly personal and is driven by emotions. For instance, an individual could choose to purchase a house due to the emotional attachment toward the place. As Oprah Winfrey mentioned, "I will forever believe that buying a home is a great investment. Why? Because you can't live in a stock certificate. You can't live in a mutual fund."

This is further exacerbated by behavioral biases, as well as a lack of financial literacy and knowledge when buying a home. For instance, individuals might be tempted to purchase their dream homes without considering their finances.

Moreover, buying a house is not a simple decision. There are many steps involved. In general, you will first engage a real estate agent to assist in your housing search. After choosing a house that appeals to you, the next step is to negotiate for a suitable price. In the event of unsuccessful negotiations, you will have to restart the search process. This could create stress and anxiety, and you might get emotionally exhausted from the search.

But this is only the beginning! Once you are satisfied with the price, you will need to make decisions about mortgages. Choices to be made include the type of mortgage, mortgage insurance, size of down payment, and also how much to pay in terms of points and fees.

Following the completion of the mortgage contract, there remain various aspects to contemplate, including the possibility of refinancing down the line. Overwhelmed by the large number of decisions to make, you might end up making many poor choices.

Frictions in the Housing Markets

A key reason why people make mistakes when buying or selling houses is attributed to the idiosyncrasies of the housing market.

While houses are assets, they are highly illiquid. There are many frictions involved in the buying and selling of houses, generating uncertainty about the time of sale.

This is because, it takes time to match a buyer and seller with the appropriate house, negotiate prices, conduct due diligence, and then obtain the relevant mortgage.

With these difficulties, individuals who would like to sell their house quickly might end up with a lower price. Thus, households must be mindful of the fact that purchasing a house entails a long-term commitment.

Owning a house also requires us to take into account depreciation and maintenance costs. The house might also go out of style, given the dynamic changes in residential preferences.

On top of that, whenever we buy or sell a house, there are many additional charges involved. This includes commission fees to realtors, taxes, as well as renovations.

We will devote the next few chapters to mortgages and the different intermediaries. In what follows, let us outline the main three steps that should be thoroughly considered before embarking on a house purchase.

Three Steps to Consider Before Buying a House

1. Set your objectives in buying a house

The first step involves having clear objectives in buying a new house. Before you even begin, take a moment to reflect and ask yourself a series of questions.

Why do you need to move? Is it because you are starting a new family? Is it because you would like to reside close to your child's school or parents' place? Or is it because you would like to impress your high school friends?

Establishing your goal in buying a house is crucial. This is to prevent yourself from getting derailed from your initial objective when you start your house hunting. Sometimes, you might also realize that you do not need a new house after all! This will save you a lot of time and effort.

At this point, you should also assess whether this is a need or want. If this is a want, are you able to afford it? Is it financially viable?

2. Document the costs of buying a house

After establishing your goal, the next step involves writing down all the costs involved in buying a new house. The breakdown differs from country to country, but the general principle is the same.

Besides the cost of the house, there is also stamp duty and legal fees charged by the government. In some cases, if you are a foreigner, you will be charged additional taxes. It is advisable for you to be aware of the extra fees that you are liable for, as the additional taxes could go up to as high as 30 to 40 percent of the selling price. This could substantially impact your budget.

On the other hand, some countries provide subsidies for first-time homeowners. In the case of Singapore, the maximum amount of grants can be as high as S$160,000 (US$110,000). Through means testing used in different countries, everyone's situation is unique. It is highly recommended that you proactively find out how much subsidies and grants you are eligible for, so that you do not miss out on any opportunities.

3. Assess your affordability

The final step relates to affordability. While most of us rely on mortgages to purchase our house, the amount of loan that is disbursed to us is heavily dependent on our own financial circumstances and the valuation of the house.

One consideration is the loan-to-value limit. This is the allowable ratio of a loan to the value of the property. Note that the interest rate might vary with the loan-to-value ratio, since a higher loan-to-value is riskier for the mortgage lender.

With a 90 percent loan-to-value mortgage, you are expected to fork out a 10 percent mortgage deposit. For instance, if the property is valued at $500,000, you will need to come up with $50,000 in cash.

We highly recommend that you devise a financial plan before proceeding with house hunting. For a start, you should check if you have sufficient liquid assets (such as cash or bank deposits) for the down payment. Thereafter, you could assess the amount of mortgage you can afford to repay each month.

Evidently, calculating loan repayments play a crucial role. But this is not an easy task and requires some form of financial sophistication.

This is compounded by changes in the macroeconomic environment in recent years, which could impact individuals' ability to finance their houses. For example, the global rise in interest rates by central banks in 2022 has led to higher mortgage rates, elevating the borrowing costs for borrowers.

Financial sophistication helps to overcome some of these challenges. For example, to account for such uncertainties, you could do a scenario analysis that evaluates possible changes in interest rates and income. Through the utilization of big data applications, you can further improve your predictive capabilities and evaluate your affordability in diverse circumstances.

Financial Sophistication

But financial sophistication alone cannot solve all problems. To have a better understanding of the role of financial sophistication in housing markets, we will take a closer look at a recent article that Sumit wrote with Crocker Liu, Walter Torous, and Vincent Yao. Titled "The Mistakes People Make: Financial Decision Making When Buying and Owning a Home," this study examined how financial sophistication influences the mistakes households make when they purchase their houses.

As a proxy for financial sophistication, schooling and work experience are used. Based on the years of schooling, homeowners are classified into different educational levels. From their occupation and experience in financial investments, they are further grouped into various categories of financial sophistication.

In this study, the financial mistakes found in the housing market include the following:

1. Paying too much for a house.
2. Paying too high interest rates on the mortgage.
3. Failure to refinance a mortgage when it is beneficial to do so.
4. Failure to default when it is beneficial to do so.

Using data from all mortgages securitized by a national insurer from 2001 to 2011, it was found that financial sophistication impacts the above mistakes differently and that there is no uniform impact across different decisions.

On one hand, financially sophisticated households pay too much for their houses, and they do not default even when it is financially beneficial to do so. The underlying factors can be attributed to the emotional nature of buying homes and the moral considerations associated with defaulting. Thus, financially sophisticated households are susceptible to various behavioral biases that impact their decisions in the housing market.

On the other hand, financially sophisticated households are less likely to make mistakes in terms of mortgage rates and refinancing choices. This is because their decisions are more analytical.

Put together, certain characteristics might allow an individual to make a good decision somewhere, but a bad decision elsewhere! This makes managing our decisions in the housing market even more challenging.

Loss Aversion and Selling Houses

Finally, similar to what we have discussed earlier in spending and investing, behavioral biases also play a significant role in the housing markets.

We now explore one form of behavioral bias in selling houses: loss aversion. As highlighted in Chapter 17, loss aversion refers to the idea that we are more sensitive to our losses, compared to our gains.

Here, we will focus on a 2001 study by David Genesove and Christopher Mayer that is published in *The Quarterly Journal of Economics*. Evident from the title of the paper "Loss Aversion and Seller Behavior: Evidence from the Housing Market," it shows how home sellers experience loss aversion.

With the original purchase price as a reference point, the analysis indicated that sellers are particularly sensitive to losses and therefore only willing to sell at a higher price.

Using data from downtown Boston between 1990 and 1997, the authors established that condominium owners who faced nominal losses set higher asking prices than the market rate.

The markup is estimated to be around 25 to 35 percent higher based on the difference between the original purchase price and the expected selling price. Eventually, they end up with selling prices which are higher by 3 to 18 percent.

Furthermore, sellers who face a smaller loss demand a higher markup relative to sellers with a larger loss. This is consistent with the convex slope of the value function in prospect theory, which has been discussed in Chapter 17.

We would like to highlight that loss aversion is not confined to a particular group of individuals. It was observed that loss aversion occurs across both investors and owner-occupants, though owner-occupants have double the degree of loss aversion as compared to investors.

Key Takeaways

The process of buying a house is a long one, which involves multiple stages. Hence, we akin buying houses to a marathon rather than a sprint. In fact, choosing a house that you like is only the first step.

In this chapter, we have outlined several steps that you might wish to consider when purchasing a house. While everyone's circumstances are different, the key steps are the same. It is about having clear objectives, cost assessment and affordability.

At each stage, we encourage you to be clear about the procedure of buying a house and come up with a systematic plan. This will allow us to steer clear of the behavioral biases that could influence our decisions.

After all, home is where the heart is. As we look to buy a house that we can call home, our heart tends to rule over our head. To strike a balance between both our heart and head, careful planning is required.

23

Mortgages

In this chapter, we will discuss mortgages. Mortgages are financial contracts that are used to purchase a house. To finance the purchases of their houses, new homeowners will have to borrow from mortgage lenders (unless they have financial assets to pay off the house straight away).

Just like how houses make up the largest proportion of an individual's portfolio, mortgages are one of the largest financial commitments they will ever make in their lifetime.

Take the United States for example. Home mortgages account for 64 percent of the US$18.4 trillion debt held by households in 2021. Besides, the value of mortgages is generally larger than the net worth of the households. This underscores the importance of the mortgage contract.

Nonetheless, managing mortgages is not an easy task. Due to the complexities involved in making multiple decisions, a large amount of information processing is required. Typically, households are presented with a range of options to select from when it comes to managing their mortgages.

For new homeowners who have already dedicated a large amount of time and effort to selecting their house, they might not have the capacity or willingness to deliberate the optimal mortgage choice.

Indeed, economic research has shown that households do not make optimal decisions in managing mortgages. Let us look at some key decisions that we need to make in the mortgage market and the lessons that we can draw from them.

Adjustable-Rate Mortgages Versus Fixed-Rate Mortgages

One important decision we need to make is to choose between adjustable-rate mortgages (ARMs) and fixed-rate mortgages (FRMs). As their names suggest, ARMs have nominal interest rates that vary over the life of the contract, while FRMs have constant nominal interest rate.

Whether we would be better off with ARMs or FRMs depends on many factors including the future interest rate.

Suppose we are given two options now: ARMs with a current interest rate of 3 percent and FRMs with a current interest rate of 5 percent. To determine which is a better deal, we must consider how the future interest rate for ARMs moves.

If we believe that the variable rate will increase steadily from 3 percent today to 7 percent in five years' time, then we will have the following scenario (Figure 23.1).

Figure 23.1: ARMs Versus FRMs

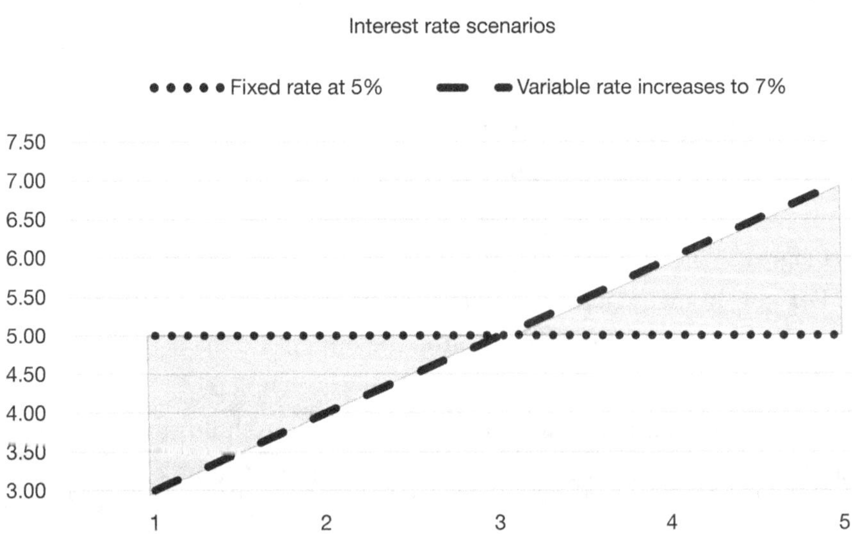

For individuals who have chosen the fixed rate, the left-shaded triangle refers to the interest lost when the fixed rate exceeds the variable interest. In contrast, the right-shaded triangle is the interest gained as the variable interest is now higher than the fixed interest.

In this example provided, the interest gain is equal to the interest loss, suggesting that we will be indifferent toward both ARMs and FRMs. However, should the variable rate increase at a faster rate, then we will prefer to have FRMs.

Hence, we can see our beliefs of future interest rates playing a vital role in choosing between FRMs and ARMs.

But this is no mean feat. To predict future changes in interest rates, we would need to forecast the future interest rates set by the central bank in our country, which in turn are dependent on future economic conditions.

The roles of interest rate expectations and mortgage choices have been examined in earlier economic studies.

Let us refer to a 2017 *Management Science* article by Cristian Badarinza, John Campbell, and Tarun Ramadorai. Titled "What Calls to ARMs? International Evidence on Interest Rates and the Choice of Adjustable-Rate Mortgages," the article examines nine countries: Australia, Belgium, Denmark, Greece, Ireland, Italy, the Netherlands, Sweden, and the United States. The study shared the following results.

To begin with, the authors documented the variation in share of FRMs across different countries and different time periods. While some countries, such as Australia, Finland, Ireland, Portugal, and Spain, have more than 80 percent of households having ARMs, other countries, such as Belgium, the Netherlands, and the United States, have less than 25 percent of households taking up ARMs.

In addition, it has been shown that short-term (one year) interest rate forecasts and the current spread between FRM and ARM, influence households' choices to take up ARMs.

On the other hand, long-term (three-year) forecasts do not play significant roles. This shows that individuals are primarily concerned with both current interest costs and short-term interest changes.

Another important factor to choose between FRMs and ARMs is future inflation expectations (which we have discussed in Chapter 3).

The role played by inflation was the subject of a 2003 article in *The Quarterly Journal of Economics* by John Campbell and Joao Cocco. Titled "Household Risk Management and Optimal Mortgage Choice," the study proposed to have inflation-indexed FRM in order to adjust for inflation risk.

By focusing on real values, the authors emphasized that FRM is a risky contract as the nominal interest rate is fixed. Much uncertainty will arise for the real interest rate when there are fluctuations in the inflation rate.

On the other hand, ARM is deemed to be the safer choice in real terms. Despite the fact that the nominal interest rate tends to fluctuate over time, the real interest rate stays constant with ARM, making it the preferable option in real terms.

This stands in contrast to some popular opinion that FRM is more dependable, as the nominal interest rate is established in advance, making financial planning easier. By this reasoning, FRM is considered to be a safer choice. While this could arguably be true for certain individuals with unpredictable real income, it is important to note that ultimately, it is the real value of money that matters.

To obtain the advantages of both options, the authors recommend the use of an inflation-index FRM, which combines the stability of FRM with the ability to adjust to inflation changes. Unlike the traditional FRM where the nominal interest rate stays throughout the life of the loan, nominal interest rate in the inflation-index FRM vary with the inflation rate. As such, we would be protected from the risks posed by inflation.

Another consideration to choose between ARMs and FRMs will be our time horizon. How long are we expecting to stay in the house that we just purchased?

If our intention is to move within a few years, we may want to consider opting for ARMs as they usually start with lower interest rates than fixed interest rates. This will allow us to enjoy lower rates for the first few years before we sell the property.

At the same time, there will be less cash outflow in the initial years. Therefore, if we have liquidity constraints in the early years, we might also prefer ARMs.

Now, suppose we have selected our mortgage, but we would like to change them a few years down the road. Is it possible? Yes! This brings us to the next issue, refinancing.

Mortgage Refinancing

With refinancing, we are able to replace your current mortgage with a new loan. There are many reasons that motivate individuals to refinance.

One possible reason is to change the size of the mortgage. If the value of our home has increased over time, we are now able to take a larger loan as compared to our existing home loan. Consequently, we will be able to receive (in cash) the difference between the new amount that is borrowed and the existing loan balance.

Commonly known as cashing out equity from homes, this will allow us to smooth our consumption over time. We can also use this to pay off other debts. As interest rate on mortgages is lower than other forms of debt, such as credit card debt and payday loans, this will reduce our interest expenses.

Another reason to refinance is to take advantage of lower interest rates. If interest rates have decreased, it is optimal for us to refinance as long as the benefits of refinancing outweigh the costs.

Benefits here refer to the interest saved from refinancing. On the other hand, costs refer to the sum of refinancing costs and the opportunity cost of refinancing too early. By refinancing too early, we will miss out on future gains when interest rates fall further.

Now, solving for the optimal refinancing rule is a challenging task (even for economists!). Traditionally, it is solved through an implicit numerical solution of a system of partial differential equations (which is highly complex).

More recently, Sumit came up with a simple optimal refinancing rule together with John Driscoll and David Laibson. The details of the refinancing rule are presented in a 2008 article in the *Journal of Money, Credit and Banking*. Titled "Optimal Mortgage Refinancing: A Closed Form Solution," the details of this optimal refinancing are shown to be tractable and can even be solved using a calculator. We invite you (and your mortgage advisor) to refer to the formula that is presented in the research article for more details.[9]

Do households make mistakes when refinancing mortgages? If so, what are the common mistakes and how do we avoid them?

Together with Richard Rosen and Vincent Yao, Sumit addressed these questions in a 2016 *Management Science* research article. This study, titled "Why Do Borrowers Make Mortgage Refinancing Mistakes?," provides evidence of how the majority of borrowers do not refinance in an optimal manner.

Two main errors were found. Firstly, it was found that households make errors of commission, which occur when they refinance at the wrong rate. Secondly, there are errors of omission, which happen when households fail to refinance at the optimal time.

Using data from one of the government-sponsored enterprises (GSE) in the United States between 1998 and 2011, it was discovered that 57 percent of borrowers refinance suboptimally. According to the findings, 50 percent chose the wrong rate, 17 percent waited too long to refinance, while 10 percent made both mistakes.

Moreover, it was revealed that the financial sophistication of borrowers influenced households to make both errors of commission and omission, as their choice and timing of refinancing were erroneous. As a case in point, borrowers with higher incomes and larger credit scores make fewer mistakes.

There is also evidence that borrowers learn from their refinancing experience. After making mistakes in their first refinancing experience, borrowers subsequently change their behavior and make smaller errors.

[9] The article provided two analytical solutions: a closed-form exact solution and a second order approximate (which is referred to as the square-root rule). In the simplest assumption, we just require 5 parameters: real value of the mortgage, tax rate, volatility, discount rate and probability of mortgage repayment. The details of the formula are beyond the scope of this book.

Sources of Inaction in Mortgage Refinancing

Why do individuals delay in refinancing their mortgages?

This has been examined in a 2020 article in the *American Economic Review* by Steffen Andersen, John Campbell, Kasper Nielsen, and Tarun Ramadorai. Titled "Sources of Inaction in Household Finance: Evidence from the Danish Mortgage Market," the study breaks down the refinancing behavior of different borrowers in Denmark.

The authors established that individuals hold back refinancing until the interest rate savings are much larger than the total costs involved.

The reason is because in addition to the presence of monetary fixed costs, psychological costs and information-gathering costs also play a significant role.

In this context, psychological costs encompass the time dedicated to making a refinancing decision and the costs related to behavioral present bias. Conversely, information-gathering costs are required to assess the costs and benefits of refinancing.

The authors show that middle-aged and wealthy households have high psychological refinancing costs, explaining their inaction in mortgage refinancing. This reflects the unmeasured value of time that is spent on mortgage refinancing.

On the other hand, older households with lower education, income, and financial wealth have a low refinancing probability. This is attributed to the high information-gathering costs for these individuals.

Mortgage Discount Points

Another mistake that households make in their mortgage decisions is related to mortgage discount points, which allows borrowers to lower their interest rate in exchange for an upfront payment.

When buying a home or refinancing an existing mortgage, borrowers are often given the option to take up mortgage discount points. With mortgage discount points, borrowers will enjoy a fall in their interest rate throughout the life of the mortgage.

It is noteworthy that by paying upfront for mortgage discount points, there is no impact on the down payment or the loan amount. We only save on interest.

Sumit scrutinizes the issue of mortgage discount points in a 2017 *Journal of Financial Economics* article with Itzhak Ben-David and Vincent Yao. Named "Systematic Mistakes in the Mortgage Market and Lack of Financial Sophistication," the analysis indicated that borrowers end up paying too much for the discount points.

The study centered on 300,000 prime FRMs between January 2001 and March 2001 that were insured by a large national mortgage securitizer in the United States. It was documented that 12 percent of borrowers take discount points. On average, they buy 1.31 discount points and lower their interest rate by 29 basis points.

There were several mistakes made by borrowers. Overall, borrowers overestimate how long they will stay with the mortgage. As mortgage discount points will benefit borrowers who stay longer in the mortgage, we will expect the point takers to have longer mortgages. Nonetheless, it was established that the length of stay for both the points takers and non-points takers with their mortgages is similar.

Furthermore, the average return earned on discount points is lower than the cost of borrowing. Hence, for these borrowers, they will be better off decreasing the mortgage balance as compared to investing in discount points. In fact, the after-tax loss (caused by taking discount points) was estimated to be around US$676.

Why do borrowers take points? There are two possible reasons.

One explanation is related to high (pre-points) mortgage rates. With high mortgage rates, borrowers become overly focused on reducing their monthly mortgage payments without considering the upfront costs involved. Accordingly, those with the highest (pre-points) mortgage rates are deemed to have the highest propensity to take up points in this study.

The availability of financial resources is another contributing factor. It was observed that those with cash-out refinancing are more likely to take up points. As they manage to obtain cash when they refinance, they are more willing to pay upfront for points.

In all, we have highlighted several mistakes that households made in their mortgages. This is not exhaustive, and it is not possible to list down all the mistakes that we can make in their mortgages.

Moving ahead, the first step forward is for us to be cognizant of these issues and mindfully seek to address them by improving our financial knowledge.

Key Takeaways

Choosing the ideal mortgage is both an art and a science. It requires an understanding of our individual requirements (such as how long we will stay with the mortgage), as well as our predictions of the macroeconomic environment.

For instance, we would need to form expectations of future inflation rates, as well as interest rates to choose between different types of mortgages. This requires us to keep abreast of market trends and financial news.

Also, there is still work to be done after choosing the mortgage. With the opportunity to refinance, remember that taking no action is an action in itself, and making no decision is a decision in itself.

Consequently, we should continuously keep an eye on our mortgages as market conditions are constantly evolving. Making this part of our routine will further reduce the additional costs involved, including psychological costs and information-gathering costs.

24

Agents, Brokers, and Appraisers

We rely heavily on different intermediaries to help us navigate the numerous decisions we need to make when buying or selling houses. Intermediaries act as middlemen to facilitate our transactions with another party. Since they are deemed to be specialists, we seek their advice in making our choices. Thereafter, they receive a fee or commission for the services they provide as compensation.

But there is a potential problem. As these middlemen are paid by commissions, they might not have the incentive to give us the best possible outcome. For instance, they might be motivated to close deals in the shortest possible time and be reluctant to seek the best deal possible. This is because their efforts do not usually commensurate with the increase in commissions received.

Therefore, it is imperative that we select our advisors with care. To be clear, we acknowledge the fact that intermediaries in the real estate market play an important role in the economy. They can be very helpful: clients are not always shortchanged by advisors.

What we hope to achieve in this chapter is to caution readers of the potential pitfalls and identify areas to look out for. Thereafter, we seek to understand how recent technological disruptions could impact the roles of intermediaries in the future, and how we could tap on them.

In what follows, we are going to examine three intermediaries: Real Estate Agents, Mortgage Brokers, and Appraisers.

Real Estate Agents

How do we buy and sell our houses? Most of us turn to real estate agents. According to the 2021 National Association of Realtors, 87 percent of homebuyers in the United States buy their houses through real estate agents. Similar numbers can be seen in other countries as well.

As intermediaries between buyers and sellers in real estate transactions, real estate agents play a critical role in our property search. In exchange for the services that they provide, we pay them commissions that are usually based on a fixed proportion of the sales proceeds. Table 24.1 presents some examples of real estate commissions in 2015 globally.

Equipped with knowledge of the local market, real estate agents can offer their expertise in helping us find our ideal home more efficiently and reach out to a larger audience when we would like to sell our house.

Moreover, real estate agents have available resources, such as access to home listings and sales data. This provides them with an informational advantage. Indeed, economic studies have documented that real estate agents are better informed.

We first examine the sell-side activities of real estate agents. For real estate agents who help to sell houses, they bear much of the associated expenses involved in selling houses. These include advertising and marketing costs, hosting open houses, and the time spent showing the house to viewers.

However, they only receive a certain percentage of the transaction amount. Hence, they have the incentive to advise owners to sell the house quickly, even when the price is below the market rate.

Do clients benefit from agents being more well informed? This has been examined in a 2008 article named "Market Distortions When Agents Are Better Informed: The Value of Information in Real Estate Transactions" written by Steven Levitt and Chad Syverson and published in *The Review of Economics and Statistics.*

In this study, the authors examine whether there is a difference in price between the houses sold by real estate agents on behalf of others and their own homes. This is because when real estate agents sell their

Table 24.1: Real Estate Commissions in 2015

Country	Real Estate Agent Commission (%)
China	2
Germany	4
Malaysia	2
Japan	6
Indonesia	4
Singapore	1.5
USA	5.5
UK	1.5
Thailand	4

Source: The Wall Street Journal

own homes, they are claiming the full surplus of the sale (and not simply a small percentage of it).

Using data from 100,000 home sales in suburban Cook County, Illinois, it was revealed that houses owned by real estate agents sell for 3.7 percent more as compared to other houses. Furthermore, they are put on sale for a longer period of time, by 9.5 days.

At the median sales price, the difference in selling price is approximately US$7,600. While this might be a large amount to the seller, with a commission charge of 1.5 percent, the additional amount received by the real estate agent is only US$114. Consequently, real estate agents might not have the incentive to wait for a better deal.

Next, we turn to the activities under the "purchasing" facet of real estate agents. Here, we review an article that Sumit wrote with Jia He, Tien Foo Sing, and Changcheng Song. Published in the *Journal of Financial Economics* in 2019, the article provocatively asked, "Do Real Estate Agents Have Information Advantages in Housing Markets?"

To answer this question, the authors examined the transactions of licensed real estate agents in Singapore.

Indeed, real estate agents who are property buyers have information advantages as well! It was discovered that real estate agents who purchase houses paid prices that are 2.54 percent lower as compared to other buyers.

This is attributed to "cherry-picking" and bargaining power. As agent-buyers have a larger choice set, they are able to "cherry-pick" and select houses with lower prices. With this advantage in information, they end up with higher bargaining power.

Mortgage Brokers

Moving forward, we investigate mortgage brokers, who are intermediaries in the mortgage market. Mortgage brokers connect borrowers with potential lenders but do not assume any of the default risks associated with the mortgage.

As experts in mortgages, mortgage brokers have the ability to help us understand the mortgage process and advise us on the different loan options. Based on their network, they can also help us negotiate with mortgage lenders on our behalf. Similarly, we pay them commissions.

Nonetheless, just like real estate agents who have informational advantages in buying and selling houses, mortgage brokers could also exploit households' lack of knowledge and experience.

Besides receiving commissions from us, mortgage brokers often receive commissions from lenders too. This creates a conflict of interest as the amount of commissions that are received from lenders usually increases with the interest rate that is being paid. The incentive for mortgage brokers is thus to recommend loans with higher interest rates, which allows them to enjoy higher fees.

In recent years, several countries have recognized this issue and have restricted mortgage brokers from receiving fees directly from lenders too. For instance, the Consumer Financial Protection Bureau in the United

States have introduced new loan originator compensation requirements to stop commission payments by lenders.

It is useful to find out if your country still allows this compensation to continue, and how this policy impacts the incentives of the mortgage brokers in your country. This will help you to make a more informed decision when engaging your mortgage broker.

In addition, economic studies have highlighted that households have historically overpaid for the services of mortgage brokers.

According to a 2012 *American Economic Review* article by Susan Woodward and Robert Hall, homeowners tend to be confused when shopping for mortgage brokers due to their inexperience and the wide range of broker fees they encounter. How do we avoid paying more for mortgage brokers?

As implied by the title of the article "Diagnosing Consumer Confusion and Sub-Optimal Shopping Effort: Theory and Mortgage-Market Evidence," we need to shop more!

In their economic model, the authors demonstrated that by shopping from too few brokers, borrowers sacrifice at least US$1,000. One reason for the lack of shopping is the inadequate understanding of the incentives associated with having origination fees for mortgages.

Appraisers

Finally, we turn to appraisers. Appraisers are professionals who are trained in determining the fair market value of different assets, such as housing.

They are indispensable intermediaries as lenders rely on them to estimate the value of our house when we apply for new mortgages or refinance our mortgages. As the house serves as collateral for the loan, it is essential that the house is valued accurately.

As discussed earlier, one important consideration for lending is the loan-to-value ratio. Hence, the maximum amount we can borrow is dependent on the value of our house. Furthermore, it will impact the interest rate we have to pay, as the loan-to-value ratio will impact the riskiness of the loan.

However, appraisers are subject to pressures from other parties to bias their valuation. For example, borrowers would prefer higher valuations of their assets so that they can borrow more or enjoy lower interest rates. Mortgage brokers would also prefer higher borrowing so that they can enjoy higher commissions.

Do appraisers exhibit bias?

This has been discussed in a 2015 article titled "Collateral Valuation and Borrower Financial Constraints: Evidence from the Residential Real Estate Market," which Sumit wrote with Itzhak Ben-David and Vincent Yao in *Management Science*. Indeed, it was discovered that appraisers do exhibit bias as well.

Based on conforming mortgage transactions that originated between 1990 and 2011 in the United States, the average valuation bias for residential refinancing is estimated to be around 5 percent. Moreover, the bias is larger when the parties involved have stronger incentives to increase the valuation.

For example, it was documented that the higher the leverage, the higher the bias. In addition, it was observed that the bias is larger for transactions that are mediated through a mortgage broker.

Since appraisal bias might exist, it is necessary that we determine the correct value, as we might get into more debt than we can afford. As discussed in the study, mortgages with inflated valuations end up defaulting more frequently.

We have shown you that intermediaries in the mortgage market know more than us, and this might not always be to our advantage. How do we reduce the informational advantage of these middlemen? With technological advancements, there are many ways to reduce informational friction now. This includes the use of online algorithms.

Online Algorithms

With recent advancements in artificial intelligence, there has been a growth in automated valuation models. These models allow us to obtain accurate prices of houses using online algorithms.

In the United States, one example is Zillow's Zestimate algorithm. Zillow is the leading real estate and rental website in the United States and possesses a large dataset on all the recent transactions. Using machine learning techniques, they are able to provide estimations that are challenging for human assessment.

The Zestimate algorithm has been studied in a 2022 National Bureau of Economic Research (NBER) working paper by Runshan Fu, Ginger Zhe Jin, and Meng Liu. Titled "Does Human-algorithm Feedback Loop lead to Error Propagation? Evidence form Zillow's Zestimate" the article demonstrated how listing and selling outcomes are highly responsive to Zestimate, and that it is updated quickly after a listing or transaction is done.

In addition, Zestimate is able to offer valuable information when it is harder to get alternative information. For instance, the listing price is more dependent on Zestimate in places where there is no mandatory disclosure of sales information or in diverse neighborhoods.

Indeed, by using online algorithms to assess home prices on our own, it can aid us in understanding the true and fair value of our homes. This will reduce the information gap between us and our real estate agent, or our appraiser.

iBuyers

Finally, we would like to highlight the emergence of a new model of selling houses: iBuyers. iBuyers (or instant buyers) are technology entrants who buy and sell real estate using online platforms.

With the use of technology, iBuyers can estimate the value of houses and make cash offers to sellers instantly. After buying the houses, iBuyers will fix them up before reselling them to others again.

This overcomes the traditional issues that are involved in the real estate market. As discussed earlier, real estate transactions typically involve multiple stages and multiple parties. The entire process is deemed to be complicated, slow, and even stressful for some.

With iBuyers, sellers can sell their houses quickly and more conveniently. This is particularly useful for sellers who are time-sensitive, such as those who would like to relocate due to new job offers or other major life changes.

Globally, there has been an increase in the number of iBuyers in recent years. This includes companies such as Opendoor in the United States, Nested in the United Kingdom, Casavo in Italy, and Kodit.io in Finland.

What are the key benefits and challenges of intermediating houses through technology? Should we turn to iBuyers instead?

The implications of iBuyers have been examined in a recent study by Greg Buchak, Gregor Matovs, Tomasz Piskorski, and Amit Seru, titled "Why Is Intermediating Houses so Difficult? Evidence from iBuyers."

In this article, the authors prove that there is a trade-off between price and speed. While iBuyers offer a lower price, they make fast offers. Thus, our decision to utilize iBuyers or not is subject to our evaluation of whether we value the convenience they offer over the lower price they extend.

By analyzing transactions of 5 largest iBuyers in the United States (Phoenix, Las Vegas, Dallas, Orlando and Gwinnet County) from 2013 to 2018, the authors established that many turn to iBuyers due to the ease of selling their houses and are willing to sell their houses at a considerable discount.

Upon analyzing the Multiple Listing Service (MLS), a database for real estate brokers, it was determined that the average listing time to sell a house is 90 days! iBuyers will allow us to skip that, providing substantial time savings. It is noteworthy that while iBuyers are able to purchase houses quickly, they do not sell houses faster than others. In fact, it was found that they take 33 days longer to sell, conditioned upon the sale of the assets.

Based on a standard hedonic pricing model, it was further estimated that we would receive 3.5 percent less when we sell to iBuyers. Based on the average selling price, it amounts to US$10,000. In contrast, iBuyers are able to sell houses 1 percent higher than the average price.

While you might be excited to rely on iBuyers, do note that iBuyers do not serve all places. Due to the unique business model, they are only focusing on liquid markets and easy to value homes. As such, they may not be available for you. Nonetheless, as technology advances, we believe the benefits of iBuyers are expected to grow exponentially.

Key Takeaways

As experts in their field, intermediaries in the real estate can guide us through the entire process of buying and selling houses.

Furthermore, we can leverage on the experience and expertise of real estate intermediaries to help us make better decisions. Indeed, we have shown you that real estate agents and brokers have informational advantages.

However, this is not always advantageous for the client. Based on several research studies, it was found that these intermediaries know more and can get a better deal for themselves relative to their clients.

Hence, it is important to engage agents and brokers with due diligence. Look at the track record of the agent and determine whether the agent demonstrates transparency and integrity in his or her past dealings.

In addition, we can increase our knowledge of transaction prices using technological innovations, such as online algorithms. This will help us navigate the different stages of the real estate market without being overly reliant on third parties.

Part VII

Risk Management

25

Navigating the Insurance Market

We are all exposed to risk of varying degrees in our daily lives. There could be a risk of flood damaging our houses overnight, the same way that there might be a risk of being in a car accident on the way to work. We could also face sudden unemployment, disability, or even premature death. All the above possibilities have the potential to cause financial hardship for ourselves and our loved ones.

That being said, how we manage risk plays a critical role when we plan our finances. In Part VII of this book, we will discuss about risk management. In general, there are several ways to manage risk. They include risk avoidance, risk reduction, risk transfer, and risk acceptance.

While risk avoidance and risk reduction seek to remove the risk to a certain extent, some risks are simply unavoidable. For instance, no matter how many vitamins we consume, we could always fall ill!

Under these circumstances, we could turn to risk transfer, with insurance assuming a central role. Insurance is an important way to manage the risk of households as it transfers the risk of financial loss from an individual to an insurance company. By receiving a payment (known as premium in insurance terms) in exchange for insurance coverage, insurance companies will pay out the benefits to the individual when an adverse event takes place. As a result, insurance has the ability to hedge our risk and protect us from financial losses.

Various insurance products are available to safeguard us against a wide range of risks. For example, there is life insurance, health insurance, motor insurance, travel insurance, property insurance, and even mobile phone insurance. Through risk pooling, the risk is shared among the participants of the insurance program.

With life insurance, we can maintain the standard of living for our families in the event of our death. In the event of an injury or illness, health insurance helps to pay for our medical costs.

In comparison, motor insurance and property insurance seek to protect vehicle owners and homeowners from damages or theft of their vehicles and properties, respectively.

Nonetheless, economic studies have demonstrated that households tend to be uninsured, exposing them to financial risk. This can be attributed to biases in risk perception and the complexity of insurance.

We will now examine how individuals make choices in the insurance market through different types of insurance: rainfall insurance, flood insurance, life insurance, and auto insurance.[10]

Barriers to Household Risk Management

Let us first review a 2013 study by Shawn Cole, Xavier Gine, Jeremy Tobacman, Petia Topalova, Robert Townsend, and James Vickery in the *American Economic Journal: Applied Economics.*

This article is titled "Barriers to Household Risk Management: Evidence from India" and examines factors that impede households' decisions to take up rainfall insurance in India.

Rainfall insurance is a type of "index insurance" that is offered to households before the start of the monsoon season. Thereafter, future payouts are linked to the amount of rainfall that is being recorded in a local weather station.

This is particularly useful for rural households where variation in rainfall plays a significant role in their household income. In the sample

[10] We will focus on health insurance in the next chapter.

population, 89 percent of the households indicated that drought is the most important risk that they faced.

While rainfall insurance has the ability to improve the lives of many by providing certainty in future income, the take-up rate of rainfall insurance is very low globally.

To examine drivers of rainfall insurance, the authors conducted a series of randomized experiments on rural households in two different states in India: Andhra Pradesh in 2006, and Gujarat in 2007.

For households in Andhra Pradesh, they were offered insurance policies by ICICI Lombard, which cover the monsoon in three contiguous phases. The first two phases focus on deficit rainfall and they will pay the insured party when the rainfall is below a prespecified amount. In the third phase, there will be a payout when there is excessive rainfall.

For households in Gujarat, they were offered insurance policies by IFFCO-Tokio and payouts were determined based on the cumulative rainfall over the entire monsoon season.

The authors vary the prices for different households in order to understand their considerations. It was observed that households were very sensitive to price changes. An increase in prices by 10 percent resulted in lower take-up rate by 10 to 12 percent.

Clearly, the price of insurance is a key determining factor. As prices are being charged higher than the expected payouts in rainfall insurance, this contributes to a lower demand by households. While this could be attributed to the nascent development of the rainfall insurance market, prices alone cannot fully explain the low take-up rate of rainfall insurance.

In fact, for households who were given very large price discounts, less than half of them took up the insurance offer. This suggests that non-price factors also play a significant role with regard to individuals' choices for insurance.

One key non-price factor is related to trust. It has been discovered that most households do not fully understand the insurance product, and hence rely on trust. To show that trust matters, the authors invited a group of trained insurance educators to visit households in Andhra Pradesh.

For certain households, the insurance educators were accompanied by a network of local agents, known as Livelihood Services Agents (LSAs). LSAs are tightly connected with the community and are deemed to be trustworthy. By accompanying the insurance educators, LSAs personally endorsed the educator and encouraged households to listen to the educator.

In comparison, for non-endorsed visits, the insurance educator visited the household on their own. The authors determined that endorsed trips resulted in an increase in demand by 36 percent relative to non-endorsed visits, underscoring the role of trust in the insurance market.

The importance of trust is fundamentally attributed to a lack of numeracy and financial literacy. For instance, only 60 percent of households answered simple arithmetic questions correctly. Hence, they depend on the advice of someone that they trust.

Another non-price factor is related to liquidity and income. In the study, those who received high cash rewards as compensation ended up taking up insurance by a factor of 140 percent! With higher compensation, they are in a better position to afford the insurance.

Wealthier households are also shown to be more likely to purchase insurance, highlighting the role of income.

Finally, the authors show that limited attention or salience could explain the low take-up rate of rainfall insurance. It was realized that one-quarter of households in the experiment ended up buying insurance as they were being informed of the insurance policy (in varying degrees). In comparison, for the general population in the same village, the take-up rate is close to zero.

Thus, exposure to the insurance policy contributes to an increase in the take-up rate. When rainfall insurance becomes more noticeable, households will pay attention to it.

Learning About an Infrequent Event

We now move on from rainfall insurance to another form of insurance: flood insurance. As the name suggests, flood insurance is designed to help individuals protect their homes and belongings when there is a flood.

Flood insurance differs from rain insurance in several ways. Unlike changes in rainfall, natural disasters, such as flooding, happen less frequently. However, the impact of floods could be more severe, as they would cause damage to one's property. In fact, one could become homeless overnight.

Hence, an understanding of individuals' choices in flood insurance will allow us to better appreciate how households make choices in the insurance market for high-impact-infrequent events.

A key driver that influences households taking up flood insurance is learning over time. Individuals change their beliefs about future floods based on their experiences. This has been examined in a 2014 article in the *American Economic Journal: Applied Economics* by Justin Gallagher, titled "Learning About an Infrequent Event: Evidence from Flood Insurance Take-Up in the United States."

The article centered on the National Flood Insurance Program (NFIP) in the United States, whereby the federal government sets the price of the insurance at a fair rate.

Each year, homeowners are given a choice to purchase flood insurance. Accounting for inflation, the price of the insurance remained fairly constant over time, and the prices remained unchanged even if the homes had been flooded.

In studying the insurance policies from 1980 to 2007, it was discovered that the take-up rate for flood insurance increases after a flood has taken place in the region. As compared to the year before a flood, there is an increase in the take-up rate by 9 percent, indicating that learning takes place.

Thereafter, it gradually declines to zero over time. In fact, it is shown that after nine years, the flood has been "forgotten" as households revert to insurance at preflood levels.

There are also spillover effects. In nearby regions within flooded areas, there is an increase in the take-up of flood insurance by around 2 to 3 percent, which lasts for five years after the flood.

To add on, the television media market also shapes households' decisions. As highlighted earlier in our discussion of rainfall insurance, salience influences the take-up rate of insurance.

For non-flooded communities that share the same television media market, there is also an increase in insurance take-up. This is attributed to the fact that when there are floods, media outlets tend to provide more information on flood risk information.

Flood information is also dependent on the size of the population that is being affected. For instance, there were 4.3 times as many new stories on floods where more than 50 percent of the population was flooded. Such information allows households to learn more about the flood risk that others face.

In sum, learning plays an important role in influencing the take-up rate of insurance.

Life Insurance and Financial Vulnerabilities

Next, we would like to discuss about life insurance. We take up life insurance to provide financial protection for our loved ones upon our death.

With life insurance, our family members will be able to obtain a specified sum of money when we pass on. This will help provide a financial safety net for the family, especially when we have dependents.

While life insurance plays an important role in our financial plans, studies have shown that individuals tend to purchase too little insurance, resulting in a fall in the standard of living for the surviving family members.

This has been demonstrated by Douglas Bernheim, Lorenzo Forni, Jagadeesh Gokhale, and Laurence Kotlikoff in an article in the *American Economic Review*.

The article, which is titled "The Mismatch Between Life Insurance and Financial Vulnerabilities: Evidence from the Health and Retirement Study," shows that there exists a discrepancy between the insurance holdings of individuals and their vulnerabilities, in the United States.

In this study, vulnerabilities are defined as the percentage fall in the individual's standard of living due to the death of a spouse. This is measured by changes in consumption using life cycle models.

By relying on data from the 1992 Health and Retirement Survey, it was documented that workers who do not require insurance for their survivors, end up with a high insurance coverage.

In comparison, individuals who require life insurance to maintain the living standards of their surviving spouses are less likely to take up adequate insurance. For instance, should their spouses pass on, 6 percent of breadwinners and 33 percent of secondary earners will end up with more than 20 percent fall in their standard of living!

Why do households fail to purchase adequate life insurance coverage?

On top of the points discussed earlier, such as price, trust, liquidity, or even learning, another possible reason is attributed to inertia. One might purchase life insurance early in life when they have fewer family responsibilities. Subsequently, they fail to adjust the life insurance coverage.

Hence, it is timely to regularly review and update our financial plans, and to find the right insurance to meet our own needs. One can also rely on insurance technology to make better decisions.

In recent years, there has been an emergence of insurance technology or InsurTech companies. As these companies make use of big data through the use of apps and wearables, they are able to provide personalized products to each individual. We will further discuss about InsurTech in the automobile insurance market.

InsurTech

Automobile insurance is required on all vehicles that operate on the roads in almost all countries. This ensures that financial responsibility is taken up by the drivers in the event that damages are inflicted.

Traditionally, automobile insurance is priced based on the perceived risk of the driver. For instance, a younger driver will need to pay more as they are deemed to be more inexperienced and reckless.

Amid technological advancements, there have been several innovations in auto insurance to better track the behavior of drivers. One example is usage-based insurance (UBI). With UBI, the insurance companies are able to observe the actual driving performance of individual drivers.

Subsequently, insurance companies can provide discounts based on the individual's driving behavior. This provides drivers with an incentive to drive more safely, resulting in a lower likelihood of getting into an accident. Hence, insurance companies will have lower payouts, resulting in a win–win situation.

Does this work in the real world? According to an article by Miremad Soleymanian, Charles Weinberg, and Ting Zhu in *Marketing Science,* it does! Their research studypaper, "Sensor Data and Behavioral Tracking: Does Usage-Based Auto Insurance Benefit Drivers?" shows that UBI drivers are indeed more careful.

Using data from a major insurance company in the United States that provides the UBI program and traditional car insurance policy from 2012 to 2014, the study documents how UBI drivers changed their driving behavior.

It was demonstrated that, after six months, the frequency in which UBI drivers hard brake their vehicles decreased by an average of 21 percent. Hard braking is defined as when the speed of the vehicle drops by a minimum of eight miles per hour (MPH) each second and the vehicle is currently traveling at more than 20 MPH.

As hard braking happens when the driver uses more force than necessary to stop the vehicle, it is commonly considered to be an aggressive driving behavior.

Overall, the authors established that individuals did not decrease their driving mileage, but became safer drivers based on the driving behavior score that is computed by the insurance company. The better scores translate to discounts for the UBI drivers!

Besides, drivers respond to feedback to improve their driving scores and to gain discounts. It was revealed that improvements took place at different paces across different demographics. For instance, younger drivers and females had the highest rate of improvement.

Hence, InsurTech has the potential to benefit households by providing lower insurance rates and overcoming challenges traditionally faced in insurance markets.

Within the insurance industry, a significant issue pertains to the presence of asymmetric information, which will be discussed in detail in the next chapter on health insurance. InsurTech offers a means to bridge the information gap between the insurance company and the insured party by providing better information of the insured party or even monitoring their behavior.

Key Takeaways

As a financial safety net, insurance can help to protect us and our family in many ways. However, we have emphasized that there are many reasons that stop individuals from taking on insurance on their own. Among others, we have discussed the role of trust, limited attention and inertia in this chapter.

To overcome these issues, we ought to make it a point to regularly check in with our trusted financial planner. For those who prefer to work without an insurance agent, we could also turn to InsurTech companies. The key point is to find someone we can trust and are comfortable working with.

It is imperative that we include risk management as a cornerstone of our financial planning. By considering different contingencies and emergencies, we reduce the possibility of derailing from our financial goals.

This will also provide security for our family. As Benjamin Franklin once said, "A policy of life insurance is the cheapest and safest mode of making a certain provision of one's family." We should build knowledge around insurance and appreciate its potential to mitigate risk in our lives.

26

Health Insurance

Health insurance is a type of insurance coverage that pays for our medical expenses when we fall sick. By safeguarding us from unexpected and expensive medical costs, healthcare insurance allows us to prioritize our health without being overly preoccupied with our finances.

While most of us could possibly have some form of health insurance in one way or another, making choices in health insurance plans is not an easy task. Health insurance plans are often filled with numerous technical jargons, making it harder for us to understand. For instance, we need to choose deductibles and co-payments. Do these terms sound familiar to you?

In order to fully appreciate these terms (and the rationale for insurance companies imposing them), it is necessary to understand the fundamental problem in insurance: the existence of asymmetric information.

As mentioned in the chapters above, asymmetric information occurs when one party has more information than the other, and has been shown to impact the functioning of different types of markets.

A classic example of asymmetric information exists in the used-car market. This is posited by George Akerlof, the 2001 recipient of the Nobel Memorial Prize in Economic Sciences, in an article in *The Quarterly Journal of Economics*.

Titled "The Market for 'Lemons': Quality Uncertainty and the Market Mechanism," George Akerlof demonstrates that the used-car market could unravel due to the presence of "lemons."

In this context, "lemons" refer to vehicles that have defects and are unsafe to drive. While the seller is cognizant of the car's quality, the potential buyer is not. This results in asymmetric information.

Accordingly, the buyer will only be willing to pay a lower price than that of a well-functioning vehicle, as there is a possibility that the vehicle is a lemon. However, at the lowered price, sellers of good-quality vehicles will not be willing to sell! At the end of the day, only sellers of lemon vehicles are willing to make a sale.

Buyers are cognizant of this situation and are thus, not willing to purchase lemon vehicles. As such, the used-car market breaks down.

Similar to the car market, asymmetric information takes place in health insurance too. In the case of health insurance, individuals who know that they are sick are more likely to purchase insurance at a higher price as they expect higher medical costs. This could drive away healthier individuals from the insurance market.

When healthier individuals leave the insurance market, there will be fewer healthy households in the market, making it unprofitable for insurance companies to continue their operations. This is known as adverse selection.

Consequently, the design of insurance includes several elements to reduce adverse selection. For instance, health insurance companies will request for medical screenings, as well as medical records of the policy buyer and their family. This will allow insurance companies to mitigate the risk that they have to undertake.

Another form of asymmetric information is moral hazard in health insurance. Moral hazard occurs when individuals seek to engage in riskier behavior when they have insurance. For example, if individuals have health insurance, they could be less careful about taking precautions to avoid falling sick.

To reduce moral hazard, health insurance plans usually require the insured party to pay some part of the costs. These include deductibles and co-payments.

With deductibles, the insured party must pay a small amount out of his or her own pocket before the insured company starts paying. With co-payments, the insured party must pay a certain amount for each claim.

As these measures are necessary for a sustainable insurance market, households would need to be prepared to deal with deductibles and co-payments in their insurance policies.

How do households make decisions when it comes to deductibles and co-payments? It turns out that people tend to make poor choices!

Dominated Options

We will first examine the work of Saurabh Bhargava, George Loewenstein, and Justin Sydnor in a 2017 article, published in *The Quarterly Journal of Economics*.

The study is named "Choose to Lose: Health Plan Choices from a Menu with Dominated Option," and evaluates the decisions of 23,894 employees when making a choice in relation to their health insurance in the United States.

It was found that when presented with a menu of options in an employer-sponsored benefit program, the employees failed to select an option that is in their best interest. Hence, they "choose to lose."

The company in question is a Fortune 100 company, which instituted a new insurance program in 2010. The introduction of the new insurance policy significantly expanded the range of available options. Prior to the new policy, employees were limited to three choices: Basic, Plus, and Premium. However, the new insurance policy has expanded their options to a staggering 48!

One key principle behind the pricing of insurance policies relates to the payout in different conditions. As the different combinations of co-payments and deductibles impact how much individuals will share the claims with the insurance company, different prices (premiums) are offered for different options. In general, the less we pay during a claim, the more expensive the insurance policy will be.

We now turn to the new 48 options given to the employees. For this health insurance, individuals were allowed to choose between different types of deductibles, maximum out-of-pocket spending, co-insurance rates, and office co-payments.

The first group of options relates to deductibles. There are four options for deductibles: $350, $500, $750, and $1,000. Here, the lower the deductible, the less the individual must pay first before the insurance company starts to pay out. As such, lower deductibles will require a higher insurance premium.

Next, maximum out-of-pocket spending relates to the maximum amount that an individual will need to pay. In this case, there are three options: $1,500, $2,500, and $3,000. Similarly, lower out-of-pocket spending will require a higher insurance premium.

There are also two co-insurance rates: 80 percent and 90 percent. This is the amount that the insurance company will pay after the deductible is met, and before the maximum out-of-pocket payment is reached.

To provide an example, suppose you have a health insurance plan with deductibles of $500, maximum out-of-pocket payment of $2,000 and co-insurance of 80 percent. Let's say, you have medical expenses of $3,000. After meeting your deductible of $500, you would be responsible for paying 20 percent of the remaining amount of $2,500. This means that the insurance company will pay 80 percent of $2,500, which translates to $2,000. In total, you will pay $1,000 (which is less than the maximum out-of-pocket payment).

Finally, there are two office co-payments: $15 for primary care/$40 for a specialist, as well as $25 for primary care/$35 for a specialist. These are the fixed payments for primary care and specialist, respectively.

Altogether, there are a total of 48 options for the individuals to choose from, with their own unique pricing attached to them. How do we choose from here? This is not an easy task! As it is, many of us would already have difficulties understanding the different options.

One could rely on the default plan, which has the lowest monthly premium, but the highest out-of-pocket spending. In all, 14 percent opted for the default plan.

For the rest of them who chose their own plans, it turned out that most of them made poor decisions. In particular, 61 percent of participants selected an option that performed worse than alternative options under all circumstances. Economists refer to this as a dominated option.

To make dominated options more concrete, we will provide you with an example. Consider two plans[11] with the same maximum out-of-pocket spending, co-insurance rates, and office co-payments. The only difference lies in deductibles.

Plan A has a deductible of $1,000 and offers a premium of $748 per annum. In comparison, Plan B has a deductible of $500 and offers a premium of $1,455 per year. In this case, we conclude that Plan B is dominated by Plan A.

Why is this so? By choosing Plan A, we are paying a lower premium of $707. In the event that there are no claims, we saved $707. What happens when there are claims? Even though we need to pay $500 more in deductible as compared to Plan A, we still save $207 by paying lower premiums ($707–$500).

Hence, with Plan A, heads, we win, tails, we win! We would be better off with Plan A under all future circumstances.

Choosing dominated plans such as Plan B over Plan A makes one worse off. The study found that by choosing a dominated plan, employees end up with additional spending of 24 percent for their premiums.

Why do individuals make such financially inefficient choices? The authors addressed this question by conducting two online experiments. The first experiment seeks to test for menu complexity by varying the number

[11] For simplicity, let us just call them Plan A and Plan B. For the record, it is labeled as plan 38 and plan 14 in the article respectively.

of plans and attributes. In contrast, the second experiment focus on how individuals value the deductibles by providing additional clarifications.

From the experiments, it was established that individuals choose dominated plans not due to menu complexity or informed preferences. Rather, it was due to the inability to compare and evaluate plans. As such, an understanding of the different options in insurance is important in our household financial management.

Another possible reason for choosing dominated plans is related to households' aversion toward deductibles. Also known as deductible aversion, households would like to reduce their out-of-pocket payment, even though it is costly to do so. This is because they feel apprehensive about having to pay a substantial amount of money from their own pocket in the event of a claim.

Deductible Choices

Deductibles are not just present in health insurance markets. It is also present in other types of insurance markets, such as home insurance. Likewise, it is discovered that homeowners are financially worse off when they choose insurance policies with higher home insurance deductibles.

This process of making such a choice regarding insurance policies is examined by Justin Sydnor in a 2010 article in the *American Economic Journal: Applied Economics* and is titled "(Over)insuring Modest Risks." Here, it demonstrates that households tend to over-insure when it comes to managing home insurance.

The study covers 50,000 policies from a large home insurance company in the United States. For this home mortgage insurance, households are being offered four different levels of deductibles: $100, $250, $500, and $1,000.

Relative to the option with the highest deductible, the majority of households (83 percent) chose to pay more to opt for a lower deductible. The most popular choice of deductible was $500, with an average additional premium of $100.

In other words, households are willing to pay $100 to reduce the out-of-pocket payments from $1,000 to $500. However, based on the claim rates calculated by the author, the additional coverage was worth less than $25 on average. Hence, they are worse off by choosing a lower deductible.

The authors provided many plausible explanations. One main factor is attributed to the high risk aversion of individuals. As individuals have a tendency to avoid risk, they choose a lower deductible. Another possible reason is due to households' mis-estimation of risks. Most often, individuals end up overestimating the likelihood of accidents.

Enrollment in Health Insurance Marketplace

Next, we would like to discuss health insurance enrollment. Not all of us have health insurance sponsored by our employers. Consequently, we will need to search for private insurance companies to enroll in health insurance.

Governments worldwide have sought to make it easier for individuals to access health insurance. One example is the Affordable Care Act (ACA) in the United States. Through the ACA, the health insurance marketplace is introduced in all states, providing a platform for individuals to compare across different insurance packages.

In order to foster inclusivity and affordability, the ACA offers progressive premiums and cost-sharing initiatives, which come in the form of tax credits and subsidies. For instance, households with income less than or equal to 400 percent of the federal poverty level and without any access to employer's insurance or public insurance program are offered tax credits to purchase insurance in the marketplace.

Nonetheless, enrollment in the health insurance market remains low. Approximately 60 percent of individuals that qualified for a subsidy did not take up an insurance. Why is it so?

In a 2021 article in the *American Economic Review*, Richard Domurat, Isaac Menashe, and Wesley Yin embarked on an experiment involving 87,000 households in California by varying the information that is mailed to them.

As implied by the title of the article "The Role of Behavioral Frictions in Health Insurance Marketplace Enrollment and Risk: Evidence from a Field Experiment," it was found that low enrollment can be explained by behavioral frictions and that there were misconceptions about program benefits.

The authors focus on Covered California, the state's health insurance marketplace, and provided households with different information relating to the enrollment. This information includes the deadline, general benefit, website, and contact number.

For low-income households that qualified for subsidies, personalized details relating to their subsidies were mailed to them. In some cases, there were also comparisons relating to the different plans.

The research showed that by simply sending a letter reminding households of the enrollment deadline, enrollment rose by 1.3 percentage points. This translates to an increase of 16 percent. Not bad!

This also means that inattention plays an important role in determining health insurance enrollment rates. As individuals do not pay attention to health insurance, they forget to enroll for it. With reminders that are sent through letters, individuals are prompted to enroll, increasing the take up rate.

Furthermore, it was observed that due to the letter intervention to enroll, the average spending risk decreased by 5.1 percent. This is due to the entry of younger individuals who are less risky in their pursuits. Accordingly, the letters resulted in a decrease in adverse selection and greater risk pooling for the insurance at the same time.

For households with personalized information relating to their subsidies, as well as those with plan comparisons, enrollment only increased slightly. This could be attributed to individuals not being fully cognizant of the benefits given to them through subsidies.

In terms of subsidy dollars, the value of the letter intervention was estimated to be around $25 to $35 per month. This underscores the importance of interventions in overcoming behavioral frictions.

It is worth noting that informational and psychological frictions, such as inattention, do not only impact the take-up of health insurance. It also results in inertia once we have selected the insurance policy.

Inertia

Besides the low take-up rate, it has also been highlighted that there is inertia in the health insurance marketplace. Inertia relates to the tendency for households to stick to the current insurance plan even though there are changes in health plan offerings or changing needs of the individual.

Let us review a study by Coleman Drake, Conor Ryan, and Bryan Dowd in a 2022 article in the *Journal of Public Economics*. Just like the previous study on enrollment in the health insurance marketplace, this study also focused on Covered California, California's health insurance marketplace.

The difference is that it examines the response of households *after* they take up the insurance. The article is named "Sources of Inertia in the Individual Health Insurance Market," and the authors investigate the causes of inertia through individuals' inaction.

For Covered California, all households that are enrolled in the program at the end of the year will have their policies automatically renewed with their default plan. In this context, the default plan refers to the plan in which households were enrolled in the previous year, or similar plans (if the households' insurers have exited the market).

At the end of the year, existing policyholders will be informed through a renewal letter by mail. When they do not take any action, the default plans will be automatically renewed.

For households that have discontinued their insurance coverage before the year end, there will be no auto-renewal. These individuals are required to return to the platform to select a plan actively.

In examining households' decisions from 2014 to 2018, the analysis indicated that 83 percent of them remained with their default plan.

To understand different factors that impact inertia, the authors decomposed them into three sources: inattention, hassle costs, and preference for provider continuity.

In this context, consumers exhibit inattention when they fail to pay attention to their choices and instead implicitly opt for a default option. In contrast, hassle costs relate to the time and effort to change health plans, while tastes for provider continuity refer to the tendency to stick to the current healthcare provider.

Through the use of a two stage model, it was found that inattention and hassle costs are the main drivers for inertia. By simply removing inattention and hassle costs, repeated health plan choice will be reduced by 53 percentage points. In doing so, it is estimated that each household in 2018 spent an additional $1,790 per year. This is significant, as it is approximately half of the premiums paid by the median household.

Key Takeaways

When we take up health insurance polices, we often need to make several decisions, such as choosing the level of deductibles or co-payments. Nonetheless, we have documented that most of the time, individuals end up choosing financially inefficient choices! We hope that after reading this chapter, you have a better understanding of these terms, and are able to make more informed choices.

In addition, we show that households have the tendency to choose low deductibles even when it is not worthwhile to do so. Before selecting deductibles, it is crucial to pose two questions to ourselves. Firstly, what is the likelihood of filing an insurance claim? Secondly, how much we will be willing to pay out of our pocket if we need to file an insurance claim?

Most of the time, we will realize that the likelihood of submitting an insurance claim is low and that we will be willing to pay more when the time comes. In fact, Nobel laureate Richard Thaler advocates for individuals to choose the highest deductibles whenever possible!

27

Annuity

Annuities are contracts that ensure individuals enjoy a guaranteed lifetime stream of income in return for a lump-sum payment today. This is a form of insurance against longevity risk, which is the risk that households outlive their savings.

In today's world, longevity risk is a pressing issue as individuals are living longer than before. Moreover, as discussed in the earlier chapters, there is a retirement income shortfall globally. This makes annuities more relevant than ever.

Just like other forms of insurance that pool risks, annuities seek to provide us with financial security. Through annuities, we have the assurance of a certain income for the rest of our lives. As such, it will allay concerns that we might outlive our savings, providing us with the confidence to plan ahead.

Various economic studies have revealed that individuals who participate in annuities fare financially better than those who invest on their own.

Let us refer to a seminal article by Menachim Yaari in *The Review of Economic Studies* titled "Uncertain Lifetime, Life Insurance and the Theory of the Consumer." This article proposes that individuals should convert all their wealth to an annuity when they retire, if they only care about their own consumption.

The intuition is as follows. By purchasing an annuity, we will enjoy higher consumption as long as we are alive. Since the insurance company does not need to compensate customers that have already passed on, those alive will be able to receive larger payments. This results in higher standard of living for surviving customers.

Additionally, we do not need to worry about the event in which we pass on earlier than expected. Our consumption is not a concern anymore when we are no longer alive! Hence, annuities have the potential to increase one's well-being as we do not need to be overly conservative in our spending habits to ensure that we can afford living beyond our life expectancy. We can spend with the assurance that we have a fixed income for the rest of our lives.

Nonetheless, few people choose to annuitize at all. This behavior has confounded economists, leading them to label the absence of participation in the annuity market as an "annuity puzzle."

The annuity puzzle is a long-standing puzzle in Economics. In fact, this has been highlighted by Franco Modigliani in his Nobel Prize speech in 1985: "It is a well-known fact that annuity contracts, other than in the form of group insurance through pension systems, are extremely rare. Why this should be so is a subject of considerable current interest. It is still ill-understood."

Decades later, things have not changed. In the subsequent discussion, we will delve further into the intricacies of the puzzle.

Bequests

One main reason for the annuity puzzle is related to building a legacy. Some of us might want to provide bequests to our family and loved ones. Or maybe, we would like to leave money for a good cause.

Hence, we might not opt for annuities as maximizing our personal consumption is not the sole objective. Are individuals motivated to leave bequests? If so, what is their motivation behind it?

In general, there could be accidental or intentional bequests. Accidental bequests occur when people leave money to others not by choice. For instance, individuals might increase their savings for precautionary reasons, such as unexpected medical expenses. However, when they pass on earlier, they unintentionally leave their savings with their next of kin.

In comparison, intentional bequests occur when people intentionally leave money to their loved ones because they care about them. Understanding the rationale behind bequests is important. While annuities can help to address ramifications related to accidental bequests, intentional bequests can explain the low take-up rate of annuities.

To investigate the types of bequests individuals have, let us review a study by Haoming Liu, Changcheng Song, and Shenghao Zhu that is titled "Intentional Bequest Motives and the Choice of Annuity."

The study revolves around households' choice of annuity plans in Singapore. As discussed in Chapter 8, Singapore's social security system relies on the Central Provident Fund (CPF), which is a compulsory savings plan for Singaporeans and Permanent Residents.

Through the CPF, how much individuals will get upon retirement is primarily dependent on how much they have in their savings. In this case, the payouts will stop once their savings run out.

Nonetheless, things changed in 2013 when the Singapore government introduced a mandatory life annuity scheme called CPF Lifelong Income for the Elderly (CPF LIFE). This transformed part of the limited-term payment into a partial annuity scheme.

There are two annuity options that are being offered: LIFE Basic Plan and LIFE Standard Plan. The key difference between the two options relates to the size of payouts and bequests.

The LIFE Standard Plan is stipulated to be the default plan. As compared to the LIFE Standard Plan, LIFE Basic Plan provides lower monthly payouts but higher bequests upon death.

Since households need to commit to either one of the plans, and are unable to withdraw money from the fund, the authors were able to distinguish whether there are indeed intentional bequest motives.

The hypothesis here is that if there are intentional bequest motives, households will end up choosing the LIFE Basic Plan, which offers higher bequests.

The authors surveyed more than 2,000 individuals around the age of 55, which is the age of enrolment for the annuity. It was observed that 20 percent of the individuals chose the LIFE Basic Plan.

This provides direct evidence of the intentional bequest motives. Besides, since the default plan relates to the plan with lower bequests, 20 percent is likely to be an underestimate due to participant inertia.

What are the reasons for intentional bequests? The authors show that better-educated individuals and individuals with children are more likely to have intentional bequests. Consequently, one important driver for having bequests is to give them to their children.

The study further provided evidence of the altruism motive, which refers to the tendency for parents to leave larger bequests to their children when they are financially worse off.

Indeed, parents will tend to have more bequests when they have children who are less well-educated or in a poor financial position.

Furthermore, parents have the "joy of giving" motive as they seek to distribute their bequests evenly among their children.

In sum, there is evidence of accidental bequest motives. As individuals have different bequest motives, this will influence their choices in annuities. Let us next examine what drives households' decisions when it comes to choosing annuities.

Understanding Annuity Choice

The choice of annuities has been explored in a 2014 article in the *Journal of Public Economics* by John Beshears, James Choi, David Laibson, Brigitte Madrian, and Stephen Zeldes.

In their research paper titled "What Makes Annuitization More Appealing," the authors surveyed households in the United States and analyzed their choices under different hypothetical scenarios. Let us discuss some of the key findings.

It was revealed that households have common concerns that relate to their decisions to take up annuities. These include having the desire to have sufficient income later in life, flexibility in the timing to spend, and worries that the insurance company is unable to pay in the future.

Does this resonate with you as well?

It is natural to have these concerns. Nonetheless, rather than avoiding annuities altogether, we can address the issue by adjusting the amount of savings that we would like to allocate to annuities. For instance, with partial annuitization, we annuitize part of our wealth (rather than completely). We can also take up different annuitization policies from different companies to diversify our risk. Annuities do not need to be an all-or-nothing choice.

This relates to the second finding that households are more willing to take up partial annuitization as compared to complete annuitization. From the survey, the authors realized that partial annuitization has higher take-up rates and a higher amount of pension invested per household.

In addition, households prefer annuities that pay an annual bonus each year, rather than ones that pay a uniform monthly payout. This relates to their preference to enjoy more flexibility and control in spending.

As such, it is crucial to bear in mind our own needs and appreciate the range of choices in annuities. When annuities can be adapted to meet our individual needs, they will be more appealing.

Behavioral Obstacles in the Annuity Market

We have discussed about behavioral biases, such as loss aversion and mental accounting behavior in earlier chapters. Recent economic studies have highlighted that these biases could also play a significant role in the annuity market, resulting in a low take-up rate of annuities.

One example relates to a study by Wei-Yin Hu and Jason Scott in a 2007 article in the *Financial Analysts Journal*. Titled "Behavioral Obstacles in the Annuity Market," the authors observed that individuals who are loss-averse tend to avoid annuities.

This is because, with annuities, we are forgoing a lump sum payment today for future streams of income. Hence, some individuals might find it painful to come up with a lump sum payment as they perceive it to be "a loss" in exchange for uncertain payment in the future. As such, they avoid annuities.

In the same vein, loss aversion can explain households' preference to have "period certain" annuities that pay out for a finite number of years, rather than those that pay out indefinitely.

To economists, the popularity of "period certain" annuities is puzzling. Theoretically, we ought to value annuities more when we get older as the longevity risk is higher. However, evidence shows that individuals are choosing annuities during periods when they have a lower risk of outliving their savings!

On top of that, there could be mental accounting in annuity markets. For instance, individuals might treat annuities separately from their total retirement spending. This is because they tend to frame annuities as risky gambles where potential losses outweigh the potential gains.

As such, understanding how individuals perceive annuities is instrumental to understanding the annuity puzzle.

Framing Effect

The framing for annuities matters. This has been examined by Jeffrey Brown, Jeffrey Kling, Sendhil Mullainathan, and Marian Wrobel in a 2008 article in the *American Economic Review*.

In their study, "Why Don't People Insure Late Life Consumption: A Framing Explanation of the Under-Annuitization Puzzle," the authors propose that annuities can be viewed in two different dimensions: the consumption frame and the investment frame.

The consumption frame relates to households' focus on what can be spent over time. In comparison, the investment frame examines the risk and return features of the asset.

While annuities are attractive from a consumption viewpoint, they are perceived to be risky investment decisions. This is due to the uncertain time period in which one is alive (and can enjoy the payouts).

If one passes immediately after the purchase of the annuities, there is a 100 percent loss in the principal value. Hence, while annuities provide insurance from a consumption viewpoint, they could be deemed a gamble from an investment viewpoint.

To examine how consumption frame and investment frame can impact households' choices, the authors conducted an experiment by presenting annuities to households using different lenses.

Through an online survey, 1,342 respondents were provided with different scenarios and asked which scenario represented a better financial decision.

For the consumption frame, the authors provide information pertaining to the consequences that annuities can have on consumption. Relying on words, such as "spend" and "payment," the focus was on how many goods and services the individual could purchase throughout his/her lifetime. The returns and value of the annuity were not discussed.

Conversely, the authors depersonalized annuities under the investment frame. Here, the focus was on the returns in different years. Words, such as "invest" and "earnings," were used with no mention of consumption spending.

Indeed, framing impacts the annuity take-up rate. When the annuities are being introduced through the consumption frame, 72 percent of the respondents prefer to have a life annuity over a savings account. On the contrary, only 21 percent of the respondents opted for a life annuity when the annuities were framed as investments.

This proves that framing could impact households' decisions in annuities. Moreover, due to mental accounting, individuals tend to focus on the two frames separately. When the investment frame dominates, annuities become less appealing.

Key Takeaways

Without proper financial planning, we are in danger of outliving our income when we retire. Annuities could thus be a valuable addition to our financial portfolio.

Nonetheless, it has been found that individuals tend to avoid annuities due to their negative perception of them. Based on our discussion of annuities above, we hope that you will have a clearer picture of annuities and are able to have a more objective view toward annuities.

Furthermore, there are several concerns, such as the desire to provide bequests to our loved ones. In this case, we could do a partial annuitization. Apart from giving us constant streams of income capable of supporting us for the rest of our lives, partial annuitization also allows us to leave bequests for our loved ones.

Speaking of bequests, have you written your will? Will writing is also an important component of household finance. Without a will, your money and property will be distributed according to the rules of the state, and not your individual preferences.

To conclude, we have discussed many financial products that you can use to manage your risks across your lifecycle. Ultimately, the type of insurance or annuity that you should take is dependent on your own specific needs. It is not a one-size-fits-all decision.

Part VIII

Gender

28

Gender Pension Gap

In the final part of this book, we are going to discuss about the role of gender when managing personal finances.

In our previous chapters, we have discussed how important it is to save and prepare for retirement. This is especially pertinent for women. Given their longer life expectancy, there is a need for women to have greater financial preparedness and to plan for a longer retirement.

Table 28.1 presents the life expectancy of individuals in selected OECD countries in 2020. We find that the life expectancy of individuals differ across different countries, with individuals in Japan living the longest. Nonetheless, one pattern remains: Females live longer in almost all societies.

Table 28.1: Life Expectancy of Individuals in 2020

Country	Life Expectancy (Overall)	Life Expectancy (Female)	Life Expectancy (Male)
Australia	83.2	85.3	81.2
Indonesia	71.9	74.2	69.8
Japan	84.7	87.7	81.6
United States	77.0	79.9	74.2

Source: OECD

As women generally live longer than men across the world, they will require more funds for retirement. Unfortunately, the opposite is happening. Globally, women receive lower retirement income than men.

Commonly referred to as the gender pension gap, the difference in retirement income between men and women, is estimated to be around 26 percent across OECD countries.

Figure 28.1 presents the gender pension gap across different OECD countries. In countries, such as Austria and the United Kingdom, women above the age of 65 received 40 percent less retirement income than men. This means that women only received 60 percent of what men received when they retire. In comparison, the gender pension gap is smaller in Germany and the United States. In these countries, women above the age of 65 received 30 percent less retirement income than men.

Figure 28.1: Gender Pension Gap Across Different Countries

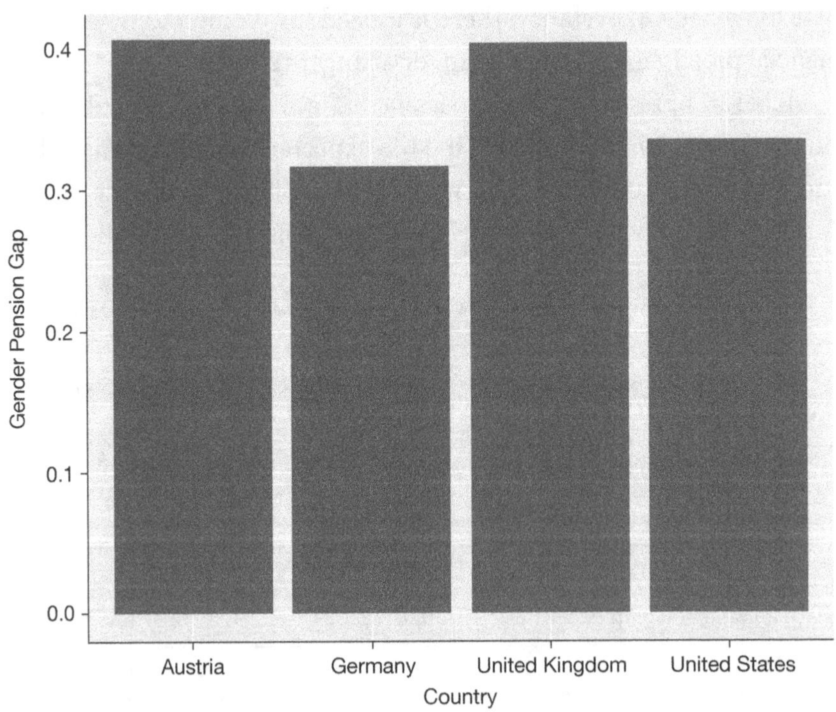

Source: OECD

The Gender Wage Gap

One main reason for the gender pension gap is that women earn lesser than men throughout their lifetime. Consequently, they receive lesser pensions than men when they retire.

The disparity in earnings between men and women is referred to as the gender wage gap. In the United States, women earn around 80 percent of the earnings of men on average.

Figure 28.2 presents changes in the median weekly earnings between men and women in the United States across time. While the wage gap has been narrowing over time, the gap is still significant.

We now look at some possible reasons for the gender wage gap. This has been well summarized by Francine Blau and Lawrence Kahn in a 2017 article in the *Journal of Economic Literature.*

In their article, "The Gender Wage Gap: Extent, Trends and Explanations," they categorize the wage gap into different components. It was established that gender differences in education and experience drive the gender wage

Figure 28.2: Median Weekly Earnings for Men and Women in the United States

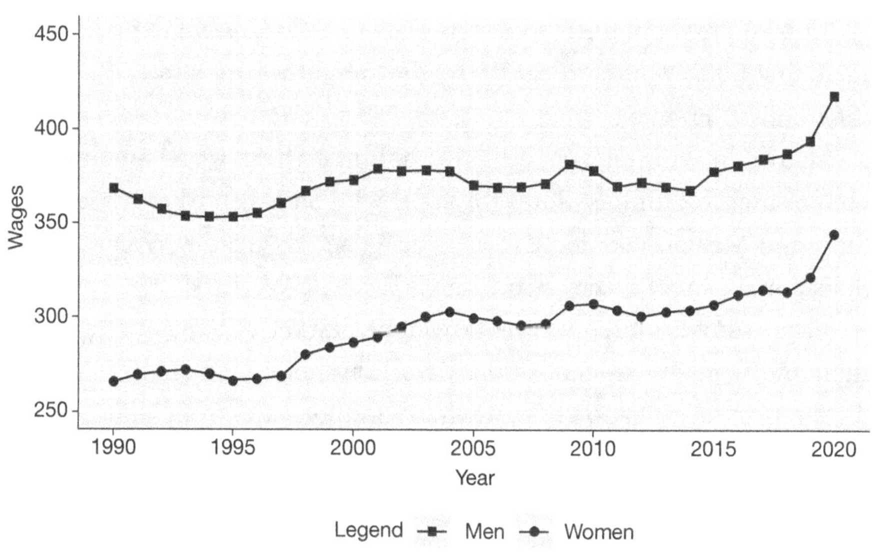

Source: BLS

gap. In fact, the diminishing gender gap in education and experience helps to explain the narrowing gender wage gap in recent years.

In addition, gender differences in occupation and industry are key factors that influence the gender wage gap. As men and women tend to work in different industries, their salaries vary according to industry. For instance, construction workers which predominantly are men, are paid more due to the higher risk involved. Currently, this contributes to the biggest determinant of the gender wage gap.

Another determining factor lies in the labor force participation rate. As women are more likely to take on childcare duties, they might work part-time or leave the labor force early. This could impact their career advancements and ultimately, their income.

There are also gender differences in caregiving. It has been shown that women are the main providers of informal care for the elderly and family members with chronic medical conditions. As informal caregivers, they might not have a stable job that provides pensions for retirement.

Women as Strategic Workers

As women are more likely to devote time to take care of family matters, including housework and childcare, they tend to work strategically and differently from men.

How do women strategically balance their work and family commitments? Sumit explores this issue with Shih-Fen Cheng, Tien Foo Sing, and Mahanaaz Sultana in an article named "Gender Wage Gap for Singaporean Taxi Drivers: Are Women Strategic Workers?"

The study centered on the taxi labor market in Singapore as both men and women can choose their working hours and timing flexibly. Through an investigation of more than 7 million rides from January 2009 to November 2010, it was revealed that the gender wage gap exists in the taxi labor market in Singapore too.

In an hour, male taxi drivers earn more than their female counterparts by more than 4.5 percent. This is due to female taxi drivers being less likely to work during evening peak hours when the demand is higher, and the rates are better.

Why do women not work during the evening? The most likely reason is attributed to family commitments. Based on anecdotal evidence, female taxi drivers allocate their evenings to prepare dinner and take care of their children. In contrast, male taxi drivers do not have these constraints.

Besides, female taxi drivers prefer to work outside the hours that they allocate for their family duties. Particularly, they choose to work during early morning and late-night shifts.

In doing so, they can kill two birds with one stone. On one hand, they can fulfill their responsibilities to their families. On the other hand, they can earn more through additional surcharges. As there are additional charges during early morning and late nights, it can make up for the better rates during evening peak hours.

To offset their shorter worker hours, female taxi drivers rely more on phone bookings (rather than flag downs). This will allow them to reduce unproductive time looking for commuters and earn additional income through booking fees.

Hence, there is evidence that women in the taxi labor market are strategic workers. They work around their constraints and maximize their income when given the opportunity.

On top of that, women also leverage on informal networks in the executive labor market. This includes golfing! As golf is inherently a social game, it provides opportunities for individuals to bond during the game.

Together with Wenlan Qian, David Reeb, and Tien Foo Sing, Sumit studies the career benefits of women golfers in a 2016 article in the *American Economic Review* named "Playing the Boys Game: Golf Buddies and Board Diversity."

In this article, it was found that women who partake in golf are more likely to serve on a board of directors in Singapore.

By analyzing 1 million golf games played in Singapore over 15 years, it was estimated that female golfers have a 54 percent higher chance of serving on the board as compared to male golfers.

This is because golf is a male-dominated sport. Thus, females tend to gain additional social capital as compared to their male counterparts when they participate in golfing activities.

In fact, females are 116 percent more likely to serve on the boards of large firms! On the contrary, there are no effects on smaller firms. This indicates that being part of the old boy's network is particularly strong in large firms.

While the study highlights that the strong influence of social capital can help to mitigate the glass ceiling in corporate boards, it has implications for the broader economy. Since the lack of a robust social network might limit women's opportunities, how do we help to bridge the gap?

Gender Gap in Access to Financial Services

Another key driver of the gender pension gap is related to access to financial services. Globally, there is a gender difference in financial inclusion. As women tend to face more barriers to borrow and save, they are less able to prepare themselves for retirement.

One example is women's entrepreneurship. In most countries, women continue to play the primary role of caregivers and will benefit from flexibility in choosing their preferred time and place to work.

The growth of the gig economy in recent years has helped to narrow the gender wage gap as it provides women with more opportunities.

From their own homes, they can also start their own business or work remotely, giving them the opportunity to earn additional streams of income.

As shown by the work of Esther Duflo, the 2019 recipient of the Nobel Memorial Prize in Economic Sciences, women empowerment and economic development are tightly connected.

At the individual level, growth in a mother's education and earnings is highly related to an improvement in the child's well-being. On a macro level, the rise in women's entrepreneurship is highly beneficial as it will further contribute to the social and economic growth of the society.

Nonetheless, it has been shown that women face greater challenges than men regarding access to finance. This includes both formal finance (such as borrowing from banks) and informal finance (such as peer-to-peer lending).

This is because women have lower income and credit scores than men and are hence deemed to be riskier by traditional lenders.

Without access to finance, female entrepreneurs remain excluded from the formal economy and are unable to develop their businesses. Moreover, female workers are unable to control and access financial services, such as savings and payments.

According to the World Bank Group's Global Findex, women have less access to formal financial services. We present some key differences between men and women in Table 28.2. Globally, there is a higher percentage of men with bank accounts and debit cards as compared to women. This translates to a higher percentage of men indicating that they have saved for old age.

It is estimated that more than 1 billion women globally do not use or have access to the financial system. This is linked to a myriad of reasons, including the gender pay gap. Without access to financial services, they are unable to grow and develop, creating a conundrum.

Table 28.2: Worldwide Use of Financial Services in 2021

Percentage of Individuals	Male	Female
With bank account	78	74
Own debit card	56	49
Used a mobile phone or the internet to pay bills	37	32
Borrowed from a formal financial institution	30	27
Saved for old age	27	25

Source: World Bank Group's Global Findex

Gender Gap in Peer-to-Peer Lending

Gender gap exists not only in traditional credit markets but also in alternative lending, such as digital lending markets. We will now shift our attention to a 2020 article by Xiao Chen, Bihong Huang, and Dezhu Ye that is published in the *Journal of Banking and Finance*.

As suggested by the title, "Gender Gap in Peer-to-Peer Lending: Evidence from China," it was shown that there exists a gender gap in the online credit market in China.

The online credit market serves as an alternative to the traditional lending institutions. By relying on online platforms that match lenders with borrowers, individuals can borrow directly from one another without relying on banks. Hence, this is commonly known as peer-to-peer lending or marketplace lending.

Just like many countries in the world, there has been an increase in peer-to-peer lending in China. To study the role of gender in peer-to-peer lending, the authors rely on data from Renrendai, a leading peer-to-peer lending platform in China.

Renrendai has more than 1 million members in over 200 cities. To borrow money through the platform, borrowers will need to post loan listings with the following information: borrowing amount, interest rate, use of loan, and monthly installment. They will also need to provide their personal information to the platform, including gender.

Once the loan listing is posted, lenders will bid on how much they would like to fund. From a minimum investment of 50 RMB, a loan listing will usually attract multiple bids before it is fully funded.

When it is fully funded, it is deemed to be a "successful" listing, and lending takes place. On the contrary, when it is not fully funded, the listing fails, and the borrower is unable to borrow any amount at all.

In examining the records from 2012 to 2014, it was observed that women are better borrowers. As they have a lower probability of default, lending to female borrowers will increase the profit by 5 percent as compared to the average.

Nonetheless, the funding success rate of female borrowers is not higher than that of males! This implies that to get funded, females are required to provide a higher rate of return to lenders as compared to men.

Hence, there is a gender gap in peer-to-peer lending. The terms and conditions of financial contracts vary according to gender. It is pivotal that we bridge the gender gap by providing women access to financial services. This will also help alleviate the gender pension gap.

Gender and Housing Returns

The gender gap in wealth accumulation can also be explained by the different rates of return enjoyed by males and females. With the role of compounding, savings that enjoy a higher rate of return can result in a significant increase in wealth over time.

It has been discovered that there are gender differences across different asset classes too. This includes having different returns in the housing market!

As discussed earlier, housing is the largest source of wealth for households, and it is challenging to navigate the real estate markets due to the large number of decisions we need to make.

Gender differences in the housing market have been examined by Paul Goldsmith-Pinkham and Kelly Shue in a 2023 article in *The Journal of Finance*. Titled "The Gender Gap in Housing Returns," the study showed that single men enjoy higher returns in the housing markets than single women.

To examine housing returns across genders in the United States, the authors make use of data from CoreLogic that covers more than 50 million housing transactions between 1991 and 2017. This allows them to compute the homeowners' annualized return by comparing the initial purchase and final sales price.

Without accounting for any mortgage borrowing, single men managed to earn 1.5 percentage points more than women. After accounting for the role of mortgages, the gender gap widens. This time, single men experienced higher housing returns of 8 percentage points.

The rate of return on mortgages is amplified due to the power of leverage. As we borrow to finance our property using mortgage loans, we are effectively leveraging others' money to purchase our homes. Since the rate of return on a property investment is based on the amount of money invested in the property, our returns will be magnified.

Given a fixed level of profits and asset value, the lower the amount invested (and consequently the higher the mortgage), the higher the rate of return will be. Hence, mortgages widen the gender gap in housing returns.

One main reason for the gender gap in the housing market is attributed to market timing. Women tend to purchase houses in locations where the prices are high and sell houses when prices fall.

Moreover, women obtained lower execution prices in housing transactions. For instance, female sellers tend to list their houses at a lower price and do not negotiate as well as men. As a result, it is estimated that women pay 2 percent more and sell for 2 percent less as compared to men.

Through repeated sales, it was found that male sellers and female buyers are related to the highest transaction prices, while male buyers and female sellers are linked to the lowest transaction prices.

The authors show that the gender gap in housing returns is attributed primarily to gender differences in negotiation. Due to different willingness and ability to negotiate, women often end up with lower discounts relative to the list price.

The gap is not due to gender preferences for different types of properties or willingness to invest more in housing maintenance and upgrades.

Gender differences in housing returns play a dominant role in wealth accumulation. Based on the estimates of the authors, it can account for 30 percent of the gender pension gap in the United States.

Evidently men are from Mars, women are from Venus. As males and females think and behave differently, they also make financial decisions differently. This will have consequences on their retirement planning.

Key Takeaways

We have shown you that women live longer than men but are less equipped for retirement. It is crucial that households acknowledge this fact and cater to different scenarios in their planning.

For instance, what happens when a wife is widowed? Will the wife have sufficient resources? Will the surviving partner be able to navigate the financial decisions on their own?

These are important questions that the family would need to discuss. The earlier the conversation, the better it is.

In addition, we have highlighted several gender gaps in the economy. This includes the gender wage gap, the gender gap in access to financial services, and the even gender gap in housing returns.

As a household, it is useful to understand what drives the gaps and equip women with the necessary knowledge and skills.

29

Gender and Self-Confidence

With longer life spans and lower lifetime incomes, women ought to be exploring different ways to save and invest to meet their retirement needs. Nonetheless, it has been documented that women participate less actively in financial markets and invest lesser in risky assets relative to men.

One main reason is attributed to women lacking confidence in making financial decisions. As compared to men, it is found that women are less self-assured in their judgment and ability when it comes to financial management.

This chapter focuses on exploring the disparities in self-confidence across different genders. As a starting point, we will delve into the factors that contribute to the gender gap in self-confidence.

Beliefs About Gender

In the article "Beliefs About Gender" that is published in the *American Economic Review* in 2019, Pedro Bordalo, Katherine Coffman, Nicola Gennaioli, and Andrei Shleifer show that self-confidence could be attributed to gender stereotypes, as well as the assessment of one's ability.

Measuring levels of confidence across genders, the authors conducted laboratory experiments to obtain data on individuals' beliefs of themselves and others and to compare their beliefs with the actual outcome.

Participants across three universities (Ohio State University, Harvard Business School, and University of California Santa Barbara) took part in the experiments by answering multiple-choice questions across different categories.

The questions were wide-ranging, encompassing topics from mathematics, verbal skills, art and literature. Questions about the Kardashians and Disney movies are also integrated into the questionnaire, reflecting interests in pop culture.

These topics were specifically selected based on the understanding that males and females display strengths in different topics. As an illustration, while males are deemed to have an advantage in categories, such as video games and sports, females tend to have an advantage in categories, such as art, emotion, and the Kardashians.

At the outset of the experiment, participants were tasked with predicting the likelihood of answering a question correctly and providing an estimation of the number of correct answers per category, based on their own responses.

Subsequently, they were asked to provide their beliefs about the performance of a randomly selected individual. In some cases, the gender of their partner was made known to them.

It was discovered that in female-type categories, women tend to overestimate their own performance. Similarly, participants end up overestimating the performance of their female partners in such categories.

The same goes for men. Both men and their observers overestimated the performance of men in male-type categories. Evidently, gender stereotypes impact the beliefs of an individual as well as those of others.

Besides stereotypes, there was also a poor estimation of ability. It was revealed that for both men and women, difficult tasks were associated with higher levels of poor estimation regardless of category.

Hence, an individual's confidence level can be explained by stereotyping, as well as the poor estimation of personal ability. When the task is more difficult, beliefs are distorted to a larger extent.

Since the financial markets are conventionally dominated by men, women become less confident to invest in risky assets. This is perpetuated by gender stereotypes.

Gender Differences in Financial Literacy

Next, we examine financial literacy. Gender gaps in self-confidence also heavily influence other aspects of households, including financial literacy.

This has been discussed in a recent article by Tabea Bucher-Koenen, Rob Alessie, Annamaria Lusardi, and Maarten van Rooij, named "Fearless Woman: Financial Literacy and Stock Market Participation."

The research study shows that lower financial literacy for women is attributed to a lack of financial knowledge and self-confidence. This results in women being less likely to participate in the stock market.

Here, the authors designed two survey modules and integrated them into the De Nederlandsche Bank (DNB) Household Survey, which is a panel study of the Dutch central bank in the Netherlands.

In the first module, the authors introduced three financial literacy concepts that involve compounding interest, inflation, and diversification. For each of the options, the respondents can also choose the option "do not know."

In the second module, the authors repeated the same set of financial literacy questions from the first module. However, the option "do not know" was removed. Instead, they were asked how confident they were in responding to the question.

The survey proved that there is a distinct gender gap in financial literacy. As compared to men, more women answered financial literacy incorrectly. Besides, women are more likely to choose the option "do not know" when given the opportunity in the first module.

When the "do not know" response was removed in the second module, the financial literacy gender gap was reduced. This suggests that females possessed more knowledge on matters of financial literacy than they had perceived. Put differently, it is likely that the lack of confidence in women contributes to the financial literacy gender gap.

To separate the financial literacy gender gap into a true knowledge gap and confidence gap, the authors compared the second module with that of the first module.

It was estimated that two-thirds of the financial literacy gender gap is attributed to a lack of financial knowledge and the remaining one-third is due to a lack of confidence.

Subsequently, the study examined how financial literacy influences households' management of their investment decisions. It was observed that higher financial literacy relates to higher stock market participation and can be attributed to both financial knowledge and confidence.

Hence, to encourage women to participate in the stock market and to increase their returns, it is imperative to improve their financial knowledge and boost their confidence at the same time.

While it is important to be more confident and assertive in making financial decisions, being overly confident has its pitfalls. In fact, several other studies have documented that when men are overly confident, they tend to make more mistakes in the stock market and take on more personal bankruptcy risks.

Gender and Overconfidence in the Stock Market

Overconfidence in the stock markets has been investigated by Brad Barber and Terrance Odean in a 2001 article in *The Quarterly Journal of Economics*.

As suggested by the title "Boys Will Be Boys: Gender, Overconfidence, and Common Stock Investment," it is found that men are more overconfident than women when trading in the stock market.

The authors came to this conclusion after examining the trading records of 35,000 households at a large discount brokerage firm in the United States from 1991 to 1997.

To gauge overconfidence, the authors relied on the frequency of stock market transactions undertaken by individuals. The higher the number of stock market transactions, the higher the perception of the confidence level of the individual.

This is because when one places an undue confidence in their stock valuations, they have a higher tendency to engage in excessive trading. In other words, when individuals overestimate their abilities, they become overly confident in their stock valuations, and tend to trade too much.

On average, the annual turnover rate of common stock investments is 70 percent, meaning that individuals buy and replace 70 percent of their stocks in a year. However, there is a wide dispersion of turnover rates among different individuals.

In this study, the authors estimated that men trade 45 percent more than women. In doing so, men end up with lower net annual returns of 0.84 percentage points. As a result, excessive trading resulted in men having lower net returns.

Furthermore, these differences are larger between single men and single women, as compared to married individuals. Single men trade 67 percent more than single women, resulting in lower annual returns of 1.44 percentage points. This suggests that married couples can influence the investment decisions of one another.

The main reason for men having lower returns is transaction costs. Trading is costly. For an average trade above $1,000, the transaction cost is around 1 percent for the bid-ask spread,[12] and around 1.4 percent for commissions. Hence, excessive trading results in men having lower net returns.

It has been further highlighted that the differences in returns are not attributed to inferior security selection. Men do not choose poor stocks; they just trade too much! In fact, both men and women earn similar gross returns (before taking into account transaction costs).

Men are also more inclined toward risk-taking as they tend to invest in smaller and more volatile stocks. Subsequently, after accounting for the risk of the portfolio, women's risk-adjusted gross returns are even higher.

[12] Bid-ask spread is the difference between the highest price that the buyer will buy (bid) and the lowest price that the seller will accept (ask). It is considered to be a transaction cost as individual investors will buy at a higher price and sell at a lower price. The moneymaker will make profits from the difference.

Put together, the combination of overconfidence and greater propensity to take risks contributed to men trading more and performing worse than women in the stock market.

Gender Gap in Personal Bankruptcy

As men and women have different risk-taking behavior, there could also be a gender gap in personal bankruptcy.

Along with Jia He, Tien Foo Sing, and Jian Zhang, Sumit explores this issue in a 2018 article in the *Review of Finance*. This is done by examining the data of bankruptcies filed from 1980 to 2012 in Singapore.

Titled "Gender Gap in Personal Bankruptcy Risks: Empirical Evidence from Singapore," it was discovered that women in Singapore are less likely to be involved in bankruptcy events by 28 percent.

To determine whether the differences in bankruptcies are driven by risk-taking behavior, the study relied on the use of prior motor vehicle accidents as a proxy for risk-taking behavior.

This is because reckless drivers with past motor vehicle accidents have a higher propensity to take risks innately relative to those without accident records. When they are more risk-seeking, they will take on more financing risk and are more likely to go bankrupt.

Indeed, it was shown that risk-taking behavior influences the gender gap in personal bankruptcy. Women tend to have lower motor vehicle accidents and lower bankruptcy risk.

The average claim for females that are involved in bankruptcies is also lower. Women file for bankruptcy claims that are 4.1 percent lower than the average claim of S$5,420 made by men.

Moreover, the study highlights that the gender gap in personal bankruptcy is not a phenomenon unique to married couples, where men tend to take on more credit risk as heads of their households. The gender gap persists when examining the relationship between single men and single women.

Consequently, gender gaps in confidence and risk-taking behavior have direct impacts on the welfare of individuals, including bankruptcies.

Gender and Annuity Choices

Moving on, we will explore the topic of gender differences and annuity choices.

In a 2008 article, "Who Chooses Annuities? An Experimental Investigation of the Role of Gender, Framing and Defaults," written by Julie Agnew, Lisa Anderson, Jeffrey Gerlach, and Lisa Szykman in the *American Economic Review*, it is observed that women are more likely to choose annuities.

The study utilized an experiment to explore gender disparities in decision-making between choosing an annuity and individual investment.

Involving 850 nonstudent respondents in the United States, the study first elicited individuals' risk aversion and financial literacy through a series of survey questions.

Thereafter, the respondents were presented with a five-minute slide show. There were three variations of the slide show. The first slide show favored annuities, while the second slide show favored the self-investment choice. The third slide show was neutral. Each respondent was presented with only one variation of the slide show.

Finally, they were asked to play a "Retirement game," in which the respondents were given $60 to either purchase an annuity or invest in a risky portfolio.

The risky portfolio consists of a safe asset and a simulated market. Participants can decide how much to withdraw, as well as how much to allocate between the safe asset and the simulated market.

Independent die rolls are used to determine whether the individual survived and could continue to the next round.

For participants who chose annuities, they would receive $16.67 in each round that they managed to survive. For surviving participants who chose to invest in a risky portfolio, they would then use the die roll to determine their rate of return.

The study realized that females are more likely to choose annuities. One main factor is attributed to differences in risk aversion and financial literacy. Females who are more risk-averse and financially illiterate prefer annuities over personal investments.

In addition, men and women respond differently to the information that is presented in the slide show.

When given negative information about annuities, both genders have a lower propensity to choose annuities. However, when given negative information about self-investment, males were more likely to choose annuities.

This could be due to the preconceived notion that self-investments are undesirable, which is present in women. Such a perception could explain their lack of response to information provided in the slideshow.

Key Takeaways

The economic studies that we have discussed in this chapter have provided us with evidence that women are less confident than men and are more averse to risk when making financial decisions.

While this results in positive outcomes, such as lower bankruptcies, lower returns on their financial assets could be crippling to their long-term financial health. Equipping women with financial knowledge is the first step toward gaining more confidence to engage in the financial market.

On the other hand, men should understand their weaknesses when it comes to being overly confident when they invest. To avoid being overly confident, it is important to be reflective and consider various perspectives when making decisions.

Only then, we can achieve the Goldilocks situation for investing.

30

Intra-Household Financial Decisions

We will conclude this book by focusing on the role of intra-household interactions in making financial decisions. Intra-household financial decisions relate to the process of making financial choices within a household or family unit.

For married couples, individuals do not make decisions on their own. Rather, household financial decisions are jointly made by both parties. Based on what is perceived to be in the best interest of the family, households will come up with fitting financial choices.

However, achieving consensus within a family is not an easy task. Earlier, we showed you that men and women have different preferences and beliefs when it comes to making financial decisions. For instance, women are less confident and more risk averse.

Accordingly, this requires some negotiation and agreement within a household. This comes in the form of intra-household bargaining power. Within the household, the extent to which a husband and wife can exert influence on each other will determine the collective decision.

Intra-Household Bargaining Power

Let us first examine an article by Jawad Addoum that is titled "Household Portfolio Choice and Retirement."

Published in *The Review of Economics and Statistics* in 2017, the article showed that because of intra-household bargaining, couples in the United States behave differently from singles when they retire.

This is done by examining data from the Health and Retirement Study (HRS). As a nationally representative study, it followed more than 22,000 Americans above the age of 50 and contained information of their financial portfolio as well as personal characteristics.

Using data from the HRS, it was established that upon retirement, couples tend to allocate their portfolios away from risky assets. On average, couples reduced their investments in the stock market by 20 percent, corresponding to a decrease of 8 percent in their total financial assets. At the same time, the stock market participation rate of retired couples also fell by 4 percent.

In comparison, singles' portfolio allocation and stock market participation rate remained unchanged.

What drives couples to change their portfolio after retirement? It is discovered that after retirement, couples are more risk averse. One main reason is related to intra-household bargaining as couples take on more collective decisions after retirement.

To estimate the risk aversion levels of individuals, the author relied on the survey questions in the HRS that pertain to their willingness to accept gambles. The more willing they are to take part in the gamble, the lower the risk aversion.

It became apparent that even though the risk aversion of men and women at the individual level could remain unchanged over time, the risk aversion of couples at the household level is likely to change. This is attributed to changes in intra-household bargaining across time.

It was observed that the larger the difference in risk aversion among couples, the greater the change in willingness to take a risk upon retirement. In other words, for couples in which the wife is more risk-averse than her husband, there is a larger shift in the portfolio away from stocks.

This provides evidence that upon retirement, wives have a larger degree of control in managing the household resources.

What then drives bargaining power? The research showed that intra-household bargaining power could be related to the share of income contributed by the husband and wife. Those with a higher share of income would tend to have higher bargaining power in the family.

Upon retirement, the husband usually experiences a larger fall in income (due to the gender wage gap), and consequently a fall in bargaining power. As a result, a shift occurs in the management of household financial resources where the wife, instead of the husband, exerts the most control. This drives a corresponding decrease in the volume of investments in the stock market.

On the contrary, when the wife experiences a larger fall in income, her husband will then enjoy an increase in bargaining power and have more control over the household finances. This change in dynamics can be observed through differences in the retirement of husbands and wives.

While there is a decrease in allocation in the stock market when the husband retires, the allocation in the stock market actually increases when the wife retires. Hence, the allocation of funds to the stock market depends on who retires.

Besides retirement events, the volume of portfolio allocation depends on which partner is widowed. Surviving husbands end up increasing their investments in the stock market while surviving wives decrease their allocation to the stock market.

Some things do not change after all.

Gender Identity Norms

Intra-household bargaining could also be influenced by many other factors, such as gender identity norms.

Gender norms differ across different countries. While women have a lesser influence over financial decision-making in some countries, they take control of the entire household budget in others.

We now examine how traditional gender roles influence households' financial decisions in a 2021 study in *The Journal of Finance* by Da Ke.

This study is named "Who Wears the Pants? Gender Identity Norms and Intrahousehold Financial Decision Making," and finds that even after we account for demographics, such as education, income, and wealth, men in the United States have higher bargaining power in the family. Therefore, besides the role of income (as highlighted in the previous study by Jawad Addoum), gender norms matter too.

The study by Ke leveraged on three different sets of data in the United States: The Current Population Survey, the Census, and the Health and Retirement Study, and came to the same set of conclusions. Stock market participation is higher in families with financially sophisticated husbands as compared to financially sophisticated wives.

As an indicator of financial sophistication, Ke makes use of individuals' careers in finance. Here, husbands who work in the finance industry are more likely to participate in the stock market than wives who work in finance by around 2 to 7 percentage points.

When husbands switched to a career in finance, stock market participation increased by 9 percentage points. In contrast, when wives switch to a career in finance, stock market participation increased by 6 percentage points.

The findings imply that gender norms influence household financial decisions. Otherwise, there will be no difference in stock market participation if the husband or wife has more knowledge and experience in finance.

In addition to financial knowledge, there is evidence that differences in stock market participation are dependent on gender norms in diverse segments of the economy.

For instance, in societies with more traditional gender roles, the stock market participation gap is wider. These groups include families in which the husband was born in the southern United States, active churchgoers, or descendants of preindustrial societies.

Conversely, societies with less conservative views on women tend to exhibit a smaller disparity in stock market participation. For instance, this can be observed in married couples raised by working mothers.

To provide more evidence on the role of gender norms, Ke conducted an experiment that involved more than 4,000 married individuals. These individuals were randomly allocated to two different groups: the gender-identity and gender-neutral groups.

In each group, participants were presented with different type of information. While the gender-identity group was given a text that talked about self-assertion for men and interpersonal sensitivity for women, the gender-neutral group was presented with a gender-neutral text on the default American lifestyle.

Subsequently, both groups were asked to advise their husband about making financial decisions. It was found that women in the gender-identity group were less likely to contribute ideas to their husbands, highlighting the influence of gender identity in the household.

Spousal Control

Several studies have further highlighted that spousal control could influence the decision of a married individual. For example, you would make different choices depending on whether your spouse can observe your choice or whether you have communicated with your spouse.

Let us now delve into a 2009 article in the *American Economic Review* by Nava Ashraf, which is titled "Spousal Control and Intra-Household Decision Making: An Experimental Study in the Philippines." By studying the behavior of married couples, this article documents the role of information and communication in intra-household financial decisions.

Working with a rural private bank in Mindanao in the Philippines, the author conducted an experiment in which married individuals were given a sum of money and were given the options to save or spend (through committed consumption or cash).

146 married couples took part in the study and were divided into three separate conditions:

Condition 1: Private Information

- In Condition 1, individuals were separated from their spouses from the beginning of the experiment. Hence, they are unaware of what their spouses are doing, as well as the decisions that they made.
- All the information is kept private to oneself, and there is no form of communication.

Condition 2: Public Information

- In Condition 2, individuals enter the room with their spouse. This implies that couples can observe each other's actions.
- However, no form of communication is allowed at any time.

Condition 3: Negotiation

- Condition 3 follows Condition 2 but allows the spouses to communicate with one another before making decisions.
- As such, the decisions are based on negotiation between both parties.

Based on the research findings, men respond differently in the three conditions, suggesting the role of information and communication in households' decisions.

In Condition 1, where there is private information, men were more likely to deposit the money into their own savings account. In Condition 2, where there is public information, men increased their consumption. In Condition 3, where there is a negotiation between spouses, men turned over their money to their spouses' savings accounts.

Why do men behave this way? It was established that the results are not attributed to gender differences, but rather the individual who controls savings decisions in the household. In the study, more than 80 percent of the households' finances were being managed by females due to the cultural setting in the Philippines.

Do women control the savings in your country too? We would like to highlight that the culture of having women manage households' savings in the Philippines is unlike other countries, such as the United States, whereby the males have larger control over managing the household finances. As such, we should expect to see opposite results in places whereby males control the savings decisions.

This is found in the current study too. Although the study in Philippines primarily focused on households in which females held authority over saving decisions in the household, the same pattern prevailed in households where males held the same authority. When there is private information, these women tend to save on their own, and when there is negotiation, they turn over their savings to their husbands.

This can be explained by the role of income monitoring within the household. With little private information, individuals tend to put less money into their accounts.

At the beginning of the marriage, husbands and wives develop a contract that relates to the financial management of the household. This can be attributed to social norms, such as in the Philippines, when women manage budgeting and decide on how much to spend.

However, this might not be in line with the husband's personal preferences all the time, so he might be tempted to withhold the money. The opposite holds true when the men control the household finances instead.

This study highlights how critical it is to establish a consensus and suitable structure in household financial management. As different genders take on different roles in the family, the way they interact could have different impacts on the finances of the households.

Key Takeaways

As the title (and cover page) of the book suggests, we seek to provide you with an introduction to household financial management. We hope that we have achieved our goals. At this point, it is important to note that a household does not constitute a single person, but rather an entire family.

Hence, we need to bear in mind that financial decisions are not made just for ourselves but rather, our families. Making household financial decisions should therefore not be an individual decision, but rather a collective one.

Moreover, the definition of household changes over time. As we move across the different stages of life, we could choose to get married and have children. This will impact our financial priorities and decisions. Consequently, even after we develop a roadmap for our household finances, we ought to remain agile and be flexible to meet the changes ahead.

As shared throughout the book, the management of household finances is a challenging but rewarding responsibility. This should not be done alone, but as a family. After all, teamwork makes the dream work. We wish you and your family an exciting journey ahead!

References

I. Introduction

1. Why Financial Literacy Matters

Agarwal, S., & Mazumder, B. (2013). Cognitive abilities and household financial decision making. *American Economic Journal: Applied Economics, 5*(1), 193–207

Song, C. (2020). Financial Illiteracy and Pension Contributions: A Field Experiment on Compound Interest in China. *The Review of Financial Studies, 33*(2), 916–949

2. Understanding Behavioral Biases

Hastings, J. S., & Shapiro, J. M. (2013). Fungibility and Consumer Choice: Evidence from Commodity Price Shocks. *The Quarterly Journal of Economics, 128*(4), 1449–1498

Ho, T. H., Png, I. P., & Reza, S. (2018). Sunk Cost Fallacy in Driving the World's Costliest Cars. *Management Science, 64*(4), 1761–1778

Larcom, S., Rauch, F., & Willems, T. (2017). The Benefits of Forced Experimentation: Striking Evidence from the London Underground Network. *The Quarterly Journal of Economics, 132*(4), 2019–2055

3. Primer to Inflation

Agarwal, S., Chua, Y. H., & Song, C. (2022). Inflation expectations of households and the upgrading channel. *Journal of Monetary Economics, 128*, 124–138

Fleckenstein, M., Longstaff, F. A., & Lustig, H. (2014). The TIPS-Treasury Bond Puzzle. *The Journal of Finance*, *69*(5), 2151–2197

Shafir, E., Diamond, P., & Tversky, A. (1997). Money Illusion. *The Quarterly Journal of Economics*, *112*(2), 341–374

4. Getting Started with Financial Planning

Agarwal, S., & Chua, Y. H. (2020). FinTech and household finance: a review of the empirical literature. *China Finance Review International*, *10*(4), 361–376

Karlan, D., McConnell, M., Mullainathan, S., & Zinman, J. (2016). Getting to the Top of Mind: How Reminders Increase Saving. *Management Science*, *62*(12), 3393–3411

II. Savings

5. Intertemporal Choices

Ashraf, N., Karlan, D., & Yin, W. (2006). Tying Odysseus to the Mast: Evidence From a Commitment Savings Product in the Philippines. *The Quarterly Journal of Economics*, *121*(2), 635–672

Laibson, D. (1997). Golden eggs and Hyperbolic Discounting. *The Quarterly Journal of Economics*, *112*(2), 443–478

Mischel, W., Ebbesen, E. B., & Raskoff Zeiss, A. (1972). Cognitive and attentional mechanisms in delay of gratification. *Journal of Personality and Social Psychology*, *21*(2), 204

Thaler, R. H., & Benartzi, S. (2004). Save more tomorrow™: Using Behavioral Economics to Increase Employee Saving. *Journal of Political Economy*, *112*(S1), S164–S187

6. Building a Nest Egg

Agarwal, S., Driscoll, J. C., Gabaix, X., & Laibson, D. (2009). The Age of Reason: Financial Decisions over the Life Cycle and Implications for Regulation. *Brookings Papers on Economic Activity, 2009*(2), 51–117

Lusardi, A., & Mitchell, O. S. (2007). Baby Boomer retirement security: The roles of planning, financial literacy, and housing wealth. *Journal of Monetary Economics, 54*(1), 205–224

Poterba, J. M. (2014). Retirement Security in an Aging Population. *American Economic Review, 104*(5), 1–30

7. Retirement Income Support

Chetty, R., Friedman, J. N., Leth-Petersen, S., Nielsen, T. H., & Olsen, T. (2014). Active vs. Passive Decisions and Crowd-Out in Retirement Savings Accounts: Evidence from Denmark. *The Quarterly Journal of Economics, 129*(3), 1141–1219

Choi, J. J., Laibson, D., & Madrian, B. C. (2011). $100 Bills on the Sidewalk: Suboptimal Investment in 401(k) Plans. *The Review of Economics and Statistics, 93*(3), 748–76

Ghafoori, E., Ip, E., & Kabátek, J. (2021). The impacts of a large-scale financial education intervention on retirement saving behaviors and portfolio allocation: Evidence from pension fund data. *Journal of Banking & Finance, 130*, 106195

8. Retirement Savings Puzzle

Agarwal, S., Pan, J., & Qian, W. (2020). Age of Decision: Pension Savings Withdrawal and Consumption and Debt Response. *Management Science, 66*(1), 43–69

Battistin, E., Brugiavini, A., Rettore, E., & Weber, G. (2009). The Retirement Consumption Puzzle: Evidence from a Regression Discontinuity Approach. *American Economic Review, 99*(5), 2209–26

De Nardi, M., French, E., & Jones, J. B. (2016). Savings After Retirement: A Survey. *Annual Review of Economics, 8*, 177–204 (Section 8)

III. Spending

9. Weather

Agarwal, S., Chomsisengphet, S., Meier, S., & Zou, X. (2020). In the mood to consume: Effect of sunshine on credit card spending. *Journal of Banking & Finance, 121*, 105960

Bordalo, P., Gennaioli, N., & Shleifer, A. (2013). Salience and Consumer Choice. *Journal of Political Economy, 121*(5), 803–843

Busse, M. R., Pope, D. G., Pope, J. C., & Silva-Risso, J. (2015). The Psychological Effect of Weather on Car Purchases. *The Quarterly Journal of Economics, 130*(1), 371–414

Chang, T. Y., Huang, W., & Wang, Y. (2018). Something in the Air: Pollution and the Demand for Health Insurance. *The Review of Economic Studies, 85*(3), 1609–1634

10. Peer Effects

Agarwal, S., Mikhed, V., & Scholnick, B. (2020). Peers' Income and Financial Distress: Evidence from Lottery Winners and Neighboring Bankruptcies. *The Review of Financial Studies, 33*(1), 433–472

Agarwal, S., Qian, W., & Zou, X. (2021). Thy Neighbor's Misfortune: Peer Effect on Consumption. *American Economic Journal: Economic Policy, 13*(2), 1–25

D'Acunto, F., Rossi, A. G., & Weber, M. (2019). Crowdsourcing Financial Information to Change Spending Behavior. *Center for Economic Studies and ifo Institute (CESifo) Working Paper*

Kast, F., Meier, S., & Pomeranz, D. (2018). Saving more in groups: Field experimental evidence from Chile. *Journal of Development Economics, 133*, 275–294

11. Digital Payments

Agarwal, S., Ghosh, P., Li, J., & Ruan, T. (2019). Digital Payments Induce Over-Spending: Evidence from the 2016 Demonetization in India. *Available at SSRN 3641508*

Agarwal, S., Qian, W., Ren, Y., Tsai, H. T., & Yeung, B. Y. (2020). The Real Impact of FinTech: Evidence from Mobile Payment Technology. *Available at SSRN 3556340*

Bachas, P., Gertler, P., Higgins, S., & Seira, E. (2021). How Debit Cards Enable the Poor to Save More. *The Journal of Finance*, *76*(4), 1913–1957

12. Online Privacy and Fraud

Agarwal, S., Ghosh, P., Ruan, T., & Zhang, Y. (2020). Privacy versus Convenience: Customer Response to Data Breaches of Their Information. *Available at SSRN 3729730*

IV. Borrowing

13. Credit Markets

Agarwal, S., Alok, S., Ghosh, P., & Gupta, S. (2019). Financial inclusion and alternate credit scoring: role of big data and machine learning in Fintech. *Indian School of Business*

Fuster, A., Plosser, M., Schnabl, P., & Vickery, J. (2019). The Role of Technology in Mortgage Lending. *The Review of Financial Studies, 32*(5), 1854–1899

Gathergood, J. (2012). Self-control, financial literacy and consumer over-indebtedness. *Journal of Economic Psychology, 33*(3), 590–602

14. Credit Cards

Agarwal, S., Chomsisengphet, S., Liu, C., & Souleles, N. S. (2015). Do Consumers Choose the Right Credit Contracts?. *The Review of Corporate Finance Studies, 4*(2), 239–257

Agarwal, S., Chomsisengphet, S., Mahoney, N., & Stroebel, J. (2015). Regulating Consumer Financial Products: Evidence from Credit Cards. *The Quarterly Journal of Economics*, 130(1), 111–164

Agarwal, S., Driscoll, J. C., Gabaix, X., & Laibson, D. (2008). Learning in the Credit Card Market. *National Bureau of Economic Research Working Paper*. (No. w13822)

Bertaut, C. C., Haliassos, M., & Reiter, M. (2009). Credit Card Debt Puzzles and Debt Revolvers for Self Control. *Review of Finance, 13*(4), 657–692

Gross, D. B., & Souleles, N. S. (2002). Do Liquidity Constraints and Interest Rates Matter for Consumer Behavior? Evidence from Credit Card Data. *The Quarterly Journal of Economics*, 117(1), 149–185

Medina, P. C. (2021). Side Effects of Nudging: Evidence from a Randomized Intervention in the Credit Card Market. *The Review of Financial Studies, 34*(5), 2580–2607

Telyukova, I. A. (2013). Household Need for Liquidity and the Credit Card Debt Puzzle. *The Review of Economic Studies, 80*(3), 1148–1177

15. Overdrafts

Alan, S., Cemalcilar, M., Karlan, D., & Zinman, J. (2018). Unshrouding: Evidence from Bank Overdrafts in Turkey. *The Journal of Finance, 73*(2), 481–522

Carlin, B., Olafsson, A., & Pagel, M. (2023). Mobile Apps and Financial Decision Making. *Review of Finance*, 27(3), 977–996

D'Acunto, F., Rauter, T., Scheuch, C. K., & Weber, M. (2020). Perceived Precautionary Savings Motives: Evidence from FinTech. *National Bureau of Economic Research Working Paper*. (No. w26817)

Stango, V., & Zinman, J. (2014). Limited and Varying Consumer Attention: Evidence from Shocks to the Salience of Bank Overdraft Fees. *The Review of Financial Studies, 27*(4), 990–1030

16. Payday Loans

Agarwal, S., Skiba, P. M., & Tobacman, J. (2009). Payday Loans and Credit Cards: New Liquidity and Credit Scoring Puzzles?. *American Economic Review, 99*(2), 412–17

Bertrand, M., & Morse, A. (2011). Information Disclosure, Cognitive Biases, and Payday Borrowing. *The Journal of Finance, 66*(6), 1865–1893

Gathergood, J., Guttman-Kenney, B., & Hunt, S. (2019). How Do Payday Loans Affect Borrowers? Evidence from the U.K. Market. *The Review of Financial Studies, 32*(2), 496–523

Melzer, B. T. (2011). The Real Costs of Credit Access: Evidence from the Payday Lending Market. *The Quarterly Journal of Economics, 126*(1), 517–555

Morse, A. (2011). Payday lenders: Heroes or villains? *Journal of Financial Economics*, 102(1), 28–44

V. Investment

17. Stock Market Participation

Dimmock, S. G., Kouwenberg, R., Mitchell, O. S., & Peijnenburg, K. (2016). Ambiguity aversion and household portfolio choice puzzles: Empirical evidence. *Journal of Financial Economics, 119*(3), 559–577

Guiso, L., Sapienza, P., & Zingales, L. (2008). Trusting the Stock Market. *The Journal of Finance, 63*(6), 2557–2600

18. Diversification

Benartzi, S., & Thaler, R. H. (2001). Naive Diversification Strategies in Defined Contribution Saving Plans. *American economic review, 91*(1), 79–98

Chew, S. H., Li, K. K., & Sagi, J. S. (2021). Experimental Evidence of Source Preference: Familiarity and Home Bias. *Available at SSRN 3870716*

Van Nieuwerburgh, S., & Veldkamp, L. (2009). Information Immobility and the Home Bias Puzzle. *The Journal of Finance, 64*(3), 1187–1215

19. Portfolio Inertia and Overtrading

Anagol, S., Balasubramaniam, V., & Ramadorai, T. (2018). Endowment Effects in the Field: Evidence from India's IPO Lotteries. *The Review of Economic Studies, 85*(4), 1971–2004

Barber, B. M., & Odean, T. (2000). Trading Is Hazardous to Your Wealth: The Common Stock Investment Performance of Individual Investors. *The Journal of Finance, 55*(2), 773–806

Cronqvist, H., Thaler, R. H., & Yu, F. (2018, May). When Nudges are Forever: Inertia in the Swedish Premium Pension Plan. In *AEA Papers and Proceedings* (Vol. 108, pp. 153–58)

Greenwood, R., & Shleifer, A. (2014). Expectations of Returns and Expected Returns. *The Review of Financial Studies, 27*(3), 714–746

Grinblatt, M., & Keloharju, M. (2009). Sensation Seeking, Overconfidence, and Trading Activity. *The Journal of Finance*, *64*(2), 549–578

Kahneman, D., Knetsch, J. L., & Thaler, R. H. (1990). Experimental Tests of the Endowment Effect and the Coase theorem. *Journal of Political Economy*, *98*(6), 1325–1348

20. Mental Accounting

Chen, Y., & Chua, Y. H. (2022). Socially Responsible Investment: The Role of Narrow Framing

Choi, J. J., Laibson, D., & Madrian, B. C. (2009). Mental Accounting in Portfolio Choice: Evidence from a Flypaper Effect. *American Economic Review*, *99*(5), 2085–95

Daniel, K., Garlappi, L., & Xiao, K. (2021). Monetary Policy and Reaching for Income. *The Journal of Finance*, *76*(3), 1145–1193

Hartzmark, S. M., & Solomon, D. H. (2019). The Dividend Disconnect. *The Journal of Finance*, *74*(5), 2153–2199

21. Interpretating Investment Performance

Birru, J., & Wang, B. (2016). Nominal price illusion. *Journal of Financial Economics, 119(3), 578–598*

Green, T. C., & Hwang, B. H. (2009). Price-based return comovement. *Journal of Financial Economics*, *93*(1), 37–50

Hartzmark, S. M., & Solomon, D. H. (2022). Reconsidering Returns. *The Review of Financial Studies*, *35*(1), 343–393

Shue, K., & Townsend, R. R. (2021). Can the Market Multiply and Divide? Non-Proportional Thinking in Financial Markets. *The Journal of Finance*, *76*(5), 2307–2357

VI. Housing

22. Buying and Selling Houses

Agarwal, S., Liu, C. H., Torous, W. N., & Yao, V. (2021). The Mistakes People Make: Financial Decision Making when Buying and Owning a Home. *MIT Center for Real Estate Research Paper*, (21/09)

Genesove, D., & Mayer, C. (2001). Loss Aversion and Seller Behavior: Evidence from the Housing Market. *The Quarterly Journal of Economics, 116*(4), 1233–1260

23. Mortgages

Agarwal, S., Rosen, R. J., & Yao, V. (2016). Why do Borrowers Make Mortgage Refinancing Mistakes?. *Management Science, 62*(12), 3494–3509

Agarwal, S., Ben-David, I., & Yao, V. (2017). Systematic mistakes in the mortgage market and lack of financial sophistication. *Journal of Financial Economics, 123*(1), 42–58

Andersen, S., Campbell, J. Y., Nielsen, K. M., & Ramadorai, T. (2020). Sources of Inaction in Household Finance: Evidence from the Danish Mortgage Market. *American Economic Review, 110*(10), 3184–3230

Agarwal, S., Driscoll, J. C., & Laibson, D. I. (2013). Optimal Mortgage Refinancing: A Closed-Form Solution. *Journal of Money, Credit and Banking, 45*(4), 591–622

Badarinza, C., Campbell, J. Y., & Ramadorai, T. (2018). What calls to ARMs? International Evidence on Interest Rates and the Choice of Adjustable-Rate Mortgages. *Management Science, 64*(5), 2275–2288

Campbell, J. Y., & Cocco, J. F. (2003). Household Risk Management and Optimal Mortgage Choice. *The Quarterly Journal of Economics, 118*(4), 1449–1494

24. Agents, Brokers, and Appraisers

Agarwal, S., He, J., Sing, T. F., & Song, C. (2019). Do real estate agents have information advantages in housing markets?. *Journal of Financial Economics, 134*(3), 715–735

Agarwal, S., Ben-David, I., & Yao, V. (2015). Collateral Valuation and Borrower Financial Constraints: Evidence from the Residential Real Estate Market. *Management Science, 61*(9), 2220–2240

Buchak, G., Matvos, G., Piskorski, T., & Seru, A. (2020). Why is Intermediating Houses so Difficult? Evidence from iBuyers. *National Bureau of Economic Research Working Paper.* (No. w28252)

Fu, R., Jin, G. Z., & Liu, M. (2022). Does Human-algorithm Feedback Loop lead to Error Propagation? Evidence form Zillow's Zestimate. *National Bureau of Economic Research Working Paper.* (No. w29880)

Levitt, S. D., & Syverson, C. (2008). Market Distortions When Agents Are Better Informed: The Value of Information in Real Estate Transactions. *The Review of Economics and Statistics, 90*(4), 599–611

Woodward, S. E., & Hall, R. E. (2012). Diagnosing Consumer Confusion and Sub-optimal Shopping Effort: Theory and Mortgage-Market Evidence. *American Economic Review,* 102(7), 3249–76

VII. Risk Management

25. Navigating the Insurance Market

Bernheim, B. D., Forni, L., Gokhale, J., & Kotlikoff, L. J. (2003). The Mismatch Between Life Insurance Holdings and Financial Vulnerabilities: Evidence from the Health and Retirement Study. *American Economic Review, 93*(1), 354–365

Cole, S., Giné, X., Tobacman, J., Topalova, P., Townsend, R., & Vickery, J. (2013). Barriers to Household Risk Management: Evidence from India. *American Economic Journal: Applied Economics, 5*(1), 104–35

Gallagher, J. (2014). Learning about an Infrequent Event: Evidence from Flood Insurance Take-Up in the United States. *American Economic Journal: Applied Economics*, 206–233

Soleymanian, M., Weinberg, C. B., & Zhu, T. (2019). Sensor Data and Behavioral Tracking: Does Usage-Based Auto Insurance Benefit Drivers?. *Marketing Science*, *38*(1), 21–43

26. Health Insurance

Akerlof, G. A. (1970). The market for "lemons": Quality uncertainty and the market mechanism. *The Quarterly Journal of Economics*, *84*(3), 488–500

Bhargava, S., Loewenstein, G., & Sydnor, J. (2017). Choose to Lose: Health Plan Choices from a Menu with Dominated Option. *The Quarterly Journal of Economics*, *132*(3), 1319–1372

Domurat, R., Menashe, I., & Yin, W. (2021). The Role of Behavioral Frictions in Health Insurance Marketplace Enrollment and Risk: Evidence from a Field Experiment. *American Economic Review*, *111*(5), 1549–74

Drake, C., Ryan, C., & Dowd, B. (2022). Sources of inertia in the individual health insurance market. *Journal of Public Economics*, *208*, 104622

Sydnor, J. (2010). (Over)insuring Modest Risks. *American Economic Journal: Applied Economics*, *2*(4), 177–99

27. Annuity

Beshears, J., Choi, J. J., Laibson, D., Madrian, B. C., & Zeldes, S. P. (2014). What makes annuitization more appealing?. *Journal of Public Economics*, *116*, 2–16

Brown, J. R., Kling, J. R., Mullainathan, S., & Wrobel, M. V. (2008). Why Don't People Insure Late-Life Consumption? A Framing Explanation of the Under-Annuitization Puzzle. *American Economic Review*, *98*(2), 304–09

Hu, W. Y., & Scott, J. S. (2007). Behavioral Obstacles in the Annuity Market. *Financial Analysts Journal, 63*(6), 71–82

Liu, H., Song, C., & Zhu, S. (2019). Intentional Bequest Motives and the Choice of Annuity, *Working Paper*

Yaari, M. E. (1965). Uncertain Lifetime, Life Insurance, and the Theory of the Consumer. *The Review of Economic Studies, 32*(2), 137–150.

VIII. Gender

28. Gender Pension Gap

Agarwal, S., Cheng, S. F., Sing, T. F., & Sultana, M. (2021). Gender Wage Gap for Singaporean Taxi Drivers: Are Women Strategic Workers?. *Available at SSRN 3996148*

Agarwal, S., Qian, W., Reeb, D. M., & Sing, T. F. (2016). Playing the Boys game: Golf buddies and Board Diversity. *American Economic Review, 106*(5), 272–76

Blau, F. D., & Kahn, L. M. (2017). The Gender Wage Gap: Extent, Trends, and Explanations. *Journal of Economic Literature, 55*(3), 789–865

Chen, X., Huang, B., & Ye, D. (2020). Gender gap in peer-to-peer lending: Evidence from China. *Journal of Banking & Finance, 112*, 105633

Goldsmith-Pinkham, P., & Shue, K. (2023). The Gender Gap in Housing Returns. *The Journal of Finance*, 78(2), 1097–1145

29. Gender and Self-Confidence

Agarwal, S., He, J., Sing, T. F., & Zhang, J. (2018). Gender Gap in Personal Bankruptcy Risks: Empirical Evidence from Singapore. *Review of Finance, 22*(2), 813–847

Agnew, J. R., Anderson, L. R., Gerlach, J. R., & Szykman, L. R. (2008). Who Chooses Annuities? An Experimental Investigation of the Role of Gender, Framing, and Defaults. *American Economic Review, 98*(2), 418–22

Barber, B. M., & Odean, T. (2001). Boys will be Boys: Gender, Overconfidence, and Common Stock Investment. *The Quarterly Journal of Economics, 116*(1), 261–292

Bordalo, P., Coffman, K., Gennaioli, N., & Shleifer, A. (2019). Beliefs about Gender. *American Economic Review, 109*(3), 739–73

Bucher-Koenen, T., Alessie, R. J., Lusardi, A., & Van Rooij, M. (2021). Fearless Woman: Financial Literacy and Stock Market Participation. *National Bureau of Economic Research Working Paper*. (No. w28723)

30. Intra-Household Financial Decisions

Addoum, J. M. (2017). Household Portfolio Choice and Retirement. *The Review of Economics and Statistics, 99*(5), 870–883

Ashraf, N. (2009). Spousal Control and Intra-household Decision Making: An Experimental Study in the Philippines. *American Economic Review, 99*(4), 1245–77

Ke, D. (2021). Who Wears the Pants? Gender Identity Norms and Intrahousehold Financial Decision-Making. *The Journal of Finance, 76*(3), 1389–1425

Index

www.ingramcontent.com/pod-product-compliance
Lightning Source LLC
LaVergne TN
LVHW052036200926
848481LV00005B/1699